The British

HERITAGE

PUBLISHED 1948

MADE AND PRINTED IN GREAT BRITAIN BY
ODHAMS (WATFORD) LTD., WATFORD
T.1048.T

THE CORNFIELD

John Constable

The British
HERITAGE

The people, their crafts and achievements

as recorded in their buildings

and on the face of the

countryside

ODHAMS PRESS LIMITED · LONG ACRE · LONDON

Colour Plates

Contents

SYMOND'S YAT, WYE VALLEY

From the rocky hill known as Symond's Yat the Wye can be seen in all its beauty between high, partly wooded hills, twisting and turning as it finds a way through the narrow gorge. Near the river's banks there is a charming mixture of ploughed fields and meadows giving way on the higher ground to a strip of woodland with rough pasture-land above. Far to the north, beyond the neck of the gorge, is the wide vale of Hereford where the fertile fields are picked out by thick hedgerows. In this one view are all the elements which make up the scenic heritage of southern England and Wales from the rich farming country of the lowlands to the coarse grazing ground of the hills.

The British Heritage

THE purpose of this book is to show how the British way of life is a compound of ingredients derived from the cultures of many races and many peoples, and how in art, in architecture and the planning of towns and villages, even in the very pattern of rural life, the debt which the present owes to the past is immense and almost incalculable.

The British landscape, the natural environment in which the British people has matured, should first be studied. Roughly speaking, Great Britain slopes from north-west to south-east. All the high ground is in the north and west, including the highlands of Scotland, the Lake District of England, and the mountains of North and South Wales, as well as the lower hills of Devon and Cornwall, with their high moors, Dartmoor, Exmoor and Bodmin Moor. These areas through the ages have been easy to defend, almost unconquerable. Again and again the people who were dwelling in the more fertile lowlands of the south and east have retreated to these mountain fastnesses, driven there to seek refuge from the advancing hordes of continental invaders who were seeking fresh lands to conquer, fresh ground to till.

This is something that happened many times in the prehistory of Britain

and has been repeated at least twice since history was first recorded, when first the Roman influence and then the Saxon spread across the southern and eastern districts of England. Thus the literature and traditions of Wales, western Scotland and the south-west of England are much older than those of the rest of England or of the east of Scotland. The people, too, are even now racially different, and the difference is one which can be easily discerned in the characteristic appearance of the mountain folk and of the lowland people. Along with this difference of physical appearance there is also a difference in outlook and tradition which not even the levelling influence of present-day communications, including the very important one of broadcasting, has eradicated. A pride in local institutions has grown up and many traditions of speech and observance are preserved self-consciously as a kind of bulwark against a growing uniformity.

Later in this chapter will be traced the course of some of the chief invasions from the Continent which have influenced the development of Britain and have accentuated this startling difference between the two parts of the country. But there is another important influence which has contributed to it, arising from the contrast in soil. The lowlands

7

of the south and east, including the rich corn lands of East Anglia, the fertile pasture lands of the south country and the Midland plain, proved ideal for agriculture, once the use of iron had been introduced, with all the improvement in agricultural science which resulted in up-to-date and more efficient machinery.

The rugged mountainous country of Wales and Scotland, by contrast, has never yielded readily to cultivation. The bulk of it is still unploughed, with rough pasture on the middle slopes of the mountains and nothing but rocky screes or rank, boggy land on the higher ground. Only in the narrow valleys which intersect the mountains and in the broadening valleys of some of the swift streams which flow westward into the Atlantic Ocean or the Irish Sea has cultivation on a large scale been possible.

Agriculture is the most important industry of Britain. Little more than one hundred and fifty years ago it was virtually the only important one, for it is only since the Industrial Revolution and the introduction of machinery on a large scale that the great industrial towns have sprung up, and there has been a drift of population away from the land and at the same time a vast increase in the total number of inhabitants. Before that, the life of the people was determined almost entirely by the wealth of the land which they worked.

MAN'S STRUGGLE WITH NATURE

So the husbandmen of the mountain country, who drew only a poor living from the unyielding soil, developed a hardiness and a dourness which many attribute to racial difference, but which really derives from their unceasing struggle with Nature. The people of the hill country are vigorous as well as conservative of old ideas and traditions. The rural people of the lowlands are comparatively easy-going and receptive of new ideas, more friendly perhaps, but with a less fiercely passionate regard for their own way of life. There is more of tolerance in the lowlands, but less of the spirit of adventure which inspired the seafaring of the later Middle Ages and the consequent building up of a great empire to which the Scottish people have contributed so much.

CHANGES IN SCENERY

This contrast in character and way of life reflects, and at the same time is reflected by, the startling contrast in scenery. In the north and west the scenic heritage remains much as Nature designed it. Just as the valleys are the only part of the land which has yielded to agriculture, so they are the only part which shows the hand of man as it modifies the natural heritage.

The bold, sharp, treeless outlines of the Pennines, of the Cambrian mountains, or of the Cairngorms show no trace of man's handiwork. Rain and storm have played their part in eroding the gulleys, and exposing the bare rock. But the last two thousand years, though they are the whole span of recorded history in Britain, represent only a minute fraction of geological time. Within them there can have been little or no change in the face of the land. Perhaps there has been little visible to the naked eye since the glaciers, which once covered all the north and west of England, receded many thousand years before history proper began. The rank grass and the heather, which are the only vegetation to be found on the uplands, quickly covered the land after the glaciers had disappeared.

During the present century a man-made change is slowly beginning to take place. New forests of pine trees are being planted, for the pine family is very hardy and resistant to the stresses of weather and poor soil. Even the mountain sides of the Lake District of Cumberland and Westmorland may soon be partly covered in the serried rows of young fir trees which mark the first stage of afforestation. But as yet the visual effect is small, the areas of barren land so vast, that it must be many decades before the highland scene is changed out of recognition.

Nevertheless, the characteristic appearance of a limited area can be changed out of all recognition in a score or so of years. That is a fact which experience has proved. In the Breckland area of Norfolk and Suffolk, many square miles of the sandy warrens which have defied the efforts of man to tame them have been changed into dark sombre forests, almost impenetrable, the rows of trees planted so close together that the interlacing branches shut out the light, and the earth, bare of undergrowth and vegetation, is carpeted with dead pine needles. So in the fullness of time may certain areas in the highlands change their nature and in the process become productive of timber,

PASS OF LLANBERIS, CARNARVON

Between Snowdon and the Glyder mountains, the Pass of Llanberis is a deeply etched valley from the floor of which the craggy hillsides rise like cliffs. The valley, like many others in the mountain districts of Britain, was first scooped out by a glacier. There is a wild beauty in the scene but the soil is too poor to be worked. As in all the mountainous regions of Britain, the poverty of the soil goes hand in hand with scenic grandeur and lonely beauty.

HARVEST ON FERTILE SLOPES

The tractor has come to even the most remote parts of the countryside and Britain today is one of the most highly mechanized farming countries in the world. Here in the Teign Valley of South Devon the corn harvest is in full swing when every available man, woman and child is pressed into service to gather in the harvest before the autumn rains begin. This lovely countryside is one of the most fertile of the south-

10

OF SOUTH DEVON VALLEY

western counties. On the lower slopes of the hills corn crops flourish in spite of the fairly high rainfall. On the higher ground there is good pasture-land divided into fields by trim hedges. Everywhere there is fine hedgerow timber and rich, scattered coppices. In all the panorama there is not a single field which is completely unproductive of either grass or crops—not a corner of waste land in the whole landscape.

11

which is one of Britain's most vital raw materials. But for the time being the highland scene is unchanging.

Very different is the story of the lowlands which comprise all that part of England which lies south and east of a line drawn from the Wash to the Severn, the eastern coastal strip of northern England and Scotland and the plain of central Scotland, in which lie Glasgow and Edinburgh. In all these areas Nature has had a part in shaping the scene, for the rise and fall of the low hills, the pleasant winding ways of the river valleys, owe nothing to the hand of man. But the clothes in which Nature is decked are entirely man-made. The trim pattern of stone wall or hedgerow, the villages, the varying colours of the landscape, the woodlands and the coppices—these are what constitute the characteristic beauty of the scene. Though Nature may determine what crops can be grown or, by the provision of a local building stone, as in the Cotswold country, affect the general characteristics of town, village and farm, it is man who has given them reality and has moulded Nature's work to his own pattern.

In a few areas like the Romney Marshes of Kent and the fen lands of Cambridgeshire and Lincolnshire, even the basic structure of the landscape is artificial. Here the land has been reclaimed by human toil from the encroaching sea, drains have been constructed and long sea walls built, the very courses of rivers have been changed, and thousands of acres of fertile land have been won, fine pastures in the Romney Marshes, black earth ideal for ploughing in the Fens.

In fact, the courses of the rivers which flow into the Wash have been changed as much by the creation of artificial channels as was the Sussex Ouse by the monstrous storm in the late Middle Ages, when, tradition relates, in a single night its mouth was changed from a point near what is now the town of Seaford to its present position where the cliffs break off at Newhaven.

Thus man and Nature sometimes achieve the same results. All over southern and eastern England their work

ROMNEY MARSH

This characteristic view across the Romney Marsh toward the tree-sheltered village of Snave shows the rich sheep pastures which have been reclaimed by the labours of man from salt marsh and intractable swamp.

CUMBERLAND STONE CIRCLE

Under the frowning slopes of the Saddleback near Keswick, this stone circle, unusually complete as it is, forms a link with Britain's prehistoric heritage. The stones of which it is composed are of local origin, and were in all probability regarded as having sacred qualities. According to tradition it was a Druids' temple, but there is strong evidence of much greater antiquity relating back to the Stone Age at least four thousand years ago. Here, as in the case of Stonehenge and other stone circles, the Druid tradition has died hard, though its only claim to belief seems to be the tendency to ascribe any strange feature of the countryside to one of two fabulous sources—the Devil or the Druids.

inextricably fuses one with the other. The countryside of the lowlands is like a gigantic garden, laid out on a vast scale, sculptured by Nature, planted and tended by man, with only here and there the pockets of squalor and untidiness which in the latter part of the nineteenth century grew up round the new industries.

To begin the story of the influences which have moulded the culture of Britain, it is essential to go back into prehistoric times, to a time, in fact, when Britain was joined to the continent of Europe by a narrow strip of land where now is the Strait of Dover. This strip of land linked the Shakespeare Cliff at Dover with Cap Gris Nez on the French coast, where the cliffs today match the white splendour of the Dover cliffs. It is these "white cliffs of Dover" which have given Britain the name of Albion; they are as significant to returning travellers from the Continent as is the Statue of Liberty to American citizens returning to their native land.

In prehistoric days two great rivers rose from springs in the isthmus, one flowing down to what is now the English Channel, the other flowing north toward what is now the North Sea. Gradually the head waters of the two rivers, aided by the force of weather erosion, ate away the soft chalk until the two rivers were united and water encircled all the shores of Britain.

Before that happened mankind had begun the process of evolution which was to prove the power of mind over matter; man had already shown that

TRETHEVY QUOIT, CORNWALL

This cromlech, or prehistoric stone structure, on the edge of Bodmin Moor, near St. Cleer, was originally the burial chamber of a Stone Age long-barrow, from which the covering of earth has disappeared.

in spite of his small stature he was capable of dealing effectively with animals ten times his size and weight. Even so the first tribes which made their way across the isthmus and settled in Britain were nomadic and remained in no place for very long. Civilization had not advanced to the point at which settled government and permanent homes were possible.

It is not until about 3000 B.C. that the succeeding waves of invasion which passed across Britain can be traced with any certainty. By then, of course, the Channel isthmus had disappeared, though the narrows which intervened between the coasts of Britain and Europe were not quite so broad as the modern Strait of Dover. Between 3000 B.C. and 1800 B.C. there was a flourishing civilization centred on Salisbury Plain, the metropolis of the Stone Age people, and a system of communications had already been largely developed over the southern half of England. The New Stone Age

people must have been quite highly civilized. They have bequeathed vast stone monuments like Avebury and Stonehenge, the building of which took hundreds of men many years to complete, especially as the only tools and implements available to them were the crude but beautifully fashioned implements made from the flint nodules dug out of the chalky ground. The building of works on so large a scale implied a settled government and a mature organization, and moreover a settled tribal dwelling place.

Here then, two thousand years before recorded history begins, is a picture of a highly developed people who, incidentally, had a religion which, whatever its nature, must have been of enormous importance in their lives to inspire such mighty works as Stonehenge.

About 1800 B.C. a fresh migration from the Continent overran the New Stone Age civilization and produced another culture which was characterized by the use of bronze. It may well be that the invention of bronze was the stimulus which produced this far-flung migration. Certain it is that the Bronze Age people, who flourished in Britain between 1800 and 800 B.C., were of a different race from that of the stone-using people whose civilization preceded theirs. It is known from excavations carried out at their burial places (the round barrows or tumuli which are so frequent all over the chalk country of southern England), that the people of the Stone Age were a long-headed race, those of the Bronze Age a round-headed one. The bronze weapons of the round-headed people were far too effective for any great resistance to be made by the long-headed Stone Age people. So these latter divided into two parts; some stayed behind and were absorbed into the Bronze Age culture, others retreated northward to Scotland, westward into

Wales, and south-westward into Cornwall, where they were safe from attack.

It is a natural inference that these Stone Age people formed the backbone of the Welsh and Cornish populations and have continued to influence the racial strains of those districts right up to the present, however slight this racial influence may be. In Cornwall especially, legends are still told of races of pygmies and giants. It is thought by some scholars that these legends represent prehistoric races who entered Cornwall and made their homes there. Certainly now, though more noticeably in the last century, there are observable in the more remote rural areas of Cornwall groups of families of unusually large stature and other groups, especially in the fishing villages, of unusually small stature to give credibility to the legends.

In a countryside mainly untouched by

STONEHENGE, WILTSHIRE

This is the most elaborate and complex of the stone circles of Britain. Excavation on the site has indicated that it was constructed about 2000 B.C. The vast stones which make up the trilithons (two upright stones supporting a horizontal slab) are of local origin, but the "blue stones" of the inner circle occur nowhere nearer than the Prescelly Hills in Pembrokeshire and must have been transported from there by manual labour.

ROMAN CITY—MEDIEVAL TOWN

St. Albans Abbey is one of the many buildings constructed largely of materials taken from a ruined Roman city, in this case, Verulamium. Remains of one of the walls of the city can be seen in the foreground. The Abbey tower is a fine example of Norman architecture and has so many Roman bricks in its composition that it gleams red in the setting sun in contrast with the grey stonework of later parts of the building.

Roman and Saxon influences and cut off by physical barriers from the rest of Britain it is only natural that early racial strains should have persisted longer than in other parts of the country. In early times man's horizon was bound by the home fields and the true unit of population was the village; in those circumstances inter-marriage between villagers is the rule rather than the exception. When in addition the people of even nearby towns are regarded as foreigners, as they are, or until recently were, in many parts of the mountainous districts of Britain, the same stock goes on from generation to generation and century to century, with only a very occasional introduction of alien blood.

In southern and eastern England about 800 B.C. another wave of invasion followed. This was consequent on the invention of iron, in just the same way as the previous one had followed the invention of bronze. The Iron Age invasions, which were in two or three waves, spread over the period between 800 B.C. and the beginning of the Christian era.

Prehistoric invasions spread from diverse parts of the Continent, some from the region of central Germany, others across France from the Mediterranean coast, deriving ultimately from the Near East, which was the cradle of early civilizations. Some of the Iron Age tribes came also from Northern Europe and brought with them a different, more virile strain, into the population.

For the greater part of the first four centuries A.D. Britain was a province of Rome. It was a period of the utmost importance in the creation of modern Britain. For the first time there was a literate civilization, a civilization of known ideals and advanced institutions. It was, too, an era of peace, perhaps the most prosperous period in Britain's history prior to the nineteenth century.

I. DISTANT VIEW OF THE TOWN OF EXETER: *J. M. W. Turner*

II. CARNARVON: *John Brett*

III. BACK OF THE NEW MILLS, NORWICH: *John Crome*

IV. COOKHAM MOOR: *Stanley Spencer*

CASTLE HILL, DOVER

Dover has been a place of importance ever since Roman days. Its long history is matched by the wealth of ancient monuments that survive today. Here on Castle Hill are grouped together links with every period of the port's prosperity. In the foreground is the Church of St. Mary in Castro side by side with the Roman pharos or lighthouse, the first lighthouse ever constructed in Britain and the only one which the Romans thought worth building in north-west Europe. The Church of St. Mary is of Saxon foundation, raised within the ramparts of the Roman camp. In the background the castle still dominates the town. The square keep is Norman and is one of the chain of Norman strongholds in south-eastern England of the same type as the castles of Rochester, Canterbury and London. These were the four castles which guarded the main Norman port of entry and the principal highway from the Continent to the English capital city. Dover Castle retains its character as a fortress.

Peace and the arts go hand in hand, so it is not surprising to find that in those four centuries Britain shared in the cultural activities of Rome. The Romans came as conquerors in the first century A.D. but they stayed as friends, and when the last of the Roman legionaries were withdrawn the British were exposed to less kindly invaders.

Modern Britain owes an enormous debt to Rome, incurred indirectly in the Middle Ages, when the rebirth of interest in classical study, called the Renaissance, spread across Europe and brought new learning and new ideas to medieval Britain. Even so, the basic ideas of Roman civilization were deeply implanted during the four centuries of the occupation, and though the barbarian invasions of Saxons which followed swept away much of the edifice, some of the foundations remained.

To the Roman lawmakers indirectly Britain owes a small part of her legal system, for Roman law has proved the foundation of most modern judicial

MOSAIC FLOOR OF ROMAN VILLA, SOMERSET

This perfectly preserved mosaic is part of the floor of a Roman villa discovered at Low Ham, near Langport, Somerset. Villas were the homes of the prosperous merchant farmers in the first four centuries A.D. They were well built and luxuriously appointed, and mosaic floors like this one in the main living-room were commonplace. The scenes depicted in these Roman mosaics varied from religious subjects to designs of purely imaginative origin.

ROMAN ROAD, NORTHUMBERLAND

Near the great Roman wall of Hadrian which divided the province of Britain from the country of the Picts and Scots a military highway was constructed to supply the garrisons of the mile castles and forts along the course of the wall. Most of this road can still be traced. Near Haltwhistle, as shown above, it has been reconstructed in modern times and serves as part of an important cross-country route. Beside it can be seen the deep ditch or trench which, with an earthen rampart, defended the road from sudden attack—a feature which does not occur in the case of Roman civil highways.

systems, not only in Britain but in all countries of Europe. To the Romans, too, are due the basic conceptions of architectural forms. These, of course, were first realized in Britain in the towns which the Romans founded and in the villas which they built in country districts. They were re-established in the magnificent architecture of the Norman period and brought back once more in the time of the classical revival, when buildings such as the Banqueting Hall of Whitehall and St. Paul's Cathedral were erected, and great names such as Inigo Jones and Sir Christopher Wren emerged in the story of British architec-

ture. Even the typical Georgian style of architecture, from which by successive modifications many of the everyday buildings of the twentieth century have evolved, was derived from the same conceptions.

It is fair to say that the whole appearance of Britain's towns owes much to the influence of Rome. Add to that the great number of modern towns, particularly the county towns and market towns, which were founded by the Romans, a few of which, though extended and rebuilt, have never materially departed from the Roman plan—we begin to see how great is the debt of

19

CHICHESTER, SUSSEX

Founded by the Celtic people whose capital was at Trundle Hill on the South Downs, Chichester became in turn Roman town and medieval city. It retains the outline plan of the Roman town, for the four main streets of the city which meet at the market cross, seen on the left of the photograph, are on the site of the four main roads of Roman Chichester. In the foreground is the cathedral, a Norman building enlarged in the thirteenth and fourteenth centuries. The spire is a nineteenth-century copy of the original, which was built in the fourteenth century, but fell in 1861. In the extreme foreground the detached bell tower, dating from the fifteenth century, is in the characteristic style of that period and is the only detached belfry belonging to an English cathedral. The whole of the business district of modern Chichester is still confined within the circuit of the medieval walls, fragments of which were so solidly constructed that some parts are still preserved more or less intact.

the present to the past and the extent of the heritage handed down from two thousand years ago.

The Roman occupation of Britain, too, is a chapter in the annals of the country, because it provided a direct link not only with the native Roman culture, but with the civilizations of Greece and Egypt, which the Romans had themselves absorbed earlier. Indeed the Roman forms of architecture were derived from the Greek forms. Even the native Roman religion which was introduced into Britain had been modified by contact with the Greek religion and mythology and with the peoples of ancient Egypt. The Christian religion, which has proved the spring of more creative work than any other factor in the western world, became established in Britain long before the Romans withdrew and there seems to have been a certain religious toleration, with perhaps Christian churches existing side by side with Roman temples in some of the bigger towns like Silchester.

Although the literature, the language, the religion and the crafts of the Roman colonists did not survive, modern commercial Britain owes a permanent material debt to the system of roads which the Romans initiated and developed, and which has proved the framework of all subsequent extensions of the internal lines of communication.

The building of roads goes along with the development of towns. The sites which the Romans chose for their towns were many of them sites already selected by the Iron Age peoples who had preceded them. In other cases entirely new sites were chosen, usually at a point where new lines of communication forded the great rivers, or straight roads connecting existing towns crossed. Thus Dover became for the first time the main port of entry for traffic from the Continent; Rochester and Canterbury were

SAXON KING COMMEMORATED

The statue of King Alfred in the market place in Wantage, Berks, commemorates the king who was the first to encourage the arts in Britain and to establish the heritage of learning and literature. It was Alfred, too, who secured the heritage of the sea by building the first British Navy.

built where the easiest road from Dover to a point at which the Thames could be crossed forded the Rivers Medway and Stour; London itself guarding the ford over the Thames; Verulamium (St. Albans) was in a direct line from London to the outpost of the Empire at Chester, and so on.

The Romans engineered highways on a large scale and because the course of these highways was well surveyed and the routes most of them followed were intrinsically good, no subsequent period of road-building has altered them. So the great road from Dover to London through Canterbury, and its extension from London through St. Albans to the north-west, the whole known as Watling Street, has remained to the present day the main artery of road traffic connecting these points.

This is only one example out of many that equally illustrate the point. The Romans built towns all over southern and central England, from York, Chester and Lincoln in the north, to Leicester in the Midlands and Winchester, Exeter and Gloucester in the south. All these are towns which to a greater or lesser extent retain something of their original Roman plan, however unwieldy they have become in modern times and however crowded they were in the Middle Ages. At Chichester, for instance, the four main roads which radiate from the medieval market cross are precisely on the site of the original Roman roads. Medieval London was almost entirely confined within the circuit of the Roman walls. The medieval walls of towns like Chester and Rochester were built over the crumbling ruins of the Roman walls. The list can be extended indefinitely.

PICTS AND SCOTS

The Roman influence did not extend much into Scotland, nor into Wales and Cornwall. These areas through the four centuries of Roman domination continued to be "native" and the population grew from the stock of the indigenous Stone Age people and those of the Bronze Age and Iron Age peoples who had retreated there for shelter. It appears that the tribes known as Picts and Scots who carried on a guerrilla warfare against the outposts of Roman Britain, were even then armed with only the primitive "weapons" of earlier ages

and were undoubtedly direct descendants of the Stone Age Britons.

The ambition of everyone who dwelt within the province was to obtain the status of a Roman citizen. The population probably never exceeded two million and may well have been much smaller, but was large enough at least to act as a civilizing influence on the people who invaded Britain after the Romans left. The British people are often called an Anglo-Saxon people, yet, as has been seen, the heritage bequeathed to the present by the peoples who dwelt in Britain before the first Angle or the first Saxon set foot there is considerable.

ANGLO-SAXON INVASION

When in the fourth century the first of the Anglo-Saxon tribes began to raid the southern and eastern coasts of England they sailed up the estuaries and made attacks on the Roman settlements which they found there. Then, and for hundreds of years afterwards, their influence was purely destructive, their legacy to the future negligible. After the last of the Roman troops left Britain to defend the frontiers of their empire nearer home there was the beginning of a real dark age from which Britain did not emerge for nearly four hundred years.

Left to their own resources, the citizens of Roman Britain were no match for the hordes of barbarian invaders which swept down upon them. Gradually the Angles began to make settlements in what is now East Anglia, the Saxons in most parts of southern and central England, and the Jutes in the Isle of Wight. The first thing they did was to destroy what they could of the existing civilization. Walled towns meant nothing to them, the fine Roman buildings stood to them for the lurking places of potential enemies and strongpoints from which they themselves

22

VILLAGE OF THE DANES

The broad stream of the River Ure flowing down from Wensleydale passes hard by the stone-built houses and tall-towered church of West Tanfield, a typical Yorkshire village. In the "Domesday Book" Tanfield appears as Danefield, Field of the Danes, and it is possible that, like other places in Yorkshire, this village owes its name to the Danish or Scandinavian invaders.

could be attacked. So whatever Roman town they captured they sacked and razed to the ground, killing many of the citizens and driving most of the others out into the fields, where they perished from exposure and lack of food.

Then for the first time, by that sardonic change of circumstances which repeats itself so often, Roman culture began to make itself felt in the outlying districts of the south-west and Wales, where some of the people of the erstwhile Roman colony were given succour by the Celtic population which had successfully defended itself against the forces of Roman armies, and which was again to prove itself immune to the Saxon invasion. Apart from the gradual

MEDIEVAL MARKET VILLAGE

Taking its name from a Norman castle, which was one of the strongest in the West Country, Castle Combe retains its air of medieval prosperity. Here the stone cottages, the Gothic church, the medieval market cross and the ancient inn make a group which is as picturesque as any village of England. In the flourishing days of the Wiltshire cloth trade local clothiers sold their goods in the shelter of the market cross. The prominent tower of the church, like so many other fifteenth-century buildings, was built through the liberality of the wealthier cloth merchants of the district.

development of native culture in those parts a new spirit began to spread through the introduction of Christianity, which came to the west and south-west much earlier than to Saxon England, through the influence of Ireland and the Celtic missionaries.

Modern England owes to the Anglo-Saxon settlers, once the destructive period was over, a complete change in the rural economy. In Roman Britain the hill villages and upland cultivation of early peoples persisted side by side with the urban development of Rome. Both were swept aside by the Saxons. Though the development of towns was only postponed for a few centuries, upland agriculture disappeared for good. In its place there began the intensive cultivation of the valleys, for the Saxon settlers, once their early nomadic life had ended, began to found villages by the banks of the rivers and by the seashore, where they could fish for food.

The vast bulk of modern England's village communities was founded in Saxon days, and the names of villages today are derived directly from the

24

names which the Saxons gave them. To the Anglo-Saxons, too, are due the names of many of the counties; Essex is the land of the East Saxons, Sussex, that of the South Saxons. Wessex, the name revived by Thomas Hardy, though no longer a geographical division, was the land of the West Saxons. Norfolk is the land of the north folk, and Suffolk the land of the south folk, in this case the Angles.

The shires came later, when under a more settled government in later Saxon times local administration began to take shape and the word "shire" means a part which is shorn off under the juris-diction of a shire reeve, forerunner of the more modern sheriff.

Meanwhile another racial and cultural influence was beginning to affect the eastern part of Britain, that of the Vikings or Norsemen who came from Denmark, Norway and Sweden. Just as the Saxons invaded the shores of Roman Britain, so these seafaring warriors raided the coas· of Saxon England and established themselves just as easily. Their fine physique, their high cheek-bones and fair hair remain predominant in the coastal villages of north-eastern England and parts of eastern Scotland. The seafaring traditions which they

KERSEY, SUFFOLK

Just as Castle Combe represents in its present buildings the medieval wealth of the cloth trade in the West Country, so Kersey stands for the wealth that came from the woollen trade in East Anglia. For the West Country and East Anglia were the two principal centres of this flourishing industry, which continued in rural centres right up to the Industrial Revolution. Here the houses are half-timbered or white-washed in contrast with the stone of the Wiltshire village, but there is the same air of quiet dignity and the same feeling of prosperity without ostentation.

brought with them formed the foundation of the great seafaring history which resulted in a vast British empire. To them, as to the Saxons, we owe the names of many villages, those ending in -thorpe and -by being of Norse origin, most of them founded by the Viking invaders. The Normans, who succeeded to the government of England in the eleventh century, were themselves descended from another branch of the Norse race who had settled in Normandy about the time they were invading England.

Among the many thousands of villages founded by the Saxons, very many of them end in terminations such as -sted, -ton (tun), -wich, -ham, all of which mean village or farm. Then there are the places ending in -ing, which derives from the Saxon Ingas, of which Hastings and Reading are typical. This group is derived from the name of the tribe which settled there, as it were the Hast people, the Read people. Most of the villages ending in -worth derived from the Saxon word "worp" meaning enclosure. Those ending in -bury are derived from the Saxon "byrig," meaning a fortified place.

Often the subsequent history of a

KENNINGHALL, SUFFOLK

This quiet Suffolk village, grouped about the four wide cross-roads, is a typical centre of rural life in one of the most agricultural of the English counties. The architecture of its cottages is pleasant rather than distinguished. Deserted though it appears to be in spite of the bright summer sunshine, its name proves it once to have been a place of great importance. Kenninghall (which is a shortened form of Kenningham Hall), means the ham or settlement of Kena's peoples, in other words, a tribal capital, like Hastings in Sussex, which takes its name from the people called the Haestingas.

PEMBROKESHIRE COAST

Some of the most magnificent cliff scenery in Britain makes the coast of Pembrokeshire an inspired choice for a National Park. In this photograph Lydstep Point is reminiscent of Cornwall's more famous Land's End. The cliffs have been battered by sea and weather into fantastic pinnacles and rugged headlands. The base of the cliffs is undermined and many large caves have been formed, their floors sloping upward into the cliff face so that, though the mouth of the cave is submerged at high water, the sandy floor of the interior is never reached by the highest tides.

place can be inferred from changes in its name. The Normans and their successors delighted in attaching to an earlier place name their own family name. This gives rise to names like Yardley Hastings, or Higham Gobion, and some with a much more Norman-French sound, particularly in Essex, such as Layer de la Haye, Layer Marney, Tolleshunt d'Arcy, and so on. In a good many cases the Normans renamed their places and to them we owe names such as Belvoir, Beaulieu, and a large number of places in many parts of the country which begin with beau or bel, including Beachy Head. Ekwall records that there was often a good reason for the change, as when the village in Essex which the Saxons called Fulanpettae (foul pit) was changed by the Normans to Beaumont (beautiful hill).

Other place names recall a great change which has overtaken the landscape in the course of a thousand years. Even after the Saxon clearance of many

ANTRIM HOMESTEAD

The mountains of Antrim rise nearly two thousand feet above sea-level and slope gradually down to the coast of the North Channel. Here in the extreme north-east of Ireland the land is fairly rich and mixed farming is the rule.

of the river valleys, great forests covered wide tracts of land which are now fertile and well tilled. Two of these great forests were the Wealden forest, or Forest of Anderida, which covered most of the Weald of Kent and Sussex and part of Surrey, and the Forest of Weltham, which covered much of southern Essex, from the valley of the Lea almost as far as the coast. Gradually clearings came to be made in these forests, and these were given distinctive names. In Kent and Sussex it was a den or dene. All the denes were originally clearings in the forest where swine were kept and the swineherds held the right to drive their herds into the forest to feed off acorns in the autumn. These clearings have become towns of today such as Tenterden, Biddenden, Horsmonden and High Halden. In Essex the clearings or enclosures are called leighs, which meant originally a meadow and explains the number of Essex place names ending in "leigh."

With the Norman occupation, the last of the great invasions was over and the last of the important racial influences which made the British people what it is. After that there were many fresh strains introduced, but always in the way of peace and always forming only a small admixture in the whole. In general, the British people in the twelfth century appear to have been racially much the same as they are today, predominantly Anglo-Saxon or Norse in the east and central districts, with these racial strains superimposed on and having absorbed many earlier peoples, but predominantly Celtic or derived from sources earlier than the Saxon in Wales, in Cornwall, and in Scotland, except near the east coast.

The peoples who since the twelfth century have contributed to the racial heritage of Britain have been mainly refugees from more warlike and less tolerant countries of Europe. Some of them, like the Flemings, contributed to the wealth of the country by adding to Britain a heritage of skilled crafts, in that case the crafts of the weaving industry. Others, like the Huguenots, have brought with them some of the culture and civilization which are regarded as peculiarly French. Others again, like the Jews coming from many countries of Europe, but especially from Germany, have not been absorbed into the population as readily as many of the peoples who came earlier to seek the hospitality of Britain. Though the Jewish pride of race has tended to keep

IN A SCOTTISH PORT

A great ocean-going liner enters the port of Glasgow, towed by powerful tugs. This is a scene which is repeated many times a day at all the great ports of Britain, as the big ships come in from the seven seas bringing goods from all the continents in exchange for British manufactures. In normal times, Britain has the largest mercantile fleet in the world; the seafaring traditions have brought added wealth to her people. London, Liverpool, Southampton, Belfast and Glasgow are still among the busiest ports of the Western hemisphere.

Jews of all nationalities as a nation within a nation, yet they, too, have contributed in full measure to the artistic as well as the racial heritage of modern Britain.

Such are the factors in terms of population which have made Britain what it is, the raw materials, as it were, from which the whole structure is built. But as was said earlier, a country is moulded not only by the people who make it their home, but by the heritage of Nature, which includes the richness of the soil, the varying nature of the landscape and, above all in Britain, the fact of being an island. For of all the factors belonging to the natural heritage, the sea is the one to which Britain owes the greatest debt.

INFLUENCE OF THE SEA

A ship first appeared on the British coinage during the reign of Edward III, on his gold noble; six hundred years later there is again a ship on the money of everyday use—on the halfpenny of today. Almost without their being aware of it, ships and the sea are inextricably woven into the pattern of British lives; phrases and metaphors of the sea have crept into the everyday speech of even those who live in smoky industrial towns. They complain that there "isn't room to swing a cat," or say that it was "touch and go," quite unconscious that they are using expressions once confined to sailors; while few schoolboys or cricketers know that their gaudy coat gets it name from the boats' crews of H.M.S. *Blazer*. There is no escaping the influence of the sea, which is not surprising in an island where no one lives more than eighty miles from it.

Although the British themselves may not be seafarers, the sailor holds first place in their affections; is it only because the blue collar and bell-bottomed trousers are an attractive rig? It is more probable that they are an embodiment of vague longings to be wearing them themselves. As if to gratify this longing, the average Briton makes for the sea on his annual holiday. Why to the sea, where he exists in crowded discomfort and is most probably seasick on a trip round the bay in the *Skylark*? But every year he answers the call to something he feels is his. Many factors have helped towards framing this state of mind, and the most important is that Great Britain is a small island. That sheet of water, now grey and threatening, now sparkling and benign, seen from a seaside lodging-house window has made men what they are—and to it they owe the national character, the course of history, even their very institutions.

Providence was kind when it placed the British Isles just off the north-western corner of Europe where they catch the effect of the Gulf Stream. The result is a temperate climate, not a continental one of fierce extremes. Rivers and harbours are open all the year round; yet on the other side of the Atlantic, Labrador, which is the same distance from the Equator as Britain, is under ice and snow for six months of the year. It is a thinly populated area of almost virgin forest.

RACE OF SKILLED FISHERMEN

The Continent of Europe is built upon a ledge that plunges suddenly down into the immense depth of the Atlantic Ocean just off the coasts of Spain and Portugal in the south, and off Norway in the north. But the British Isles nowhere quite overlook these deeps; they are placed instead upon a shelf where the surrounding water is comparatively shallow—seldom over a hundred fathoms in depth. The enormous advantage of this is that these waters teem with different kinds of fish.

And if that were not blessing enough,

UNLOADING HERRING AT GREAT YARMOUTH

The catch is landed and packed into wicker baskets or crans. Most of the fish are sent by rail for distribution in the large towns of Britain. The remainder is kept back for curing on the spot. By a process of smoking and drying, kippers are produced. Some of the herring ports have their own traditional method of curing; for instance, Yarmouth bloaters have a more than national fame. Much of the handling and curing of the fish is done by teams of Scottish girl workers who move on from town to town as the herring shoals come south.

31

some five hundred years ago, for reasons known only to itself, the herring which had until then lived in the Baltic, suddenly changed its habitat to the North Sea. In the Middle Ages salted herring was a staple article of diet in Northern and Central Europe; it was the only food which would keep in those days before preservatives and refrigeration. The powerful confederation of Baltic towns—the Hanseatic League, Hamburg, Lübeck, Rostock, Reval—had built up their prosperity largely on the herring industry, and English boats were forbidden the Baltic. This change in the habits of the herring marked the beginning of the gradual decline of the Hansa and the rise of Grimsby, Lowestoft and Aberdeen, whose drifters throng the Dogger Bank and "Broad Fourteens" to bring in those silvery cascades of fish. So the British people includes a race of skilled fishermen, and fishermen make valuable reserves of seamen for war, as Queen Elizabeth realized when she instituted two fish days a week—Wednesdays as well as Fridays, not out of religious scruples, but to encourage fishing.

SHELTERED HARBOURS

Britain is lucky, too, in possessing a coast-line whose many gulfs and tidal estuaries make sheltered harbours with deep water; the Firth of Clyde and Glasgow; the Mersey and Liverpool; the Bristol Channel and Bristol; Plymouth and the Tamar; Portsmouth and Southampton sheltered by the Isle of Wight. And note how they all face the Atlantic Ocean, one of the great highways of the world. Equally important is what lies behind those ports, rich agricultural land and good grazing country. Great oak trees to build the ships grew all over England, but they were used so fast that Admiral Collingwood began to fear for the future of the British Navy.

Whenever he went on a country walk, he always took a pocketful of acorns, planting them on the way so that the Navy after him should not lack good English oak. But long before his acorns had grown into trees, the need for oak had disappeared; wood had given way to iron, and sail to steam. Yet when the need for it came, there at hand under those glistening furrows, along those quiet green valleys, were iron and coal to build the ships, and the finest steam coal in the world to drive them.

STRATEGIC POSITION

Cargo boats from Britain penetrated into every sea in the world, and in the shipping clustered at whatever port there were always more Red Ensigns than any other flag. These natural advantages all helped to mould British history, but the strategic position on the map had an even greater effect.

The British Isles block the way to Northern Europe from the wide oceans of the world. A ship on its way to the Baltic, to the rich Low Countries, to Germany or Denmark, had to sail for miles up a narrow channel in sight all the way of that annoying island with its bulwark of white cliffs. The ship could have gone round the north of the Orkneys, but the gales and bad weather to be expected up there, particularly in the days of sail and clumsy ships, practically barred this entrance to the North Sea. The timber, hides and tallow flowing out of the Baltic, the rich argosies of spices, silks and products of the East pouring into Antwerp, all had to pass under the very noses of the British who sat like guardians at the gate. This trade could pass only as long as Britain did not object.

While the Portuguese were feeling their way round Africa into the Indian Ocean, and Columbus was discovering the New World for Spain, England was a minor power too poor to afford expensive state-financed expeditions. An agricultural country with a small population, she might have drowsed on as a small unconsidered island, if she had not been weaving far more woollen cloth than she could absorb herself, or find markets for across the narrow seas. Long trains of packhorses laden with woolsacks or bales of cloth meandered through the length and breadth of the land, "like shuttles for ever moving," wrote G. M. Trevelyan, "across the warp and woof of English life drawing distant regions and classes together in a solid national texture."

EXPANSION OF TRADE

Britain could produce the cloth, but where to sell it—that was the question. The Baltic was closed by the Hansa monopoly, the Netherlands had imposed a heavy duty, while Spain and Portugal kept their new discoveries for their own trade. So an attempt was made to find a way to China round the north of Europe. In 1553 three tiny ships set out into the gales and cold of the Arctic. One of them, the *Bonaventure*, tossed like a cork in the very waters through which Arctic convoys battled so often in the Second World War, reached Archangel. Her noble captain, Richard Chancellor, travelled by sledge to Moscow and the Court of Ivan the Terrible, and the first British trade with Russia was started. But still markets were needed, and now men's thought turned to those dazzling new discoveries. Why be content with adjacent markets for cloth? The trade routes of the world had shifted from the landlocked Mediterranean to the wide oceans and here was England in an ideal position facing the Atlantic. Beyond the line of the horizon lay rich markets. "Our chief desire," wrote Hakluyt, one of the propagandists of the day, "is to find

out ample vent of our woollen cloth, the naturall commoditie of this our Realme." What matter if Spain and Portugal barred the way to these halcyon seas and the bazaars of the East? The need had arisen—the men and ships were at once forthcoming.

MASTERY OF THE SEAS

More compelling even than the hope of profit was—a state of mind. There was a wistful urge among Elizabethans to find out what lay on the far side of that ever receding horizon, the unknown was a challenge to be taken up. And this curiosity worked like a ferment in the minds of Englishmen until it drove them out of their sheltered island to find, some fame, a few fortune, but the greater number, lonely deaths in strange seas. "There is no land unhabitable, nor sea unnavigable," said Robert Thorne of Bristol, crystallizing into one sentence the heroic temper of the age. While the Spanish and Portuguese seamen were sailing in pleasant tropical seas Britons were learning their seamanship among the gales and hardships of the north in search of a north-west passage to China and Japan. Ships were built to sail these waters, staunch, handy ships that could go anywhere. The pure ship of war was evolved, as opposed to the armed merchantmen, a ship built for speed and manœuvre, armed on the broadside with the new heavy gun. Led by men of the quality of Drake and Hawkins, Frobisher and Grenville, this small country of five million inhabitants all told set out to dispute the mastery of the seas with Spain, one of the mightiest empires the world had yet seen. Francis Drake, eldest of the twelve sons of a poor West Country preacher, attacked the enemy Spain, thousands of miles from the British coast out in the Caribbean, or even on the coast of Spain.

For all their tough common sense,

Elizabethan seamen were romantic at heart. Among their dreams—and they had many—were two which recurred with more persistence than any others, command of the sea and an overseas empire. By coupling the two they showed their practical wisdom, for neither is attainable without the other. By dreaming of them at all, they displayed the courage of visionaries, for in their day Spanish power at sea was stronger after the Armada than before it, while their only attempts at founding

TRIBUTE TO A GREAT SAILOR

Nelson's Column in Trafalgar Square is a memorial to England's greatest sailor. The column took twenty-seven years to build and was completed in 1867. It is a copy of a Corinthian column of the temple of Mars at Rome, is 170 feet high, with a statue of Lord Nelson on the summit. The square is named after Nelson's greatest battle at which he lost his life. The photograph shows the view down the Strand looking east, with the church of St. Martin-in-the-Fields in the background on the left of the column.

"Plantations," as they called colonies, were failures. But the ideas were firmly planted in British minds, and if at that time they were only seeds, it was from them that British supremacy finally grew.

The British Empire, which grew out of that Elizabethan dream, was founded upon sea power and trade, both invisible, intangible. The ship leaves no furrow upon the sea, trade appears to be no more than rows of figures in ledgers, yet the web which they spin, seemingly so frail and tenuous, is durable and lasting; its resilience makes it unbreakable, which is why the British Empire is unique in history. There have been many empires: Alexander's, as brilliant and short-lived as a shooting star; the Spanish Empire, which flowered like some exotic tropical bloom until its overblown petals fell off one by one; the Ottoman Empire of Suleiman the Magnificent, who held sway from the Crimea almost to the Strait of Gibraltar, from Vienna to Teheran, but of which in a generation only the memory remained; as well as the empires of Napoleon and Hitler. None of these empires lasted and for the same reason. All were built upon conquest. Conquest breeds feuds and smouldering hatreds, whereas trade is a matter of accommodation and mutual benefits.

English ships sailed away from that small island to wherever there was water to float them. They swarmed in the Caribbean, they forced their way into the Indian Ocean and beyond, and all the time they were seeking outlets for trade. "The use of the sea and air," Queen Elizabeth had insisted, "is common to all." The Davis who was off the coast of Greenland looking for the short cut to China when the Armada was in the Channel and who was eventually murdered by Japanese pirates off the Malay Peninsula, was exploring all the

HERITAGE OF THE SEA

In the dockyard of Portsmouth, one of the chief naval ports and dockyards of today, lies H.M.S. "Victory," the flagship of Lord Nelson, once the pride of the British fleet. The "Victory" was the ship on which Nelson met his death at the Battle of Trafalgar, falling mortally wounded on the quarter-deck. Now she is Britain's chief link with the Navy of one hundred and fifty years ago and the symbol of the British sea power which was the means of crushing the threat of invasion from the Continent. Nelson's death was not in vain. The Battle of Trafalgar ended in the complete defeat of the combined navies of Napoleon and his allies, making invasion impossible.

time for trade outlets. The ships took out British cloth until it was known all over the world, until the products of a sleepy little East Anglian village like Worstead gave its name to a commodity which is worn everywhere today. And on their return voyages the holds of these ships were bulging with the products of the East, with spices, and silks, and valuable woods. Settlements were founded across the seas, precarious footholds on the fringes of continents, where ships could obtain provisions and water, or be refitted when necessary.

In other words overseas bases were established until they stretched round the world. Some, like the Cape and Ceylon, were ceded by a defeated enemy; Tangier and Bombay were added as part of a queen's dowry; Singapore was bought at the insistence of Sir Stamford Raffles; while Malta and Fiji

DEEP-SEA FISHERMEN MAKE FOR PORT

Most of Britain's supplies of fresh fish are won from the sea by fleets of steam trawlers and drifters, based on ports such as Aberdeen, Fleetwood, Grimsby or Yarmouth. Their trips often take them far afield into the rich fishing grounds towards Iceland and Scandinavia. In the season they follow the herring shoals southward from Aberdeen to Lowestoft. As the fleets of trawlers approach the land on their return voyage, flights of seagulls, attracted by the smell of fish, hover round and often swoop down on them.

themselves asked to come under the British Crown. However they were obtained, all were strategically well placed; if a sailing ship whose motive power was the wind needed no fuel, she could not remain long at sea without replenishing her fresh water and provisions. Eventually British overseas possessions were spaced round the globe like stepping stones across the oceans and her fleets could keep the seas in any part of the world.

The British people had found, across the sea, an outlet for their boundless energy. In war or peace, workers in the fields of Kent were quite accustomed,

as they came to the end of a furrow, to gaze out at three hundred ships or more, anchored in the Downs waiting for a wind. And the sight of them when they spread their sails and moved off down Channel like so many stately swans, never failed to thrill even the ploughboy. Out in the Atlantic the great concourse split, one section standing on to the West Indies, while the remainder stretched away on their long journey southward round the Cape to India. When Napoleon arose with his dreams of world dominion he found that Britain had built up a huge overseas trade; and it was the trade represented by those ships which enabled Britain to outlast Napoleon and beat him in the end. The goods they carried in their holds proved more powerful than all his land armies with their eagles; for they brought gold and supplies with which to sustain the people and maintain the coalition on the Continent against him. Britain drew freely on the resources of the whole world, he was confined to Europe; and when he tried to break through the entangling web he found British sea power in the way.

Trafalgar was the great climax of all sea battles fought under sail. It was won by a man who was heir to all the traditions and accumulated wealth of experience of a great sea people; a man who was, as Mahan, himself a captain in the United States Navy, put it, the "embodiment of sea power." "The Combined Fleet is defeated, but Nelson is no more," the news flew round London; while the seamen of the *Royal Sovereign*, "who had fought like devils, sat down and cried like wenches," when they heard their admiral had been killed.

From his column in the very heart of the Empire's capital, Nelson looks down today on a street of offices devoted to shipping companies—concerns which were founded and thrived because of the freedom of the seas he brought them; while on either side his column is flanked by the buildings of Canada and South Africa, great dominions whose main link with Britain is the sea.

The sea has made Great Britain what it is and it is impossible to escape its influence. There is scarcely a home or a household in the land which has not some connexion with the sea—a son or relative who served or is still serving afloat, relations who live beyond the sea in one or other of the Dominions. And even if no such link exists, then the individual has only to eat a meal or to finger the clothes he wears to realize

that he, too, has a close connexion with the sea—his existence.

The sea has given much; but its gifts have not been abused. By the use made of the sea the British were able to spread their ideas of law and freedom round the earth. All that has been achieved in the course of centuries has been due to predominance as an ocean power. But, in the solemn words of Froude, "Take

INSHORE FISHERMAN

Side by side with the modern fishing fleets of trawlers and drifters, the village fishermen of England still ply their craft. This stalwart boatman of Lulworth Cove, Dorset, is one of the tens of thousands who have been born and bred to the sea in the quiet fishing villages on every coast of Britain. Fishing remains their chief livelihood, though the fashion for seaside holidays in remote places has brought a welcome addition to their incomes by hiring out their boats to holiday-makers. Even in populous towns like Hastings or Scarborough there is usually to be found today a fishing community which hands down its skill from generation to generation.

CORNISH FISHING VILLAGE

*This is one of the quiet fishing villages which abound along the much-indented
coast-line of South Devon and Cornwall. It is picturesque in position and design
alike, well grouped about the tall-towered church, its harbour almost landlocked and protected from the westerly gales. A port and fishing town from
time immemorial, Fowey has in recent times become a popular summer
holiday resort and yachting centre, though its fishing industry remains active.*

away her merchant fleets, take away the
Navy that guards them; her Empire
will come to an end; her Colonies and
Dominions will fall like leaves from a
withered tree; and Britain will become
once more an insignificant little island
in the North Sea."

It is not only the national heritage
that owes so much to the sea. Again and
again events have proved that local
prosperity is built up on the bounty of
the sea—equally that prosperity once
established is at the mercy of the sea's
caprice. There are many sleepy villages
on the south and east coasts which were
once flourishing seaports. Rye and
Winchelsea have been left high and dry
miles from the sea, which once washed
their waterfronts. Their ports have been
closed, that of Winchelsea long ago, that
of Rye only recently when it proved no

longer economic to keep open the
channel of the Rother. Aldeburgh and
Dunwich were flourishing ports in the
Middle Ages. Today their harbours are
no more. The town hall of Aldeburgh,
which was the centre of the medieval
town, now overlooks the sea on the
modern promenade. The whole town of
Dunwich like many others has gone
"down cliff." The sea has washed away
the very cliffs on which the town was
built.

If the herring brought unexpected and
almost overwhelming prosperity to the
east-coast fishing towns, the pilchard,
which is the other traditional fish of
British waters, has provided compensation by its capricious treatment of the
south-western peninsula. A hundred
years ago the many fishing villages of
Devon and Cornwall were quietly

prosperous and their prosperity depended almost entirely upon the pilchard, whose shoals came inshore regularly and provided an easy and profitable catch. In fact, at one time the value of the pilchard fishing industry was greater than that of the herring.

Then mysteriously and for a reason which is even now not fully known, the pilchard virtually disappeared. Soon after the turn of the century, Cornish fishing boats began to come home with catches so small that the standard of living of the fishing families was threatened and the prosperity of the Duchy began to decline.

Cornish people have always been resilient, and it is fortunate, indeed, that they have in their land a heritage of natural beauty, particularly in the coastline, surpassed by no other coast of Britain. Cornwall—and Devon, too—seem marked out by providence to be the resort of holiday makers, seeking quietness and rest by the sea in surroundings of great natural beauty. And

so it turned out. As the annual holiday habit grew, due partly to easier travel and partly to increased wages in the factories, the former quiet of south- and east-coast towns was shattered. Devon and Cornwall came into their own and much of their twentieth-century prosperity has been due to the service they give to holiday makers.

In south-Cornish fishing villages, between the two wars, almost every cottage and house took guests, so that it mattered less that the income of the villagers derived from the fishing was so sadly diminished. More recently the pilchard has begun to revert to its old haunts and some notable catches have been landed at Looe, Fowey and Mevagissey, to name only three of the scores of Celtic villages which once derived a fine living from the pilchard fisheries.

There are compensations for almost every calamity, and not a few Cornish families feel grateful to the strange caprice of the pilchard. If it had been otherwise they feel some of the charming

IN THE OUTER HEBRIDES

Looking from Carnish across the Red River where it meets the sheen-white sands of Uig Bay in western Lewis, Outer Hebrides, the little sheep farm of Ardroil can be seen in the distance. In the background is Suainabhal.

little villages would have become bustling towns like Yarmouth and Lowestoft. As it is, only Penzance of all the places which lie to the west of Plymouth has grown into a town which might reasonably be called industrial. Certainly this one instance bids fair to take from Mousehole and Marazion, two neighbouring villages, much of the charm which made them world famous. Already they are virtually suburbs of a commercial town.

The sea, then, is the most important part of Britain's natural heritage, or at least, that part of it which has changed most dramatically the course of Britain's history. But the sea alone is not enough to make a nation great. The land also must be capable of producing food for a vigorous population. And, indeed, Nature has smiled on British people in the provision of land sufficiently tractable to produce in modern times a harvest not large enough to feed the fifty million or so people who are crowded into the narrow confines of Britain, but at least enough to restrict the import of foodstuffs to a reasonable figure.

After the Industrial Revolution, when Britain's wealth seemed assured and the country was referred to as the workshop of the world, there was a great drift from the land, agriculture became undermanned. There was little encouragement

BILSDALE, YORKSHIRE

Sheep farming is the chief interest of the Yorkshire dales since the limestone soil produces fine pastures. Though not one of the most famous of the dales, Bilsdale is beautiful and distinctive: from its southern end near Rievaulx this mountain valley of the North Riding runs for nearly ten miles into the north Yorkshire moors to its head some five miles south-east of Stokesley.

to the farmers and more and more fields which had been ploughed from time immemorial were turned into pasture-land or even allowed to deteriorate so that they would produce nothing.

With the help of its factories and its overseas investments Britain could import anything it chose from the whole world and by the beginning of the twentieth century the shops were full of foodstuffs, necessary and unnecessary, brought from every corner of the civilized world. It required two world wars to reawaken the British people to the importance of agriculture, which remains even now the most important industry of the country not excepting coal mining. The dissipation of overseas investments on the defence of freedom, with growing competition from other "workshops of the world," and the emergence of the U.S.A. and Russia first as self-sufficient and then as exporting countries, combined to threaten the standard of living of the British people. So the spotlight was once more turned on agriculture and millions of acres of land were brought again under the plough. Under the guidance of War Agricultural Committees ditches were dug, the land drained and enriched, the traditional acreage under corn crops and roots was increased, and the newest crop of all, the sugar beet, spread out from its first home in East Anglia into the Midlands.

It is a combination of soil and climate which determines the productivity of

MEDIEVAL ESSEX VILLAGE

An ancient village of Essex, in which numerous medieval cottages are still to be seen and black-timbered thatched barns of the farmsteads are cheek by jowl with the village homes, Blackmore is a centre of one of the most fertile districts of the Home Counties. The whitewashed walls are in keeping with the Essex tradition. Beneath their coat of whitewash many of the smaller houses are timber built. Nearby is Jericho House, where Henry VIII was wont to take refuge from the cares of kingship, a fact from which is derived the familiar expression "Go to Jericho."

HAMPSHIRE FARMSTEAD

All over southern England there are innumerable farmsteads such as this—a modern unpretentious farm-house replacing a medieval house that has fallen beyond repair, old thatched or timbered barns and a granary raised on stone supports to prevent damage from damp or by rats. Most of these farms, on an average about two hundred acres in size, depend on mixed farming for their living with some ploughed fields producing corn crops and winter feed for the cattle which graze over the home pastures.

the land. Especially is this true in Great Britain, where one component of climate, rainfall, varies enormously from one side of the island to the other. In the south-eastern half of England there are numerous places where the rainfall is less than twenty-five inches a year, while in the north-west there are a few stations which record an average of more than a hundred and fifty inches a year. Generally rainfall decreases from west to east, for the rain comes with the

prevailing mild south-westerly winds, which are forced upwards by the mountains and hills of the north and west and precipitate much of their moisture before coming down on the plains of Scotland and central and eastern England.

Again, in the west, summers are cooler and the winters milder than they are in the east. It is ironic that the hardest frosts and some of the longest periods of cold weather occur in the south-eastern corner of England nearly eight hundred miles nearer the Equator than the extreme north-west of Scotland, where in the Hebrides frost is rare and snow seldom lies. Similarly, most of the periods of great and prolonged heat occur south of a line from the Humber to the Severn and this, too, has a great influence on the ripening of crops. We shall see in the following pages how these climatic factors affect the pattern of British farming.

In general, the heritage of the soil is good rather than outstanding. The richest soil of all is probably that reclaimed from the sea in fenland districts; there is rich land, too, in the valleys which lie between the many ranges of low hills in southern England, including the chalk of the North and South Downs and of Salisbury Plain, the old red sandstone of Devonshire, the sandstone hills of Surrey, and the limestone of the Cotswolds. The whole of the Midland Plain, watered by several great rivers, is fertile, as is the Vale of York and the lowland plain of central Scotland.

MOORLAND AND FOREST

It has already been said that the highland country of the north and west of Britain does not lend itself to the plough. To the definitely mountainous country must be added the moorlands of the Pennine Chain, which stretches down the centre of England from the Border Country and the outliers of the Lake District to the Derbyshire Peaks. There is, too, the barren country of parts of Northumberland, the north-Yorkshire moors, and scattered fragments of heather country and bracken-covered common in many parts of the Midlands and the south. Names such as Ashdown Forest, Leith Hill, Blackdown, and, farther north, Charnwood Forest, are all linked with some of the finest features of Britain's scenic heritage. But in all of them, as in so many other parts of the world, scenic beauty is not linked with fertility. Together with their surrounding country they are exceptions to the general rule of good farming country which predominates outside the mountainous areas.

For the rest, the low rainfall and hot summers of the east favour the cultivation of corn crops. The higher rainfall and the cooler summers of the west are more favourable to cattle breeding. And, indeed, there has been this distinction between the two phases of English agriculture through the ages, the east always being the traditional granary of the country, the west being the area of its cattle lands.

MIXED FARMING

Ever since the break-up of the feudal system there has been a tendency to mixed farming without that specialization which distinguishes the great ranches and farms of the New World. This is a method of agriculture peculiarly suited to a land of small farms, though it must be remembered that there has never been in Britain a race of yeoman peasants as there has been in France. In Wales and Scotland many of the farms are very small and the standard of living of the farmers relatively low. But in England the average size of the modern farm is from a hundred and fifty to four hundred acres, with the result that, for all their traditional grumbles, the farming community has been a prosperous one, whether the farmers are, as in some parts of the country, predominantly freeholders, or whether, as in the country of the great estates, they are tenant farmers.

It surprises many visitors to Britain to find pasture fields among the East Anglian corn farms, and cornfields amid the green pastures of the West Country, yet so it is and so it always has

44

COUNTRY LANE IN LONDONDERRY

This roadside farm-worker's cottage is near Downhill, about seven miles north-west of Coleraine in County Londonderry, Northern Ireland. Dwellings of this type have been made from time immemorial: the walls of stone which have been lime-washed, and roof of thatch, are of materials available locally, but the brick-built chimney is a later addition, solving the medieval difficulty of heating the dwelling without risk of fire spreading to the thatched roof.

been. In East Anglia most of the fields grow wheat, oats and barley, with the accent on wheat, and clover and root crops, in a three- or four-year rotation. But many farms in this area also have their dairy herd, their pigs, their chickens, and in Norfolk, their turkeys. In the west cattle graze over the middle slopes of the hills and there are dairy herds in the valleys, but on the lower slopes away from the lush meadow-lands, yet under the shelter of the hill-sides, are fields of oats and barley. In Scotland oats is the traditional corn crop, for in general oats can withstand a moister climate than wheat and requires less heat for ripening.

It is all very much the same as when the Saxon settlements in the valleys had developed and the feudal system was being evolved. Then there was common pasture-land near the river and culti-vated strips on the ground above the flood level, with rough grazing on the higher ground. The whole of agriculture was centred round the manor-house, with its church and growing cluster of labourers' cottages. So it is now with only slight variation. The manor-house has become a farm-house, but the farmer has inherited much of the influence of the medieval lord of the manor. Village life is still effectively centred on the farm and the church.

Sheep rearing is one of the great traditional features of British agriculture. It is one in which the heritage of the past has greatly influenced modern

was the spate of noble churches built during the fourteenth and fifteenth centuries in the Perpendicular style of Gothic architecture, each with a tower which vied with the tower of its neighbour, towers which are still landmarks for miles around, from Cirencester and Northleach in Gloucestershire to Tenterden in Kent, Thaxted in Essex, and Lavenham in Suffolk.

Gradually the woollen industry lost some of its prosperity though it never entirely died, but the sheep remained as a permanent feature of agriculture. Right through the later Middle Ages there were famous sheep-walks over the

MILL STREET, WARWICK

A large number of houses and cottages dating from the sixteenth and seventeenth centuries make Warwick one of the most picturesque old towns of England. It is a place which grew up round the medieval castle, which has been rebuilt again and again and is still inhabited. Warwick lies between the belt of stone-built houses which belongs to the Cotswold country and the fantastic timber framing of Shropshire and Herefordshire.

EAST ANGLIAN PARGE WORK

Parge work, or pargetting, is one of the traditional forms of decorating the dwelling house, especially in East Anglia and Essex. Starting in the Middle Ages the craft developed until by the latter part of the seventeenth century houses were being decorated with elaborate designs. This specimen from the White House, White Colne, Essex, is dated 1685.

practice. Edward III was the first king to encourage the woollen industry and foster the rearing of sheep in southern England in large quantities. There followed an era of unprecedented prosperity, to which the sheep-walks were the key. All over the Cotswold country, in East Anglia, and in Kent particularly, sheep rearing and the allied home industry of weaving brought great prosperity to the farms and many small towns which grew up and thrived on the resulting trade. One still-present result

HISTORIC ARCHITECTURE OF SCOTLAND

Culross, Fifeshire, contains a number of old buildings recalling many periods in Scottish history. In this picture is the mercat or market cross on the left, dating from 1558. On the right is a house called the Study, an early seventeenth-century building which illustrates well the national characteristics Scottish architects grafted on to Jacobean buildings. Between them is the tower of Tolbooth, also dating from the seventeenth century.

North and South Downs, in the Salisbury Plain area, and in the Midland counties, in addition to the areas already mentioned. It was found, too, that sheep were very hardy and could withstand rigorous climates and find sustenance in country which previously had been considered as useless for agriculture. So the rough pastures of the higher Pennines, of the mountains of Wales, and even the highlands of Scotland began to be grazed over by specially developed breeds which experience showed were most suited to those unfavourable conditions.

British sheep have proved the finest wool and meat producers in the world. Some breeds, like the Southdown, have penetrated to the farthest corners of the globe and have provided the stock from which many of the millions of head of sheep in the pastures of Australia and New Zealand are derived.

One interesting effect on the scenery was the close-cropping of all the upland pastures and the resultant springy turf like that of the South Downs, which, but for the sheep, would never have reached its present perfection. Again experience has shown that when the sheep are withdrawn, as they have been in parts of Salisbury Plain to make

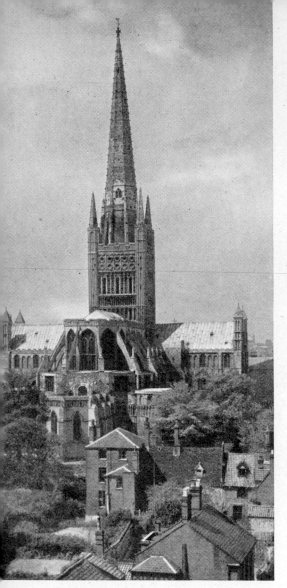

NORWICH CATHEDRAL

Dominating the old quarter of the city, Norwich Cathedral, here photographed from the tower of St. Helen's Hospital, is a fine mixture of Norman and Gothic architecture. In the chancel, nearest the camera, and in the transepts are round-headed windows which are a characteristic feature of Norman workmanship. The present spire was erected in the fifteenth century.

way for military training grounds, the close-cropped springy turf soon reverts to rank grasslands of an entirely different character. That is one more instance of how methods of agriculture change recognized and well-established features of the landscape.

Granted that Britain's modern way of life is derived chiefly from the heritage of the sea and the heritage of the land, there is one other factor which has had a scarcely smaller effect, the mineral heritage of the country. It is the coal measures of Scotland, the Midlands and South Wales which have proved the basis on which the modern industrial complex has been built. Without coal, Britain's Industrial Revolution would have been impossible. Its working produced the first large-scale shift in population, from the old towns to new centres near the coalfields, and from the country to the towns. Along with it the mining of ironstone, especially from the range of hills that extends from the Cotswolds to Lincolnshire and runs quite close to the coal measures, changed the face of the Midlands out of all recognition. The Black Country is the result, a result which lovers of beauty may well deplore, but which nevertheless represents a milestone in British prosperity and the means of sustaining a population in Britain out of all proportion to the size of the island.

It has been noted previously that the elaborate fourteenth- and fifteenth-century churches reflect the cultural and economic circumstances of the age in which they were built. The same is true of the forms of architecture through the ages. Of all the arts, architecture in Britain reflects most faithfully the varying fortunes of the country and the varied cultural influences which have contributed to modern Britain.

To many, architecture appears as the supreme part of the British heritage and, indeed, Britain is one of the few great civilized countries of the world with an architectural heritage complete enough even now to allow comparisons between one period and another and to permit of a reconstruction of the functional artistic character of buildings from the very earliest times.

The first "architects" in Britain were the citizens of the country at the end of the New Stone Age, two thousand years B.C., and perhaps longer ago than that. Theirs was by modern standards a rude architecture. It has come down to us by the name of Megalithic (from the Greek words meaning "big" and "stone") because all these earliest essays in architecture were built up from great slabs of stone, part of a crust of sandstone overlaid in prehistoric times on the downland plateaux. Many of these vast monoliths are still undisturbed on the ground. They are the "grey wethers" of the south-western highlands and of the Salisbury Plain area, so called because at a distance they are easily mistaken for sheep.

Stone Age man took these vast stones, shaped and tooled them, and set them up in the form of temples, like Stonehenge, or made from them burial chambers for their chieftains, afterwards

EXETER CATHEDRAL, THE NAVE

One of the few large churches in Britain which is built in the Decorated style of Gothic, Exeter Cathedral is famous for the beauty of its interior and of its outer fabric alike, for it is built of Devon's own building stone, the old red sandstone, which has mellowed with age to a lovely dark red-brown. This view of the nave, looking east to the screen and organ loft, with the vaulted roof of the choir behind, illustrates well the magnificence of its architecture. The stone screen was built by the fourteenth-century Bishop Stapledon.

covering these chambers with earth in the shape of the traditional Long Barrow.

That several of these primitive structures, in however ruinous a condition, should have survived the ravages of four thousand years is remarkable enough. There would have been many more of them but for the fact that the stone monuments and temples were an easy source of road-building materials in the later Middle Ages. It was left to unconscious vandals rather than time to destroy the handiwork of those faraway ancestors of the British people.

The story of architecture proper begins with the Roman occupation of Britain and the growth of the Roman province called Britannia. The buildings which the Romano-British people put up reflected truly the wealth of culture which gave birth to a tradition of fine craftsmanship carried down through the ages and broken only for a time by the inroads of the Saxon invaders.

The heritage which then came to Britain in the first century A.D. was not solely the product of Rome itself. It embraces the cultural achievements of all the peoples who had been enveloped in the Roman Empire. In architecture this meant the Greek and Egyptian traditions, which by the time the Romans came to Britain had been grafted on to the native Roman workmanship.

In a sense, Roman building of later times is more Greek than Roman. The buildings which have been reconstructed from Roman Britain show, for instance, the grace of the Greek orders of columns, the Doric, the Ionic and the Corinthian,

SHEEP-WALKS OF THE SUSSEX DOWNS

The close-cropped grass of the South Downs is grazed over by tens of thousands of sheep. The Sussex sheep-walks have produced a breed of sheep, the South-down, which has become famous in Australia and New Zealand as much as in its native Britain. This view shows one of the long "whale-backed" ridges above Alfriston where the skyline is unbroken for miles on end and trees are confined to the lowest slopes and the valley of the River Cuckmere.

MOATED MANOR-HOUSE

In eastern England many of the older farm-houses and manor-houses like this fine half-timbered hall near Ongar in Essex retain their medieval moats at any rate in part. The moat was an essential factor in the defences of medieval castles; in later manor-houses it was partly for defence but more particularly for show to retain the appearance of the magnificent early castles. The lord of the manor of feudal days has become the farmer of today; many of the Tudor and Elizabethan manor-houses have become the farm-houses of the twentieth century, while the freeholder or tenant-occupier combines the work of active farming with many of the traditional functions of the squire.

though they also include masonry of immense passive strength. And this— the construction of masonry designed to withstand attack and siege—was something which the Romans themselves perfected and which owes little to Greek influence.

On the one hand, there are the walls of Verulamium, of Colchester, of London, and, above all, the vast fortification which is called Hadrian's Wall, and which extended from the Tyne to the Solway Firth. These are all examples of the vast passive strength of Roman architecture. Their purpose was a utilitarian one; whatever beauty they have is only incidental. To that list may be added the fourth-century castles of the south-east coast, which were built by the Count of the Saxon Shore when Saxon invasions were imminent. There is nothing in Europe stronger in defence than the fortifications of Anderida, the Pevensey of today.

In a country which was only an outlying province of the Roman Empire, one might expect that the triumphs of military architecture would be the sum total of the heritage, but that is far from the truth. There is subtlety and beauty in many of the remains of Roman villas which time has spared. There is for instance the Roman villa at Chedworth, Gloucestershire, buried for centuries beneath a landslide and still complete enough for a picture to be built up of the comparative luxury and the charming surroundings in which prosperous British citizens lived in those times. Tessellated pavements which formed the floors of the main living-rooms are decorated with scenes partly drawn from mythology and partly the product of pure imagination. The design and colouring alike are of the highest order. They speak more vividly than anything else of the high standard of art which is such an important part of the national heritage.

There is beauty, too, in the remains of the Roman baths at Bath, and the promise of lovely architecture in the fragment of the Roman theatre at Verulamium. The excavations which have been carried out on the site of the town of Silchester suggest beauty as well as utility. Authentic reconstructions show temples, public buildings and private dwelling places, all built with an eye to aesthetic values as well as to everyday use.

The splendour of Roman Britain fades in retrospect into the grim, unhappy bloody period which heralded the advent of Anglo-Saxon civilization. When next the British people started building on the grand scale hundreds of years had passed, and the Roman Empire had broken up. Even so, traditions of architecture on which

ANCIENT WESTERN CITY

The city of Bath lies on both banks of the Somerset Avon. Successively Roman city, Saxon burgh and medieval town centred about its abbey, it retains much of the spirit and appearance of its long and illustrious history. Its many Georgian streets and terraces rise in tiers towards the surrounding hills. This photograph shows one of the lesser-known beauties, a stone bridge, one of the few in England which carry buildings still in use today.

NORTHERN INDUSTRIAL TOWN

Preston, Lancashire, has all the qualities of dozens of manufacturing towns in the northern counties. On the fringe of the Lancashire cotton industry, it is an important commercial and market centre and a river port. Its stone-paved roadways, its serried rows of workers' houses rising to the spire and tower of its churches and the tall chimney-stacks of its factories combine to give the effect of a sombre workaday world. But grey though the northern industrial towns may be, they all lie on the verge of green unspoilt country, the Lancashire cotton towns near the western Pennines, the Yorkshire woollen towns clustering on the eastern slopes of the Pennine Chain.

later Saxon and Norman workmanship was based were still derived from Rome and infiltrated into Britain through Norman-French influence. Nothing basically new in architecture had emerged by the tenth and eleventh centuries, and the two styles associated respectively with Saxon and Norman Britain are both rightly called Romanesque, because they were based on the classical principles of Greece and Rome.

Religion inspired the rebirth of building vigour in Britain, as on the Continent. Britain today is richer by virtue of the imaginative genius of the Saxon and Norman churches which were raised to the greater glory of God in an age which was moulded simply by two elements, on the one hand the fervour of

Christian endeavour, on the other the destructive power of war.

The earliest Saxon churches in Britain were of wood. There is still one church, Greenstead-juxta-Ongar, which preserves much of its original wooden nave, for the walls are composed of the split trunks of oak trees. The date of this oaken church cannot be much later than A.D. 900, so that these selfsame walls have seen over a thousand years of continuous use. Why build in stone when wood is so durable? Yet for the most part the Saxons rebuilt their wooden churches in stone, more, it is supposed, as a protection against fire and for the sake of greater dignity than for any other purpose. That single factor marked the new attitude to the

53

arts and civilization. And it is interesting to see how Saxon churches of stone still imitated styles more appropriate to timber buildings. The decorations of many Saxon towers show stone pilasters and horizontal bands in relief. The stone of the fabric is comparatively rough and unmoulded. In some cases the classical semicircular arch defied the Saxon builders and we find instead a pointed arch, as at Holy Trinity, Colchester.

ARCHITECTURAL DEVELOPMENT

Obviously the Saxon builders sought to carry on the tradition of classical columns, but the few supporting columns dating from Saxon times are very unlike the columns of Greek temples. Even later ones dating from the early Norman period like the columns of the nave of St. Albans Abbey deserve the name of column only because they have the traditional capital and base. Otherwise they are barrel-like piers of immense strength and thickness, admirably suited to sustaining the great weight of the roof, but showing little effort to beautify them.

It is fascinating to watch the development of Saxon and Norman architecture and to note the refinements which an increasing consciousness of art brought into the building of the great Norman churches and village churches alike. Yet the themes which ran through all this great period of the architectural heritage remained constant. They are the rounded classical arch and the classical column. Refinement is introduced by moulding such as the lovely chevron moulding of many Norman doorways and arches, and by the sub-division of the arch form into two or more minor semicircular arches, as at Chichester Cathedral, an effect which tends to lighten the whole conception and to take away the feeling of solidity which is typical of early Romanesque building.

In this period, almost all art, including architecture, was an expression of religious spirit. But even in military architecture there was a growing appreciation of the need for beauty in everyday life as is well shown by the form of the Norman castles. All these buildings, from Richmond and Norwich in the north, to the White Tower of the Tower of London and Rochester in the south, fulfilled the first need of their construction—to provide a strong bulwark against attacking forces. Many of them proved incapable of being taken by storm with the weapons which were available in the eleventh and twelfth centuries. Yet some of them are beautiful by any standard of comparison. The main living-room, for instance, of Rochester Castle, set on an upper floor so as to avoid the risk of arrows penetrating the window openings, has a real, even though a substantial and rather bare, classical beauty.

GOTHIC STYLE

The motif running through the architecture of the castles is the same as that revealed in the churches; there is the same rhythm of the repeated arch form and the same regularity of execution which marks all buildings in the classical style.

By the second half of the twelfth century in Britain Romanesque architecture had reached something very near perfection. The churches and abbey ruins of that time bear silent witness to the marvels of artistry of which it was capable. Towards the end of the century a new influence was making itself felt, a mysterious influence which revolutionized the style of building, particularly of the churches and abbeys, but the origin of which no one clearly knows. The new style came to be called Gothic, but this was a term of derision said to have been coined by Sir Christopher

THE TOWER OF LONDON

This photograph, looking downstream, shows the Tower of London in the foreground, a corner of Tower Bridge and a part of the extensive London docks, which form the greatest port in the world. It has been proved that a part of the Tower of London, the Wardrobe Tower, of which a portion still remains, stands on the base of a Roman bastion. The White Tower, seen in the centre of the defences, is one of the Norman castles built to defend the point where Watling Street crossed the River Thames and to act as a protection for the large and growing town of London, which had been a walled city since the Romans first fortified it. The wall round the Tower was built in the reign of William Rufus and it is probable that the moat dates from the time of the erection of the White Tower. The name of the White Tower is derived from the repeated coats of whitewash which were given to it in the Middle Ages. It is the prototype of all early castles in Britain; though it has often been restored, it still retains practically its original appearance. The first Astronomer Royal, who was appointed by Charles II, had his observatory in the round turret at the north-east corner of the White Tower (that on the left in this photograph) before Greenwich was ready for use as the official observatory.

MEDIEVAL MANSION IN KENT

A moated Tudor and Elizabethan grange, Ightham Mote is here seen from an unconventional angle. The splendid timber work of the upper storey contrasts strangely with the stone of the ground floor, here largely covered by creeper but clearly to be seen on the side facing the moat. In a county famous for the number and magnificence of its medieval mansions, Ightham Mote stands out as one of the most beautiful and perfectly preserved. The graceful shape of the stacked chimneys, a feature of all buildings of the sixteenth and seventeenth centuries, is particularly noticeable.

Wren when he referred to it as Gothic, or barbarian, in contrast to the pure ideals of the classical forms of the Romanesque. It was certainly not called Gothic in contemporary times. It was probably not called anything at all. The revolution in building which it represented must have gone almost unnoticed in a gradual development from the Romanesque style.

Previously the height of the roof of a church had been determined by the width of the building, for clearly if a semicircular arch is used, the height of any arch cannot be greater than its width. With the introduction of the pointed arch this limitation was removed. Now the roof of the nave of a church could tower to any height. The result is the magnificent series of Gothic churches which enriched the British

heritage and which comprehend the vast majority of the ecclesiastical buildings through the length and breadth of Britain.

The Gothic style was the predominant one from the end of the twelfth century until the end of the fifteenth century. It was never a rigid style. Through these three centuries it developed just as the Romanesque style of architecture had done before it. Starting from relatively small beginnings in a style which is usually called Transitional, when the only difference from the late Norman was the slight pointing of the arch over doorway or chancel, it developed until its final expression was reached in the great wool churches to which reference has already been made.

In this store of beauty there are three principal divisions, the Early English, the Decorated and the Perpendicular. Any wayfarer in Britain can pick out, almost at a glance, the distinction between these three, which are respectively more or less contemporary with the three centuries which the Gothic style comprehends. Salisbury Cathedral is the supreme example of the Early English style. The west front of Wells is another outstanding triumph of the period. Simplicity and austerity throughout are the keynotes of the design, line rather than ornament is the theme which inspires the whole creation.

The Decorated style was a reaction against the austerity of the Early English. It is represented by the imaginative conceptions of the stone tracery in windows. As its name suggests, decoration took the place of sheer beauty of line. In place of the long, narrow window openings of earlier styles—the lancet windows of Early English churches—there were several lights gathered together in a single composition, and the space above the lights but within the window "arch" was occupied by tracery which ranged from geometric

FIFTEENTH-CENTURY INN

This historic inn is one of the oldest buildings in the cathedral city of Gloucester. The inn's long history begins when it was built by the monks of St. Peter's Abbey to accommodate pilgrims overnight. In 1456 it was rebuilt and renamed the New Inn to distinguish it from the earlier hostelry and has retained that name ever since. In coaching days it was on the route to South Wales and was one of the leading coaching inns of the West Country. The courtyard shows the gallery on to which upper-deck passengers of coaches alighted.

forms to intricate curvilinear designs of very great complexity. It was not in the windows only that decoration ran riot. In every phase of church building the same tendency could be seen. In the font, in the altar, in the roof, and in the great entrance doorways. The lightness which had distinguished work of the Early English period gave place to a more rotund style. While it avoided the austerity of the earlier buildings, it never recaptured the grace of Salisbury Cathedral.

There is no doubt that the third period of Gothic building, the Perpendicular, was a reaction against the extravagance of the Decorated period. Decoration as such in the stonework of the building disappeared, except for gargoyles and other grotesques which in a few churches relieve the plainness of the interior. As the name of the style suggests, all the lines of the church were severely perpendicular. In place of fanciful window tracery, the lights were divided by stone strips which reached from top to bottom of the window opening. The height of the nave of the church became greater. As the window openings were larger, there was more light, but something of the beauty of the original was lost. External buttresses corresponding with the several bays of the nave came into prominence; and the flying buttress is peculiarly characteristic of the period.

Only in the tower and the roof did later Gothic architecture retain the tendency to over-decoration which had marked some of the greatest creations of the previous century. The fifteenth century generally was the era of great British craftsmen in wood and stone. In no other single way was this craftsmanship so admirably realized as in the carving of the elaborate timber roofs which even today grace churches such as Mildenhall and Bury St. Edmunds. In other ways there is a return to something very like the austerity of the churches of

SOUTH FRONT, HATFIELD HOUSE, HERTFORDSHIRE

The Old Palace at Hatfield was built by Cardinal Moreton, chief minister to Henry VII and completed about 1497. Here Queen Elizabeth spent much of her childhood. The Palace was given by James I to Robert Cecil, first Earl of Salisbury, in exchange for his great house at Theobalds, also in Hertfordshire. Robert Cecil pulled down all but one wing and used the materials in the present structure, Hatfield House, built between 1607 and 1612. It is Elizabethan in conception, its two wings being joined by a central block to form the letter E. Its thin walls, big mullioned windows and general impression of light and space are Jacobean in spirit.

two or three centuries earlier, as is well seen in the bare interior of the parish church of Saffron Walden, a beautifully light building.

So in a blaze of magnificence, partly inspired, as has been seen, by the economic prosperity of the fifteenth century, the golden era of British architecture drew to its close. Just as the original Roman style of building and the medieval Saxon were introduced into Britain by cultural infiltration from the continent of Europe, so again in the sixteenth century a fresh style of architecture, which had its origins in Italy and spread out across Europe, reaching Britain rather later, began to dominate building of all kinds.

The sixteenth century was a period of great adventure, a period when modern Europe began to take definite shape in the world of the arts and of learning. The Reformation and the Renaissance are the two great events linked with it. They were the two events which inspired a new intellectual interest among the people and at the same time a revival of admiration for classical art and classical letters. A classical revival in architecture was only to be expected and this, in fact, was what determined the course of building in Britain. It was the last great revolution of design and taste which set its stamp on the British heritage. From the sixteenth century to the present day there has been a more or less continuous development. There have been Gothic revivals. There have been many attempts to mould a style of building entirely new, but these revivals and attempts at complete revolution have been marked rather by the ebullience of the designers than by sustained artistic success. The twentieth century is too near in time for a mature judgment to be made upon its work. Throughout the eighteenth and nineteenth centuries Gothic and classical styles were used

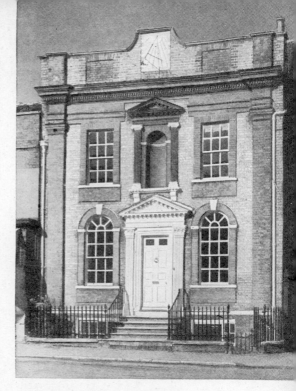

GEORGIAN ARCHITECTURE
This house in Dedham, Essex, is characteristic of the graceful lines of Georgian architecture applied to modest country residences. Very different in style from the great Georgian houses of London or Bath, it shows the same classical forms with the accent on square- or round-headed windows and unadorned classical columns.

side by side, the Gothic style usually being preferred for churches, the classical for public buildings of a secular nature.

The Renaissance was slow in coming to Britain, perhaps all the slower because with the Reformation and the dissolution of the monasteries in the reign of Henry VIII the great era of church building had come to an end. Henceforth except for one brilliant period it is the private house and the public building rather than the church which most inspires the architects and designers. It is the Tudor and Elizabethan manor-house rather than the few churches built in those times which represent the highest creative expression of the age. Even in the magnificent chapel of King's College, Cambridge, one of the latest essays in the Gothic style, the influence of revived classicism can be seen. In the manor-house it is more explicit; the pointed arch is flattened out, the entrance doorways are more severe, flanked by classical columns, and the windows become more square and classical in design. Comparison of three or four typical manor-houses ranging over a hundred years of building, reveals the gradual increase in the accent placed on classical design and forms, and the gradually decreasing influence of Gothic forms. Cotswold manor-houses such as Compton Wynyates, and the magnificent series of manor-houses in Kent—Penshurst, Knole and Ightham Mote—all show the changing fashions.

CLASSICAL BUILDING

The change is seen to even greater effect in a few castellated manor-houses (more manor-houses than castles), such as Tattershall Castle, which were begun when Gothic building was at its height, but were altered and enlarged during the reigns of the Tudor kings and Elizabeth.

All this was a kind of prelude to the full flowering of the classical styles in Britain. With the work of Inigo Jones, typified by the Banqueting Hall in Whitehall, classical architecture had truly "come to town." In this, and in the many great country houses built by Inigo Jones and his successors and imitators, there was no pretence at preserving the traditional English forms. Gone was the courtyard house, gone the traditional gatehouse, gone, too, the tradition of the great hall. Instead there were square or rectangular buildings based on Italian models, with long parallel lines of rectangular windows and often porticoes incorporating rows of classical pillars after the style of ancient Greek and Roman temples. The Italian architect, Palladio, was the prophet of the breed; the style of architecture in Britain known as Palladian was named in his honour. It was a style foreign in its conception and in its execution.

RENAISSANCE INFLUENCES

A little later, towards the end of the seventeenth century, the Great Fire of London gave the opportunity to rebuild a number of churches that had been destroyed by fire and brought to light the genius of Sir Christopher Wren. All Wren's churches and the many large houses which were attributed to him are severely classical in style, yet show some regression from the Italian forms compared with the true Palladian building.

They make a very interesting contrast with the Romanesque of the eleventh and twelfth centuries. The semicircular arch had returned. So, too, had the insistence on the alternation between the square and the round. But there the resemblance ends, for the genius of Wren lay in adapting classical models so that a true national architecture evolved, a spirit of compromise and native adaptation which is noticeable in much of the British heritage. Entirely British, too, was the craftsmanship of workers in wood like Grinling Gibbons and his many pupils, a tremendous contribution to the heritage scarcely inferior to that of Sir Christopher Wren himself.

It is an over-simplification to say that the Georgian styles evolved from the work of Inigo Jones and Sir Christopher Wren, because in fact they incorporated many features that were novel. But it is true to say that Georgian architecture represents a further adaptation of ideas

BRIGHTON PAVILION

The Pavilion at Brighton shows the fantastic lengths to which architects went at the end of the gracious period of Georgian building in England in order to produce novel effects. The style of the Pavilion is influenced by Moorish examples and though estimates of its architectural quality have varied, no one has ever denied its bizarre effect. "Inverted turnips" is the name which William Cobbett gave to the domes, but modern criticism tends to regard this, like many other extravagances of the Regency, as a successful essay in a style of building essentially foreign to Britain.

which were continental in origin, to the needs and temperament of the British people, though its classical origin is easily lost sight of, and Georgian architecture is rightly accepted as a British contribution to the story of world architecture and one on which the genius of Britain might well be judged. The direct descent of Georgian building from Renaissance prototypes is clearly marked.

It is interesting also to note how various fresh continental influences laid but a fleeting hand on the new British styles. There are the "Dutch" windows, which distinguish many early Georgian adventures in architecture. The influence of the Flemish immigrants can be seen in some of Kent's buildings, notably in the city of Canterbury. Some-

thing of the rococo brilliance of Moorish architecture can be seen in pretentious Regency buildings such as the Pavilion at Brighton, with its many domes, "inverted turnips," as William Cobbett called them.

For the most part, however, development was on conservative lines. After the first quarter of the nineteenth century, little or no real distinction was added to the national heritage, yet up to that time there was so much beauty and so little work of poor design that Britain's heritage of architecture is inferior to that of no other country, not excluding Italy itself which was the fount and origin of so many of the ideas that provided the foundations on which building in Britain was raised to the splendid heights it has attained.

HEREFORDSHIRE VILLAGE

Church Lane, Ledbury, leads from the town to the parish church, seen in the background, its stone spire a landmark for miles around. The buildings in the black-and-white style date from the sixteenth and seventeenth centuries.

Britain's Storied Past

A VISITOR to Britain, suddenly and unexpectedly confronted with Church Lane, Ledbury, must imagine that Time had tricked him and plunged him into the Middle Ages. Across the narrow, cobbled street, half-timbered houses, with overhanging gables, seem but an arm's stretch apart. At the end, a climax of beauty, the church gives the curious impression of a cluster of abbey buildings. One feels that there would be nothing strange in the appearance of a knight in armour, or of a group of Grey Friars. Nearby are the Malverns, where Langland's Piers Plowman dreamed, whence, from the Beacon, news was flashed of the coming Armada, and where the British Camp was a Celtic stronghold before England had been born.

In thousands of such scenes, scattered over Britain, the story of the past can be read. Fishmongers' Lane, Bishops' Walk, Priory Close, the Lord Mayor's Show, Guildhall, Black Rod, the Woolsack, Will Brewer, Jan Stewer, the barber's pole, a Gothic window— all have their tale to tell. But no chance meandering can reveal the story as it unfolded itself through the changing ages. Rather has history to be imposed on the visible relics, as guide and interpreter, to bring life again to the dead, and to people again the tumbled ruins. The difficulty is that some things have so much to tell, for a cathedral church may reveal the history of a thousand

EXCAVATION AT SUTTON HOO

Much of the evidence for the world's ancient history literally has been dug out of the earth, the exact meaning of some discoveries being difficult to determine. This impression in sand of a ship, for example, was found during excavation at Sutton Hoo; its date is uncertain. Ship burial was a Viking custom but this vessel is not of their pattern; it may have been Saxon.

years, and this brief pilgrimage can afford but fleeting glances of days gone by.

Within walking distance of Torquay is the famous Kent's Cavern, once the home of Palæolithic Man, a refuge from the savage animals of the wild land that was not yet Britain. In the cave have been found a recognizable fragment of the terrifying sabre-toothed tiger, and tools and weapons of the unpolished flint of an age which had not yet learned the use of metals. There are many such caves in Britain. At Langwith Bassett Cave in Derbyshire, and in the Paviland Caves in Glamorgan, human bones

LINK WITH TWO CIVILIZATIONS

This air photograph of the Trundle near Goodwood shows the remains of two distinct civilizations. The central ring clearly shown is the earthwork of a Stone Age hill fortress constructed over four thousand years ago and reduced to its present almost level condition by time and weather. Towards the end of the Stone Age the site was deserted, but about 500 B.C. the Iron Age people who colonized the South Down country afresh built the fortified hill village which is represented by the clearly shown outer concentric rings of bank and ditch.

have been discovered, thought to have belonged to men of the Fourth Ice Age some fifty thousand years ago. The caves were the only shelter from the Arctic cold, and as, during the thousands of years, the ice receded northwards, the woolly mammoths, the reindeer, and the Arctic foxes went north, too, while men and animals from the south trekked northwards in their place.

To journey to Weeting in Norfolk, to visit there the chalk pits known as Grime's Graves, is to open another chapter of history. It was on the moorlands and the chalk uplands of the south-east that Neolithic men, the men of the New Stone Age, preferred their homes, away from the dangers of the forests which then covered the Midlands and other low-lying regions. Grime's Graves are what is left of the flint mines which they dug some five thousand years ago, through the clay and soft chalk to the hard beds where the flint could be found. Some of them are thirty feet deep, with galleries and connecting passages. There are three hundred and forty-six and they cover more than twenty acres. In them have been found horn picks, flint axes, lamps made of chalk, part of a human skull, and the bones of oxen, sheep, deer and pigs, with the remnants of cooked meals. There are similar pits at Cissbury, Sussex.

These relics tell of an age when men in Britain first learned to till the fields, to domesticate animals and, in consequence, to live in settled communities. They had learned, too, to spin and weave, to grind corn and to make pottery; and the crude decoration of some of their surviving vessels shows a developing sense of beauty and the existence of some leisure.

On the way from Devon to Norfolk it would have been well to linger in Wiltshire, where at Avebury sufficient

NEW STONE AGE PROCESSIONAL ROAD

Excavation has proved that Avebury, the largest stone monument in Britain, was constructed about 2000 B.C. or a little earlier. From Avebury this avenue of giant stones leads to another monument at Overton Hill; it was re-erected in 1934 during a prolonged search into the origins and purposes of the monument. It is now felt that the avenue is almost certainly a processional way connected with the primitive worship of the New Stone Age people.

survives of the largest of the "rude stone monuments" in Britain to suggest something of its original structure. A few stones remain of the hundred huge slabs which formed the outer circle, a thousand feet in diameter, of this ancient shrine. The largest stone is thirty feet in circumference and thirteen feet high. There were two inner circles and some great slabs in the centre. Silbury Hill, near by, is the largest artificial mound in Western Europe, and on Hackpen Hill is a double row of stones, approached through an avenue of similar rough-hewn slabs.

But a short distance across the Wiltshire Downs is Stonehenge, perhaps the most astonishing of all prehistoric relics. Protected by a ditch and an earthwork, three hundred feet in diameter, and approached through an avenue of great stones, is the broken ring of the outer circle of upright stones supporting huge lintels. Sixteen remain as they were originally placed, massive, rough-hewn. Within an inner circle were five sets of three great stones, arranged horse-shoe fashion, each group consisting of two big stones and a great horizontal slab. In the centre, lying prostrate, is the altar stone, on which, possibly, human sacrifices were made. To stand at dawn on Midsummer Day on the altar stone, and to look over the great stone known as Friar's Heel, would be to face the rising sun, whose first rays reach the altar through the long avenue of stones. This fact has inspired many guesses as to the religious beliefs of these ancient peoples, such as that they possibly worshipped the sun as the source of light, life and fertility.

SILBURY HILL, WILTSHIRE

The only thing known for certain about Silbury Hill, one of the great wonders of the ancient world, is that it is the largest artificial mound in Europe. The hill is one hundred and thirty feet high and covers five acres, and is entirely of artificial construction, though from the Bath Road, which passes near, it looks very much like a natural feature. It is almost certainly more than two thousand years old, for a Roman road makes a digression in order to go round it. In form it is rather like the round barrows—the burial chambers of the Bronze Age folk who lived in Britain from about 1800 B.C. Many trial excavations have been made, but its secret will remain unknown until total excavation is possible—and since that would involve considerable expense and the labour of hundreds of men, there is little likelihood of it.

Near by are a hundred and sixty "barrows," or burial chambers.

A further great leap in human progress has been recorded by the surviving relics discovered in the Heathery Burn Cave in the county of Durham. The cave was once the home of men of the Bronze Age, Gaelic peoples whose barrows, scattered along the eastern coast of Britain, have yielded ornaments, tools and weapons of bronze. In Heathery Burn Cave was found a mould for casting bronze-socketed axes, rings and pins, tongs and a chisel, a patched cauldron, all of bronze, and an armlet and a hoop of gold. The family kept horses, for a bridle-bit of antler was discovered, and other remains show that the family hunted and fished, and kept

flocks and herds. It is an interesting commentary on the relative significance of wealth that this ancient family must have been a wealthy one. At Wookey Hole in Somersetshire similar relics have been found.

Another Celtic race brought the Iron Age to Britain, and imposed its language and supremacy over the peoples who were conquered or absorbed. These Celts were settling in parts of Europe about 1000 B.C., and when the Greek explorer Pytheas visited the island—the "Prethanic Isle"—in the fourth century B.C., there was already a trade in Cornish tin, there were scattered villages with cultivated arable land, and some organization under chieftains. A visit to Dorchester (Durotriges, "The

Dwellers beside the Water"), will reveal one aspect of life at this time—the need for defence which fear and greed, born of a possibility of relative wealth, had inspired. Metal was as yet scarce and its possession was coveted. The possession of metal arms and shields, of horse chariots and the like, meant power, and already there were soldier-chieftains, with retainers and peasant dependants, the germs of a feudal society. At Dorchester may still be seen the remains of the great camp which Thomas Hardy described as a "many-linked organism of an antediluvian time." Four hundred and seventy feet above sea-level, along the edge of a plateau, a great earthwork, a thousand yards long and five hundred wide, formed an outer protection. There were towering ramparts, with maze-like approaches, and platforms within from which the defenders could hurl stones or spears. Near by, at Poundbury (pronounced locally as "Pummery"), was another Celtic fort.

There are many relics of such forts in Britain, and from some of them the first towns grew. Built in naturally defensible places they provided obvious foundations for many of the Roman encampments which developed into Roman cities.

Before leaving pre-Roman times, however short the historical pilgrimage, one ought to visit the site of the ancient lake-village, three miles from Glastonbury. Driven perhaps by a similar fear, or perhaps as a refuge from conquering settlers, an ancient group of peoples built their homes on piers or platforms, supported by stakes driven into clay beds in the marshy ground or water.

THE RIDGEWAY, BERKSHIRE DOWNS

A characteristic part of the Ridgeway near White Horse Hill on the Berkshire Downs, this ancient trackway, which extends from the Marlborough Downs to the Thames by Goring, is certainly earlier than the Roman occupation, but is probably later than the Stone Age Pilgrims' Way of the North Downs and the Icknield Way which follows the northern slopes of the Berkshire Downs and the Chiltern Hills. Today the Ridgeway is reserved for travellers on foot or on horseback, and is one of the finest long rides in the south of England.

There were ninety such dwellings and a causeway of stepping-stones connected them with more solid ground. Excavation has brought to light ornaments, tools, weapons of bronze and iron, tubs, spoons, bowls of wood, and beautifully fashioned and decorated pottery, especially of the later Celtic peoples. Evidence of their astonishingly developed art, with its beauty of design and perfection of craftsmanship, may be found in most British museums of any significance.

One interesting and still visible relic, though there is some doubt as to its origin, is the great white horse cut on the slopes of White Horse Hill at Uffington, in Berkshire. Another famous hillside figure is that of the Giant of Cerne Abbas in Dorset, a figure of 180 feet high, wielding a club 120 feet long. The Long Man of Wilmington, in Sussex, a

WHITE HORSE OF THE BERKSHIRE DOWNS

One of the most striking of the ancient chalk monuments of southern England, the White Horse which is cut in the downs above Uffington, to the west of Wantage, is a highly impressionist figure representing equine speed and grace. It is probably one of the earliest of the hill figures which have been carved at intervals from prehistoric times until the present day, the lion of Whipsnade Zoo being one of the latest. On the summit of the hill on which the White Horse is cut there is a prehistoric encampment and it may be that its purpose was to mark the position of this fort: if so, it is three thousand years old.

ROMAN VILLA

The Roman villa at Chedworth, Gloucestershire, built as the home of a rich merchant farmer of Roman Britain about the third century A.D., was covered for hundreds of years by a landslide, so that when it came to be excavated the greater part of it was intact, in contrast with many other Roman villas which had been destroyed by vandals or to provide road-building materials. This photograph shows the foundations and part of the lower storey.

figure 230 feet long, cut in the downs is probably of later date.

ROMAN BRITAIN

Along the Northumberland uplands for many miles, the ruins of the old "wall," which formed part of the boundary of the Roman Empire, may still be seen, stretching five or six feet high, a barrier against the Celtic "Picts" of the barbarous north. On the north side a ditch, twelve yards wide and five yards deep, was the first obstacle to invasion. Further advance was checked by the wall itself, originally twelve feet high and seven and a half feet thick.

Seventeen forts, at intervals of about five miles, housed the Roman garrison, and detachments were stationed in the smaller towers known as "mile castles." Communication between these was made easy by the wide road built on the south side of the wall.

At the forts were officers' quarters, barracks for the troops, stables, granaries, cooking ovens, parade grounds, and, indeed, everything necessary for the efficient maintenance of military headquarters. Still to be seen are remains of the hypocausts which provided central heating for the officers' quarters by leading hot air from a furnace through flues in the walls and under the floors. There were baths, a cemetery, shops, gambling houses and a religious shrine. It is not difficult to picture the lives of the Roman soldiers who held this most distant outpost.

Neither this garrison nor any other Roman outpost was isolated, for an astonishing system of roads, constructed with characteristic thoroughness, connected each with London and Dover, and thence, by a similar European system, with Rome itself. Until the eighteenth and nineteenth centuries there were no roads in Britain to compare with the Roman ones, which still survive in the pattern of our modern transport system. The scheme illustrates the logical nature of Roman planning. Watling Street, one of the four main roads, ran from London to the centre of Britain (to Venonæ or High Cross), thence west to Uriconium (Wroxeter, which is well worth a visit), and north to Chester, where a garrison kept in check the wilder tribes of North Wales. A continuation reached the straits which faced Mona (Anglesey), the Druids' headquarters. A branch from Uriconium went south to Caerleon, the camp necessitated by the tribes of South Wales, and Exeter, an outpost against the wild Celts of Cornwall and Devon. Ermine Street, the Great North Road, connected London with the northern wall, passing through Lincoln and York. Fosse Way was a cross-country road, running from Exeter, through Bath and Cirencester, to Leicester and Lincoln. A southern road connected London with the coastal ports and Exeter.

Excavation on the sites of Roman cities continues to reveal a wealth of detail of Roman life and of the structure of their communities. The most complete investigation is that of Calleva Atrebatum or Silchester, north of Basingstoke in north Hampshire. Clearly the town was planned in its entirety, with six parallel straight streets running north and south, and six similar ones crossing them at right-angles. In the centre of the town were the forum or market place and the basilica or town hall. There were the usual baths, shops, temples (and a Christian church near the south-east corner of the forum), and well-spaced villas, some with open fireplaces, others centrally heated, and with gardens. Later, when Roman security was threatened, a ditch and a wall with gates were added for protection.

Before leaving the Roman period of occupation one must visit Bath, the Aquæ Sulis of the Romans, where there are still extensive remains of the swimming baths into which the Romans diverted the still-steaming natural spring. Legend has it that Bladud, son of Hudibras and father of King Lear, was miraculously cured of disease through the accident of having fallen into the mud, and that in 863 B.C. he founded a city on the site of his adventure. It is certain that the famous Roman city was built on some previous settlement centred round the hot spring.

A less direct or dramatic reminder of the Roman occupation of Britain than these concrete relics, but of more permanent significance than most of them, are the cherry trees, the geese and common fowl, the chestnuts, thimbles, dice and many similar things which the Romans brought over for their comfort or pleasure, and which came to stay.

THE ENGLISH CONQUEST

With the withdrawal of the Romans in A.D. 407, and the official end of the occupation in 410, Celtic invaders began to pour over the undefended northern wall, while English tribes, the Angles, Saxons and Jutes of the class books, began to invade, settle, and penetrate

TYPICAL ROMAN ROAD

Several Roman roads cross the Midland counties, among them the main road from London through Huntingdon and on to Lincoln, a road which from Norman Cross northwards is largely followed by the modern highway. Most of the Roman roads in Leicestershire and Rutland were originally links with this Roman trunk road, and several of them, like the one pictured above, are still used as modern roads. The picture illustrates how the Roman roads followed an absolutely straight line from hilltop to hilltop. When they changed direction it was always on the crest of some high ridge, as is the case with this road, which can be seen veering to the right in the far distance. In Roman times the countryside was less widely cultivated and so more overgrown than today and it was by means of beacon fires on the hilltops that the road builders maintained direction which otherwise could easily have been lost.

from the south and east. As the English made village settlements, and either destroyed, or permitted to fall into decay, the towns from which they drove the Romanized Britons, it is obvious that for some centuries they could not leave much that would survive through the centuries as concrete evidence of their lives. Of their destructive activity there is plenty of evidence, in the hacked sculpture, the smashed tesselated floors, and the broken fragments which excavation reveals. Yet it is not that they were mere barbarians. Museums reveal the skill and craftsmanship of their metal-workers, in the swords, shields, jewels and various surviving implements.

With the conversion of the English to Christianity begins the period which provided more definite records for the historical pilgrim. Few with any historical imagination would regret the climb of the one hundred and ninety-nine steps which lead to the surviving relics of the grey, seventh-century abbey at Whitby, high on the east cliff. The north transept, the chancel and part of the nave of the old church remain. Here Caedmon dreamed his poetic dreams, and here Oswy presided over the Synod which, in 664, united the

HISTORIC ROMAN CITY

One of the great historic cities of the north of England, York was a vigorous and flourishing town in Roman times, its name then being Eboracum. It was here that the Romans quartered their legions to defend north-east England from the attacks of the Picts and Scots. The walls of the Roman city were rebuilt and enlarged in the Middle Ages, when the life of the town centred round the great minster, which was planned and designed by the Normans, and embellished and several times enlarged until the fifteenth century.

TWELFTH-CENTURY ABBEY

Building of Melrose, the oldest and finest of four abbeys founded in the reign of David I, was begun in 1136 by a party of monks from Rievaulx Abbey, Yorkshire. After its destruction in 1320 it was rebuilt through the energy and devotion of Robert Bruce, and there is a legend that Bruce's heart was buried under the high altar. This photograph shows part of the ruins of the cloisters and conventual buildings, and the lovely and extensive ruins of the abbey church, which mostly date from a rebuilding in the fifteenth century. By many, Melrose Abbey is judged to be the most beautiful ruin in the whole of Scotland.

British Church. The Britons whom Rome had converted had been separated for two centuries from the European Church, when Augustine converted the English. In the interval differences had arisen and the Medieval Church would not tolerate dissension. The union of the Church in Britain, and its incorporation into the general fabric of the Church which Rome dominated, brought Britain into closer contact with the more culturally advanced peoples of south and west Europe; the organization of the Church helped to create a sense of unity and of national dignity; and the increased concentration of peoples round abbeys and cathedrals implied the growth of a new urban society.

At Canterbury, whither Augustine had come in 597, a new church was

NORMAN ABBEY

The gateway of Battle Abbey was built in 1338, but the foundation of the abbey itself goes back to 1067. It was founded to commemorate the victory of William the Conqueror in the previous year, for the tradition is that the battle of Hastings, at which Harold and the Saxons were defeated, was fought on the site occupied by the abbey. Until the dissolution of the monasteries, Battle was one of the richest abbeys in the south, but only the gateway, parts of the wall and some minor buildings escaped destruction in the centuries which followed.

begun in 598, and later it became a cathedral. In the south transept of St. Augustine's Priory the remains of four tombs of Saxon kings have been found. St. Martin's Church was probably that in which Bertha, Ethelbert's Christian queen, worshipped; and its font is supposed to be that in which Augustine baptized the king. The beautiful three-spired cathedral of Lichfield is built on the site of a Saxon cathedral which was for a time the see of an archbishop. York Minster is a history in itself. At York the Roman Emperor Severus lived for a time and died. Constantine, who proclaimed Christianity as the recognized religion of the Empire, was proclaimed emperor there. In 627 Paulinus was made bishop of York in a small wooden chapel that was York's first cathedral. Many Saxon churches, and Saxon parts of churches, survive.

One of the finest examples is that at Escomb, three miles west of Bishop Auckland in Durham; it was built in the seventh century.

During the English (or Saxon) period of settlement, Great Britain gradually emerged as a land of three groups of peoples, each of which began to harden into a national entity. The English were concentrated in the south-east lowlands; in the north the mountains and moorlands of northern "England" became a lawless borderland beyond which the Celtic peoples forged the kingdom of Scotland. In the west the mountains of Wales formed a formidable stronghold for the Britons or Celts unconquered by the English. Probably few golfers who visit Prestatyn in Flintshire recall that Offa's Dyke, the rampart held by some authorities to have been built by the Mercian king as a frontier defence, begins near the town. It continued to the estuary of the Severn at Sedbury Park. Much of it may still be seen.

By far the most impressive evidence of this ancient tripartite division is the still surviving nationalism of the Scottish, Welsh and English, strengthened by surviving language and national literature. A visit to a Welsh eisteddfod will reveal much of significance to the historically imaginative. There, for example, one would meet again the Druids, still retaining one characteristic of the ancient priesthoods in that poetry and the written language were their concern, as they were in ancient Egypt.

VIKINGS AND NORMANS

Britain had not yet finished with invasion. First, Viking adventurers from the fiords of Scandinavia, and, later, Normans, the descendants of Vikings who had settled in northern France and adopted the superior culture of France, crossed the seas and settled in the land. The Viking penetration resembled that of the earlier English conquest, and the "Danes" were gradually absorbed into the population. Their river strongholds grew into towns, and many place names, especially those ending in "-by," "-wick," or "-wich," bear evidence of their origin, or at least, of Viking occupation. More important was the Norman conquest, for this established a military, feudal hierarchy at least over the English, and imposed a central organization and administrative unity on the kingdom.

At the little town of Battle, near Hastings, are the remains of the abbey, consecrated in 1095, commemorating William the Conqueror's victory of 1066 over Harold and the English. The nature of the feudal authority which the Normans imposed over the conquered English is revealed in the ruins of the castles which they built as baronial strongholds in almost every part of the country. The imposing ruins of the great keep of the castle which Ansculf built to establish his authority over the manor of Dudley which William had assigned to him are still to be seen. In the shadow of such castles the English were reduced to a virtual serfdom, and the evidence of the social relationship established still survives. For instance, an English word is still used for a sheep, when alive and needing a herdsman, while a French word is used for the *mouton* prepared for the table.

Near by are the ruins of a priory, symbolizing the close relationship between Church and monarchy in early medieval life, when bishops and abbots were feudal magnates, and when Europe was, in fact, Christendom.

The Normans were great builders of abbeys, priories, churches and castles, and a great wealth of their work remains. Norman buildings and parts of buildings are readily recognizable. Built for strength, for even the church had to be a fortress and a refuge, they are characterized by the massive bulk of their great heavy pillars, by round arches and by simple decoration. One of the most interesting examples of this typically strong, solid architecture is the round church of the Holy Sepulchre, near St. John's College, Cambridge. It is one of the four surviving Crusaders' churches. The cathedrals, whether secular or monastic, many of which the Normans began, grew under later hands into poems of architecture, and a pilgrimage round the British cathedrals provides an incomparable record of British history during a thousand years of evolving national consciousness. A glance reveals the solid foundation with towering stronghold which the Normans laid. With increasing security and developing wealth, with greater leisure and repose, solidity gave way to a slender beauty. With the coarsening of increasing commercialization, refinement gave way to over-elaboration and decoration, and, at last, to the destruction of abbeys that their stones might be used for the houses of a new commercial aristocracy.

Probably the most imposing single symbol of Norman power is the Tower of London, commanding the Thames, the open door into Britain from the Continent, and guarding "the City." Its massive walls, battlements, portcullises, moat, drawbridge, inner wards, and its donjon, or keep, speak of an age when war was a matter of arrows, battering-rams, and hand-to-hand fighting. It was at once fortress and state prison, and for centuries was an impregnable stronghold.

Another stronghold begun by the Conqueror is Windsor Castle, near the Thames. The castle was at once fortress and palace. There Henry I held his marriage feast. Henry II held Great Councils there, and it was from Windsor that John sailed, in 1215, in a boat down the Thames to set his seal at Runnymede island to the Great Charter.

With the advance through the centuries the difficulty of selection from an ever-increasing store of the memorials of the past increases, and, in so brief a narrative, it is possible only to indicate different types of historical shrine to the pilgrim. Evidence of two very different aspects of Norman and early medieval life may still be seen. The New Forest, for the creation of which William I was said by chroniclers to have destroyed sixty villages, wasted their land, despoiled their churches and expelled their inhabitants, recalls the harsh Forest Law which the Normans introduced, whereby, for disturbing the King's Game, a man could be blinded and mutilated in other ways before being hanged. In great contrast was the new development of culture and learning for which French rule was a great stimulus. At Oxford, where the Conqueror built a castle in which Matilda, daughter of Henry I, was besieged by Stephen, students were encouraged by the Norman kings to settle, and some four thousand of them, representing many nationalities, are said to have been established there by the end of the twelfth century. The university was founded in the next century when three colleges were established.

THE LATER MIDDLE AGES

During the three centuries which end with the Wars of the Roses and the accession of the Tudor king, Henry VII, in 1485, the period which roughly constitutes the later Middle Ages in Britain, the outstanding characteristic is the change from a feudal form of society to a commercial one. The centre of interest changed from fields to towns, from castle to home, from baron to merchant, from armour to rich clothing, from the tournament to the fair. The

MEDIEVAL STRONGHOLD

A modern royal residence, Windsor Castle is one of the chief remaining medieval strongholds which have handed down their tradition as castle and palace combined. In the foreground is the circular keep or fortress raised high on an earthen mound dating from Norman times. Around it are grouped the battlements of the medieval castle reconstructed by Wyatville in the last century.

surviving memorials of this period of social change give to any journey through England today (and, in this instance, to England, rather than to Britain as a whole) its unique character and much of its charm. In most of the old towns and cities medieval features peep unmistakably through the more recent superstructure. Narrow streets, some still cobbled; half-timbered houses with overhanging upper storeys; fragments of walls and gates; stocks and pillories preserved in old market-squares; hump-backed bridges and bridges with spaces for refuge from passing pack-horses; and a wealth of surviving names—in such is the storied past revealed.

At Exeter and at Taunton are two fine examples of surviving guildhalls, once the seats of authority from which the masters of the merchant guilds controlled the commerce and general government of their respective towns. In Taunton the guildhall is in the old market house and nearby are blocks of medieval almshouses. One of these, thatched, was originally reserved for lepers and the abbot's arms it bore may still be seen. A similar urge for mutual and self-protection created the craft guilds, the brotherhoods of apprentices, fellow craftsmen and master craftsmen of specific trades. Many of these, too, had their own halls. At Salisbury, for example, are three such halls still surviving, the woolstaplers', the joiners' and the shoemakers'.

The most important item of medieval trade was wool, for English wool was the finest in Europe, and the demand for it was insatiable. Barons, abbots, bailiffs and finally even the more successful and imaginative peasants, turned to sheep-farming, to derive wealth themselves from the main source of British prosperity. It is, therefore, no meaningless symbol that the Lord Chancellor should still sit on a wool-sack in the House of Lords.

Visitors to Weymouth may be reminded that at the little town of Melcombe Regis, which is now incorporated in the municipality, is supposed to have begun the dread pestilence known as the Black Death, one of a series of plagues which, in this instance, destroyed in a few years from a third to a half of the population. The pestilence hastened the development of sheep-farming, increased the capitalization of agriculture and helped to widen still further the growing gap between wealthy and poor. Extravagant costume, elaborate menus and a general luxury began to distinguish one class from another increasingly depressed and impoverished. At Blackheath, the wide common from which the Danes once threatened London, John Ball preached his famous sermon on the text: "When Adam delf and Eve span, Who was then the gentleman?" All those who "pounded the law" for love of "penyes" rather than for "love of oure Lorde," all tyrants, lords and lawyers, were to be put to death. It was, however, Ball himself who suffered death, after the suppression of the Peasants' Revolt, in 1381, after its leader Wat Tyler had been slain.

There is little opportunity in a survey so brief for more than a passing glance at the visible memorials of Welsh, Scottish, or Irish elements in the general story of Britain, for inevitably the central pivot of progress lies in the lowlands which Rome helped to urbanize and in which the English settled. The grim mountains of Snowdonia were for long an impenetrable fortress for the princes and peoples of Gwynedd, until Edward I defeated them, and Llewelyn was slain in the cave which may still be visited on the lovely hill opposite Builth in Brecknock. At Caerphilly, in Glamorgan, is the biggest castle of Wales, now being

THE HOUSE OF LORDS

The Houses of Parliament are officially part of the Palace of Westminster, and there has been a building on this site since before the Norman Conquest. This, the most ornate of the many chambers of the palace, has stained glass windows depicting figures of all the sovereigns from William I to William IV. It is traditionally the meeting place of the Upper House, though used by the Commons after the House of Commons was destroyed by enemy action. In the left foreground is the Woolsack, seat of the Lord Chancellor.

restored. Built in Norman times, it is one of the long chain of fortresses which stretched from the Wye to Milford Haven and their ruins symbolize the penetration of Norman adventurers into the fertile valleys of South Wales.

Of the later castles, built by Edward I to make permanent his conquest, that at Harlech is the most impressive, commanding from the high rock on which it stands much of Cardigan Bay. At Rhuddlan, in Flintshire, is Parliament House, where Edward I is said to have held, in 1277, the parliament which established the English system of law throughout Wales.

The imperishable mountains of hard rock and the gale-swept valleys which are the highlands of Scotland express all the essentials of Scottish history and truly Scottish character better than can any man-made monument. Rugged independence, an open-air honesty, an untamable hardness softened by a lovable simplicity, and a vast poverty, these are terms which apply equally to mountain and to the people. The development of tribal clans under chieftains was inevitable and the total population of Scotland, necessarily confined mainly to the glens, the coastal plains and the lowlands of the rift valley, had probably not reached half a million by the sixteenth century. In the regions

CONWAY, NORTH WALES

One of the castles built for Edward I, Conway is similar in type to the castles of Harlech and Carnarvon. Concentric in form, it was a real breakaway from the traditional method of castle building. Within ten years of its construction in 1294, Edward I, with a part of his army, was besieged there. Reinforcements reached him only just in time to prevent his capture. In the centre of the picture is the Stephenson tubular bridge across the estuary of the River Conway. This handsome bridge, more than four hundred feet long, was opened in 1848, its architecture a successful effort at harmony with the austere lines of the castle.

SCOTTISH ROYAL RESIDENCE

This mansion is the traditional palace of the Scottish kings. Most of the present buildings date from the seventeenth century, and the palace is still the official state residence in Scotland of the King and Queen. On the left in the photograph is the ruined church of Holyrood Abbey, which formerly occupied the site on which Holyroodhouse was built. Founded by King David I, it is by tradition supposed to have been built where the Scottish king was saved from being gored by a stag by divine intervention in the form of a fiery cross. The ruin shown is of the thirteenth-century nave. In the background are the rocky hills known as Salisbury Crags, which lie south of Edinburgh and west of Arthur's Seat.

of Norman-English penetration many lovely abbeys were built, as those of Holyrood, Melrose and Jedburgh, and there towns and commerce began to grow. Edward I, bent on conquering Scotland as he had conquered Wales, after defeating the Scots at Dunbar took back with him to England the Stone of Scone, the ancient stone which was placed under the coronation chair of English kings at Westminster. But Scotland was not yet conquered and for centuries the bitter national hostility continued to rage unabated.

UNDER THE TUDORS

For a first glance at Tudor England it may be as well to visit Hampton Court Palace. Built by Henry VIII it symbolizes much that was essentially Tudor. The days of castles and fortresses had gone with the barons and with the advent of gunpowder. In their place were appearing stately homes and palaces. The decorated brick chimneys of Hampton Court symbolize the rapid development of British industry, while the maze and gardens suggest the growing leisure of the new commercial aristocracy and the new sense of pleasurable indulgence in a security born of a reimposed reign of law and order. It is a characteristic of the sixteenth century that men in this country began to build houses that were homes and to take pride in making them beautiful. This truth helps to make intelligible the patriarchal element in the Puritanism that was a characteristic of the next century.

A visit to the lovely Cotswold district reveals many of the fine homes built, in the beautiful pinkish stone of the district, by wealthy merchants, to the memory of many of whom there may still be seen interesting tablets in neighbouring churches. More typical of the general class of Elizabethan house are those half-timbered ones, of which so many are still standing. There is a beautiful example at Bridgnorth, with the inscription, "Except the Lord build the Owse, The Labourers thereof Evail not." Built in 1580, it was to be the birthplace of Thomas Percy, Bishop of Dromore, the author of *Reliques of Ancient English Poetry*. A less imposing home, "a small mean-looking dwelling of wood and plaster," is Shakespeare's birthplace in Stratford-on-Avon.

HALF-TIMBERED HOUSES

Above is the house in which Thomas Percy, distinguished Bishop of Dromore, was born. The date 1580 appears under the central eave and the front of the building is a fine example of Elizabethan and Jacobean architecture. Notice in particular the small-paned windows and the gigantic oaken beams which form the framing. The timberwork design is similar to that found in many houses in the counties that border on Wales. Sometimes known as magpie architecture, this type of half-timbered front is even more ornately developed in some parts of Cheshire. The house on the left is an interesting contrast with that above. It shows the characteristic timber design as applied to smaller houses and cottages. The similarities and differences are equally striking and the decorative effect is even more attractive in the smaller and less elaborate building.

All over the country may be seen the ruins of priory and abbey, ruins which are themselves a monument to the dissolution of the monasteries by Henry VIII, and the end of the long period of unity and authority of the medieval Church. The second Roman Empire died with feudalism and the empire of commerce took its place.

It is fitting that the Tudor costume should still be worn by the Beefeaters of the Tower of London, for the old fortress had ceased to be primarily the outer bastion of England's defences, and had become the symbol of monarchic despotism. There Henry sent, at will, wives, friends and servants to the headsman.

The concentration of tobacco factories at Bristol, noticeable on any journey through the port, reminds one of the great geographical discoveries of this age, discoveries which changed the destiny of the British people. A map, Mappa Mundi, which may still be seen in the library at Hereford, shows Britain as a negligible fragment on the edge of the world. So, in fact, she had long been—a veritable Land's End. The discovery of the New World placed Britain in the centre of world commerce which rapidly began to develop from the discovery. A new oversea route to India led to the formation of trading companies by the western nations, and, in time, to the acquisition by the British company of the virtual sovereignty of India. Ships from Bristol and Plymouth began to sail with cargoes of Negro slaves to the Spanish Main, to Central America and to the West Indies, and to bring back tobacco and other tropical produce grown by European planters, who formed settlements some of which were to grow into colonies. Liverpool was as yet little more than a village.

Few can stand on Plymouth Hoe without recalling the story of Drake and the destruction of the Spanish Armada, which was Britain's first really national victory, a victory which expressed the birth of a new and widespread patriotism, new commercial opportunity and a new zeal for Protestantism.

STUART BRITAIN

If the century of Tudor rule may be regarded primarily as the age in which monarchy helped the consistent development of Britain by strengthening a commercial aristocracy and completing the destruction of the baronage, so the Stuart age may be regarded as that in which the process was completed by the seizure of the government by the wealthy classes and their destruction of monarchic authority. The name of Scotland Yard recalls the transference of the Scottish court to London, as Bonfire

OLD STOCKS AT SULHAM

The stocks and whipping post are a feature of the traditional English village. These at Sulham in Berkshire are of the same design as the famous stocks of Aldbury in Hertfordshire. They represent a medieval means of punishment for petty crimes.

TOM TOWER, CHRIST CHURCH,

Below is the entrance gate to Christ Church, Oxford, more generally known as "The House." It reveals an unusual mixture of styles, for the gateway was built in the time of Wolsey, when the greater part of the college was constructed, but the tower is the work of Sir Christopher Wren. The tower is the belfry of Great Tom, the bell which still rings the medieval curfew of 101 tolls at five minutes after nine o'clock every evening.

Night recalls the early attempt of Guy Fawkes and the Roman Catholics to blow up the first Scottish king and his parliament. James I had the knack of displeasing everybody and the inscription on many editions of the Authorized Version of the Bible recalls his abortive Hampton Court Conference, when he alienated the Presbyterians, and from which the only positive result was that fine translation. The quarrel developed under Charles I, and the ceremony of Black Rod, at which the King's Messenger is refused entry into the House of Commons, commemorates Charles's violent attempt to impose his authority on its members.

Of the Civil War itself there is little point in looking for relics. The ruin of almost every castle is attributed locally, and often wrongly, to Cromwell, though many which had served as royal garrisons were destroyed at his command. Many villages claim the Royal Oak in which the young Charles hid after his flight from Worcester, though the genuine one is probably that at Boscobel. Whiteladies, where he hid and from which he escaped to seek shelter in Wales, may still be visited.

It was in Westminster Hall, the building of which was begun by Rufus and which now serves as a vestibule to the Houses of Parliament, that Charles was tried and condemned to death. Here, too, Cromwell dissolved the remnant of the Long Parliament known as The Rump, and, pointing to the mace, said: "Take away that bauble." The two events have interesting significance.

HALL OF CAIUS COLLEGE

Though Gonville and Caius College, Cambridge (opposite), was founded in the fourteenth century by Edmund Gonville, most of the fabric dates from the sixteenth century, when it was enlarged by Dr. John Caius.

Whitehall, of which only the Banqueting Hall remains, had been Wolsey's London residence and after his death it became a royal palace. Through an opening in one of its walls Charles I went to his execution on a scaffold erected in the street. Afterwards Cromwell lived there, as did Charles II.

Drury Lane Theatre reminds one of the return to the enjoyment of drama and the arts generally which accompanied the restoration of the monarchy in 1660, for it was built in Charles II's reign and was his favourite theatre. The present building was opened in 1812 on the site of the seventeenth-century playhouse.

London, the streets of which were still narrow and undrained, with houses which lacked any regular supply of clean water or general sanitary conditions, was troubled in 1665 by the last severe outbreak of the Great Plague, which for centuries had periodically swept over the country. It was followed in 1666 by the Great Fire, though this did not, as is sometimes stated, destroy the worst and most plague-ridden parts of London. It was most destructive in the City, and plans were proposed by Sir Christopher Wren for the rebuilding of London. Wren was responsible for the designing of some fifty new churches, including the present St. Paul's Cathedral.

At Brixham, the little fishing town of Devon at the southern extremity of Torbay, is a statue commemorating the landing there of William of Orange, on November 5, 1688. At Newton Abbot, near a stone wall in Wellborough Street, he made his first proclamation to the people of Britain. The joint acceptance of the crown by William and Mary and the flight of James II mark the end of the struggle which the Civil War had begun and the virtual control of the government by the wealthy. Parliament took over the responsibility of the nation's finances and for the first time it was possible to lend money to the nation, or at least for national enterprises controlled by parliament, instead of to a sovereign on short term loans for which there was no security.

In 1694 a loan of £1,200,000 began the National Debt, and the promoters were compensated by the granting of a charter which enabled them to found a bank with extensive privileges and the security of government support. This was the Bank of England, "the Old Lady of Threadneedle Street." It is in the heart of commercial London, with the Mint, the Stock Exchange and the Custom House nearby, and surrounded by streets famous in financial history. Lombard Street recalls the medieval bankers and merchants of northern Italy, who with other merchants had offices there and in Cornhill and Leadenhall Street.

Heavy demands for money were made in the reigns of William III and of Anne, the last of the Stuart sovereigns, because of the long wars against the France of Louis XIV, and it was in the last of these wars, that of the Spanish Succession, that the great Duke of Marlborough won his famous victories, and that Britain gained Gibraltar. At Woodstock in Oxfordshire, the great palace of Blenheim was built by Vanbrugh to commemorate the first of these victories and in the park is a statue of Marlborough (in a Roman toga!).

The Cross of St. Andrew, which forms part of the Union Jack, was added to that of St. George after the union of England and Scotland in 1707. If the union satisfied the peoples of the more urbanized and commercial Scottish Lowlands it roused bitter resentment amongst the peoples of the Highlands, who still loved independence and hated "the auld enemy." When in 1713 Anne died, and the Hanoverian George

HENRY VII'S CHAPEL, WESTMINSTER

The chief features of interest in this world-famous building are the beautiful carved-stone screen and the fan tracery of the vaulted roof, the latter one of the most perfect examples of its kind. When the great period of medieval church building was drawing to its close in the fifteenth century, window tracery and other decoration common in earlier periods of building ceased, as illustrated here by the rather severe lines of the window in the background.

ascended the throne, many Scots remained loyal to the Stuart line and in 1715 and 1745 rebelled in favour of James Edward and Charles Edward respectively, the son and grandson of James II. The attempts were in vain, and after the Duke of Cumberland's English victory at Culloden Moor, the clan system was abolished and the Highlands were brought under the central system of government. The magnificent courage and fighting ability of the Scots found opportunity both in the Highland regiments which Pitt formed in the British Army and in great colonial activity.

UNDER THE GEORGES

Georgian Britain begins to resemble much more closely the country of our own time. The period marks the climax in the economic evolution which made Britain the leading commercial and industrial nation of the world. The process of agricultural capitalization was completed and some hundreds of enclosure acts ended the old open-field system of farming. The mechanical revolution followed, paving the way for the rapid growth of the industrial towns on and near the coal-fields and the concentration of wage-earning industrial workers round mills and factories. In one of Shropshire's industrial "islands" a long row of tiny houses known as Mechanics' Row, and another even worse, known as The Barracks, still bear witness to the conditions in which workers had to live. In the towns where crowding was less avoidable the still existing slums tell their own story.

In many of the towns which grew rapidly in the eighteenth century, as did Birmingham, Liverpool, Manchester and the neighbouring cotton towns, and the wool towns of the West Riding, wide streets, flanked with massive Georgian houses, are backed by small paved courtyards, with high walls, which open on to narrow, dirty little streets of dark and miserable houses. Georgian houses are unmistakable and symbolic. The typical ones combine a pretentious classical arrogance with a hard-headed utilitarianism. Most of them have a dark and gloomy basement reserved for the use of the domestic staff. Steps and a pillared porchway led to the entrance hall. Usually they were built in rows which were often long, and more elaborate ones were built as crescents. The finest, and sometimes the ugliest and most pretentious, of the Georgian houses may be seen in the spas which became popular under the early Hanoverians. Bath became a popular resort, and a statue to Beau Nash, in the Pump Room, recalls his long rule over the fashions of his day. The mineral springs of Cheltenham were discovered in 1717, and soon attracted Georgian residents and visitors as did those of Buxton, Harrogate and other spas. The Crescent at Buxton, built 1780-84, is said to have cost the fifth Duke of Devonshire £120,000.

Developing industry and increased mobility demanded better roads than the rut-filled tracks which for centuries had made travelling a hazardous adventure, and by the turnpike system and the employment of such men as Macadam, or Telford, improvements were made which permitted the development of a regular system of travelling by stage coaches. Country inns, where horses could be changed and where refreshment and rest often meant a later encounter with highwaymen, began to flourish. Many such survive, with cobbled courtyards and stables converted into garages, still bearing evidence of their earlier use. At Broadway, one of the most beautiful villages in Britain, is a fine example of an old posting inn, the Lygon Arms, dating from the seventeenth century.

BROADWAY, WORCESTERSHIRE

The national heritage of towns and villages is rich in the Cotswold country, where Chipping Campden, Stow-on-the-Wold, Burford and Broadway are a group of places all of which have numerous late medieval stone buildings and a mellow beauty derived from the use of the local Cotswold stone in buildings of every kind. On the right in this picture of Broadway, Worcester, is the Lygon Arms, a famous old hostelry and coaching inn which dates from 1620, though its architecture shows more of Elizabethan than Jacobean influence.

As Hogarth's paintings and the writings of Fielding or Defoe reveal, eighteenth-century life, especially in the English towns, was cruel, gross, selfish and materialistic. There was a tendency to scoff at idealism in the days when it was believed that "every man has his price" and when individualism was the basis of accepted philosophy. It was in reaction to this view of life that Wesley preached and was twice stoned. The Methodist churches which began to appear after his death are a monument to one of history's greatest truths, that the flame of man's spiritual conviction and selfless devotion to a cause he believes to be the right one is often reduced to a glimmering flicker but is never extinguished.

It was in the reign of George III that Britain, often alone, bore the brunt of the twenty years' struggle against revolutionary France and against Napoleon's bid for world power. The danger was greatest in 1797, with the Navy in mutiny and three nations, Spain, Holland and France, preparing to invade Britain. The fort on Berry Head, Brixham, and the Martello Towers built at various points on the coast, still bear witness to Britain's preparations for defence. Then, as since, the Navy, restored to order and efficiency, kept Britain secure, and Nelson's final victory in 1805 is commemorated by the monument in Trafalgar Square. Though the war lasted for another decade it left Britain supreme on the seas, with a vastly increased commercial and colonial opportunity. It left, too, the authority of parliament, and the modern political mechanism firmly established.

WESTMORLAND FARM

In hundreds of narrow valleys between the mountains farming is carried on successfully. The valleys are divided by stone walls into long, narrow fields, the farm-houses sheltered by clumps of trees or small plantations. The climate is too wet for corn to be cultivated extensively, but the heavy rainfall helps grass crops so that there is good grazing and usually a fine hay harvest.

Heritage of Soil

IN no other country in the world is there so great a variety of rocks and soils in so small a space as in Great Britain. The country is only small, yet it has taken part in almost all the chief geological changes and still shows their marks. Setting off in a car in the morning in the eastern counties where new soils are being formed, as one goes westwards one passes over older and older formations; before evening the Wrekin and a chain of ancient volcanoes now happily extinct are reached and the traveller can end up in south Shropshire at the Long Mynd, one of the most ancient rocks in the world.

The country has not always been dry land; at least three times most of it has been submerged under the sea, while under water the old land surface was covered with thick deposits of sand, shiny mud known as ooze, and so on, which, by the great weight of the upper layers, were compressed into solid rock. After each submergence earth movements brought the sea bottom up as a new land surface. But this did not remain fixed: erosion, or wearing away, at once began and went on continuously, the softer rocks were carved into valleys while the harder ones remained as hills. In some epochs the climate was tropical, sometimes much of the land was desert and sometimes much was covered with swamps. Had it been left level at the time of the last uplift the result would have been a soil of the same geological age over most of the country. But it was not; it tilted to the North Sea and the Channel so that the formations became exposed towards the west.

This eastward tilt gives Britain its great variety of soils and scenery. However, the landscape as it is known today was not yet formed; a great climatic change occurred and Great Britain became arctic; almost the whole country north of the Thames was covered with huge glaciers coming from the north. In their slow southward journey they transported rocks, stones and soils over which they passed, grinding some of them to boulder clay as they went.

This was the last great change; the present landscape is much as it was modelled by the glaciers, though it has been modified by the slow, imperceptible and continuous erosion brought about by wind and weather.

This breaking up of the rocks is the first stage in the formation of the various soils to be found in the country. It provides the mineral basis, though it is not yet a complete soil. The eastern and southern counties are dominated by the chalk which in the south extends as far west as Devonshire, then strikes north-eastwards and includes parts of south Dorset, Hampshire, Berkshire, Buckinghamshire, Hertfordshire, south Bedfordshire, Cambridge and on into Lincolnshire and the Yorkshire Wolds, running into the sea at Flamborough Head. Its northern and western edge forms a bold escarpment which includes

SOUTH DOWNS LANDSCAPE

This hillside harvest field looks across the valley of the Ouse to the ridge of the South Downs which lies between Lewes and Seaford. Harvesting with combined cutting and binding machines is a swift task. Two tractors with four men do in a day the work which would take a week or more with horse-drawn cutters and several labourers to bind the sheaves. The play of sunlight and shadow in the distance throws up the recently ploughed fields, the newly turned chalk gleaming white against the darker pastures.

the Chiltern Hills and the splendid ring of downland with its smooth massive contours fringing the former Wealden sea of Kent, Surrey and Sussex.

Owing to its low level the eastern part of the country includes a considerable fringe of land liable to be flooded by the sea, so that it has to be protected by banks or walls. A perpetual fight with the sea goes on; in some places man wins and gains new land; in other places man loses and the sea swallows a slice of the country. The most notable gains have been round the Wash, where a great stretch of low-lying land, the Fens, was formed by the estuary of three rivers, the Ouse, the Nene, and the Welland. During its long period of submergence it has accumulated much organic matter and now, after reclamation, it constitutes one of the richest agricultural regions of Britain.

Passing eastwards and northwards of the chalk one traverses a belt of sandstone forming a small but pleasingly wooded escarpment, then over a clay plain, at times, as in Northamptonshire, scored with valleys which go down to a lower formation, but on the whole it slopes upwards towards the west. The southern part of the plain forms the basin of the Thames, and it includes as important tributaries the Oxford group of rivers. Some of the beds of the underlying rock, as in Bath and Portland, are freestone which is excellent for building and carving; others form good thin slabs for roofs though they have the disadvantage of being heavy. The inhabitants have always been able to live comfortably, especially in the Cotswold region, and this is dotted with beautiful old stone villages mostly lying away from the roads, some of the most attractive in England and at the moment unspoiled. The soil of the plain is good, sometimes a reddish clay, sometimes very stony, but it is responsive to the farmer's efforts. Then, continuing westwards, the plain ends abruptly in a high, steep escarpment from which a magnificent view suddenly appears over the broad valley of the Severn or the Avon; in the blue haze of the distance lie the hills of Herefordshire and Wales. Here is some of the most typical and pleasing scenery in England.

The comely land of Teme and Lugg
And Clent and Clee and Wyre.

The low land beyond the escarpment includes the heavy lias clay which stretches diagonally across England and in places such as Leicestershire and Rutland forms famous hunting country. In the Avon sector there is much lighter soil forming the Vale of Evesham.

FENLAND LANDSCAPE

The Fen country is one of the richest agricultural districts of Britain. The black earth, in many areas sunk some feet below sea and river level, bears magnificent harvests of corn and root crops. The fields are divided largely by dykes which take the place of the more usual hedges or the stone walls of the Pennine and Cotswold districts. Most of the farm villages are recent and the traditional mellow sixteenth- and seventeenth-century farm-houses of other parts of Britain are absent. The photograph shows corn fields with the harvest stacked for gathering, fallow fields and a modern farm-house in the background.

Across the Severn, the good country continues for a while, where life has always been comfortable and oak abundant, and there are many pleasing timbered villages and some beautiful wood carving in the churches. Here are to be found some of the most delightful little towns in England—Ludlow, Knighton, Much Wenlock, Church Stretton and others.

Farther west, in Wales, lie the older rocks, so hard that in spite of their vast age they are still respectable hills, though only shadows of their former selves. They give rise to poor soils, so

DRAINING THE LAND

Drainage and reclamation have played a major part in attaining increased agricultural production. Here is a ditch along the side of a Gloucestershire lane after deepening and cleaning. Without regular attention the ditch would become choked and would no longer carry away surplus water from the surrounding fields.

that the country has never been rich, they are little use for building and carving, so there is none of the beautiful stonework one sees in the Cotswolds. The country is entirely different from anything to the east, having all the characteristics of a land of mountains, of narrow, fairly productive valleys and a sturdy, intensely patriotic race of farmers overflowing up the hillside and wresting a living out of an unresponsive soil.

This sequence is reproduced if one travels from south to north; the chalk escarpment and the overlying soils disappear into the sea at Flamborough Head and the limestone escarpment ends in the moors behind Whitby.

The prevailing wind is from the southwest and it comes heavily charged with moisture from the Atlantic. Much of this is caught by the high country of the west; there the rainfall may in places be seventy, eighty or more inches per annum. Passing eastwards it becomes less, partly because the land lies lower and partly because the wind has become drier; in the central section the rainfall is about thirty to forty inches; in the eastern counties it may be as low as twenty inches.

A very important agricultural division of the country is made by the line of thirty-inch rainfall which stretches from Berwick-on-Tweed to the Isle of Wight. East of this line most of the country has less than thirty inches, and west of it most has more, except in the centre where there is a western loop-like extension including parts of Warwickshire and Cheshire where the rainfall is less. The rain has no seasonal character but may come at any time; in the eastern counties the wettest months on the average are July, August, October, November and December; the driest are February, March, April and May; but this means only that spring is likely to be

SCENE ON THE YORKSHIRE WOLDS

The Yorkshire Wolds are the most northerly extension of the chalk hills of England and end at the bold cliffs of Flamborough Head. In soil, as in contour, they are similar to the Lincolnshire Wolds and the chalk ridges of the East Anglian heights. Most of the land is farmed, and where the flinty soil is mixed with clay there are good harvests on lower ground, though the uplands are usually too cold and bleak for corn crops to be grown successfully.

dry, autumn and winter usually wet and summer either wet or dry.

The temperature is not usually high; it rarely exceeds 80 degrees Fahrenheit, nor does it fall low; much of England, especially the west, has only occasional snow and ice, though there is considerably more in the north.

The climate of Great Britain is peculiarly favourable to plant life; in most places in England grass remains green for almost all the year; only the very lightest sands are devoid of vegetation.

Over most of England deciduous trees, that is, those which shed their leaves annually, form the native vegetation except on the heaths, the chalk downs and the wind-swept upland moors. It has not always been so; the first vegetation that appeared must have been humble forms of plant life that could get nitrogen from the air, for this essential element of plant food was not present in the rocks. Step by step, however, a richer plant life was built up and finally the trees became dominant.

HARVEST TIME ON THE BERKSHIRE DOWNS

The chalk downlands of England were the first area to be cultivated in prehistoric times and right up to the Roman occupation bore a harvest of food crops. After that until the beginning of the twentieth century the accent was on cultivating the lowlands and almost all the downland was given over to sheep-walks and cattle pastures. Once again, however, artificial enrichment of the soil has made it possible to cultivate wheat and other cereals in the chalk country, as this scene on the Berkshire Downs, near Blewbury, demonstrates.

Some trees are indigenous, or native to the locality; some have been introduced. They are now so persistent that long after traces of them have been removed and the land used for agriculture they speedily come back again if the ground is left derelict.

The vegetation differs markedly with the conditions. On the chalk soils of the south, beech predominates with juniper and numerous flowering shrubs; on the clays, oak, thorn and ash, or oak and hornbeam preponderate; and on the intermediate loams elms are common. All these are deciduous trees and so fertilize the soil by shedding their leaves and help the undergrowth.

In the north, however, the prevailing trees are conifers; firs, pines and spruce, which retain their leaves in winter, and when they finally fall, the dead leaves do not manure the land. But these conifers will grow on sandy wastes where other trees fail, so they have been introduced on the Bagshot sands of Surrey and Hampshire, on the Norfolk heaths and elsewhere; they speedily begin to flourish. In recent years they have been planted on other soils because they quickly furnish saleable timber, but they are alien to the landscape and not beneficial to the soil.

Between them, the rock, the climate and the vegetation cover have made the soil of Britain. The rock fragments split off by the action of the rain, heat and cold, or ground off by the glaciers, constitute the skeleton; they are coarse or fine according as the rock is hard and resistant, or soft and susceptible to chemical change. The coarser fragments are called sand and in England are commonly composed of quartz, though in the older rocks of the west and north they may be more complex in composition. Smaller particles of the same composition are called silt; the finest particles are called clay.

When the plants die, their roots and leaves mingle with this mineral matter, the process being greatly facilitated by earthworms. These plant residues are decomposed by innumerable micro-organisms to which they serve as food.

The vegetation cover serves another purpose besides completing the soil: it protects it from the rapid erosion that would otherwise take place. Hot, arid countries are apt to be very brown and dusty in summer when the thin vegetation cover becomes parched and ineffective. The soil is lost, gulleys and ravines are scooped out by the wind and the rain, and only with difficulty can the vegetation cover be established. This mild, wet climate, with many cold, wet days, gives England its freshness and its greenness and it has saved the soil in spite of a thousand years of cultivation.

When the earliest farmers—people of the New Stone Age—came to England about 2500 B.C., the wild forest was so

CULBIN SANDS, MORAYSHIRE

For centuries the shifting sand dunes of Morayshire have engulfed field after field of fertile land. There is a tradition that a whole village was engulfed in the Middle Ages. Today the sand dunes still cover thousands of acres but their threat is being diminished by scientific methods. Here is a section of the dunes planted with rough grass and small conifer trees which are capable of growth even in this arid soil. As they grow, their roots help to bind the sands.

dense and overgrown that they could not clear it, and so they settled on the open downs of the southern counties. Here the land was sufficiently easy to clear for the sowing of wheat and other crops, while the short downland herbage gave food for their livestock. They were

THE SHEPHERD AND HIS CROOK

The shepherd works on in this mechanical age much as his ancestors did in the fifteenth century when the era of sheep farming was at its peak. With his dog as his only companion he spends most of his life following his flock over the upland sheep-walks of Britain's mountainous country. In the lowlands the shepherd is less cut off from his fellow men and lives on the farm or in the village in contrast to the shepherd of the hills whose shelter is often a lonely shack on the mountain side. Like most other country crafts the skill of the shepherd is handed down from father to son.

succeeded by the Bronze Age and Iron Age peoples.

It was the Saxons who first seriously tackled the clearing of forests. They did not settle on the tops of the Downs but in the river valleys, from which they spread all over the country: many towns and villages still have Saxon names. Most of the cultivated land of the village was divided into three fields, one of which was put into winter corn, one into spring corn, while the third was left fallow, i.e. uncropped. In the following year the winter-corn field was put into spring corn, the spring-corn field was left fallow, and the fallow land was sown with winter corn. So the rotation went on year after year. In some regions, however, the two-field system had to be adopted: corn—fallow; and in Celtic regions another system was followed.

If one could have flown over England in the first half of the fourteenth century this is what would have been seen. The background of the landscape was forest, in which the lords of the land hunted and the cottagers fed their pigs. There were many clearings and in these were the villages. The three fields divided into strips looked rather like a great patchwork quilt. There was a common on which the cottagers had grazing and other rights, some of their animals—sheep kept for wool and manure were their mainstay—could be seen in charge of a shepherd. The commoners also had grazing and other rights in the forest.

In addition to the cottages there was the manor-house and the lord's demesne, which might be either divided into strips or cultivated as one unit, like a modern home farm but with a dovecot. There was also a mill and a church. But there would be no signs of a big main road, for each village was self-contained and farming was for subsistence only. In places there were majestic castles and elaborate monastic establishments.

COTSWOLD SHEEP-WALKS

Sheep were the foundation of the prosperous medieval woollen industry in the Cotswold country. Something of the tradition of common grazing land has remained, for the many farmers who have grazing rights in the hills still join forces in organizing sheep drives. Here sheep are being driven over the downs near Winchcombe, Gloucestershire, to a valley farm.

The three-field system had an element of social justice and technical stability but it was wasteful of labour and the yields were low: they could hardly ever have exceeded ten bushels per acre, and the sowing had been about two bushels; usually they must have been much less. Except perhaps on the lord's demesne it was difficult to effect improvements.

The agricultural system was tied up with the elaborate social system of feudalism. Changes, however, were slowly taking place and they were hastened by the Black Death of 1348-49, which greatly reduced the population and wiped out many villages. Much of the land was left derelict. The situation was met, as often since, by developing livestock, especially sheep kept for wool; this brought much wealth to the countryside. In the favoured sheep districts such as the Cotswolds, magnificent churches and beautiful towns like Burford were built. This wool industry necessitated enclosure and turning men off the land, a process which at times caused much suffering, but in the end proved beneficial because it was soon found that a well-managed single farm could produce much more food than scattered strips.

Improvements were brought in from the Low Countries. Refugees from the Civil Wars, especially Sir Richard Weston, saw there clover, grasses and turnips. A great advance was made when Jethro Tull introduced the drill and the horse hoe. These improvements were popularized in England by Lord Townshend and others from the early eighteenth century onwards and worked into a four-course rotation: wheat, roots, barley, clover. Improvements

GREAT MASSINGHAM, NORFOLK

The village of Great Massingham is eleven miles to the north-east of King's Lynn. The grouping of church and cottages around the village pond is paralleled in many other villages of the eastern counties. The best-known example is Finchingfield in Essex. Great Massingham is in the East Anglian corn belt, where some of the world's finest barley is grown, yet only a few miles away is the edge of the sandy and relatively unfertile countryside which includes many of the great parks such as the King's Sandringham estate.

were made, too, by Coke of Norfolk (1754-1842), and the rotation long remained the basic plan of farming in Britain.

More and more land was brought into cultivation, including some released by the heavy felling of the forest to meet the demands of industry. Money became more plentiful in the countryside.

Fortunately Englishmen always loved country life, and this second half of the eighteenth century saw the adornment and extension of the big country houses, the building of many new ones and the laying out of some beautiful parks tastefully planted with trees. Much reconstruction went on in the villages, and the rural England of the end of the eighteenth century was more beautiful and richer in domestic architecture than it has ever been since. Meanwhile farms

and farm buildings were gradually taking their present shape.

Best of all the changes, however, was that the farmers were beginning to improve themselves. They were now better off than their predecessors and travel was easier; they could go off on horseback to see what their neighbours were doing. Thanks to the influence of King George III, farming became a popular, even an aristocratic pursuit. "The farming tribe," wrote Arthur Young during this period, "is now made up of all ranks, from a duke to an apprentice." The Duke of Bedford, Coke of Norfolk, later Earl of Leicester, and others opened their farms for inspection and lavishly entertained their visitors; the annual sheep-shearings at Woburn and at Holkham drew crowds of farmers to see better animals, larger crops, new and improved implements, better buildings and new methods which they might try to adopt. Agricultural writers became busy and some excellent accounts of agriculture were written by Arthur Young, Marshall, and the authors of the County Surveys that the Board of Agriculture were then conducting. There was no lack of advice to farmers.

Then came the Napoleonic Wars which brought much money into the countryside, though the farm labourer unfortunately did not get a fair share. The wars were followed by a period of great distress; "the Hungry Forties" have become a by-word.

Gradually things mended and improvements of the soil continued. The older farmers had had no difficulties with the loams, but they could not tackle the very light sands and they had great trouble with the heavy clays which obstinately retained water, becoming very sticky and difficult to plough and which, in dry weather, were hard as a brick and cracked badly. The damp affected the human beings: rheumatism and especially ague were common.

COTTAGE HOMES OF RURAL ENGLAND

In this quiet corner of Essex is typified the story of life on the arable lands of Britain. Many of the farm workers live in old thatched cottages, often far removed from the nearest village settlement. The high road may pass near their homes, but their horizon is bounded by the farm-house, the fields and the nearest shopping centre. In Essex, where there is no local building stone, cottages are built of timber or lath and plaster; many like those below date from the eighteenth century or earlier. There is real charm in this old cottage architecture and in the gay covering of white-wash or colour-wash on the walls.

HORSES ON A KENTISH FARM

The tractor has not meant the end of the horse's usefulness on the farm. Most farmers in the lowlands keep a pair or larger team. For carting away the timber along deeply rutted forest tracks when trees have been felled, a team of horses is still most often used in all parts of the country.

Only three crops could be grown with any certainty: wheat, beans and grass; of these, wheat was the most important. Fortunately it did not suffer in dry weather—the old proverb ran "Drought never bred dearth in England"—but in wet weather wheat suffered badly. A wet harvest was disastrous.

To allow the excess of water to escape, the land was laid up in high ridges, separated by deep furrows; many of these still survive in the clay fields of the Midlands and West Country, though time has somewhat flattened them. The drainage was very inefficient. Then in 1850 came the first pipe drains made by machinery, and drainage was extensively practised, often with more enthusiasm than discretion, for at first the drains were laid too deep. Later efforts, however, were very successful. Meanwhile the great agricultural societies were stimulating interest in agricultural improvements.

The period 1855 to 1875 was the most brilliant in British agricultural history. The town population was increasing and demanding more and better food. Prices were good, labour was plentiful and efficient, but unfortunately ill-paid, and there was a run of good seasons. The standards of farming were high, village craftsmanship was at its peak and experts came from overseas to study, admire and copy British methods.

Going round the countryside one would have found it to be pulsating with life, dotted with stately mansions, well staffed—for they were hospitable times —good farm-houses and attractive villages, though the cottages were small and as yet there was no sanitation. The old subsistence farming had mostly gone and with it all the uniformity of the

SCYTHEMAN AND THATCHER

The field of corn is nearly ripe and the scytheman prepares to cut round the edge of the field. Even today it is usual for the first cutting round the edge of the field to be made by scythe. Among the crafts handed down from the Middle Ages is that of thatching, and the thatcher is always in demand for the upkeep of the hundreds of thousands of thatched roofs which survive in rural districts as well as for covering stacks at harvest time. More of these craftsmen are needed.

medieval scene; instead, farming for the market was the rule, specialization was more common: arable farming dominated in the east and south, and grass farming in the west and north. The old structure of the feudal village had gone and was replaced by the three-class society—landlord, tenant farmer and farmworker—still to be found to-day. The fields were admirably kept and well cropped; there were green meadows, pleasing woods and beautiful parks which blended into an harmonious landscape. While the villagers had little money, they had plenty of joy in life; the old feasts and holiday customs still survived, there was food and shelter; the village was a close-knit community with squire, parson, farmer and labourer, each knowing his God-appointed place and playing his part. For all that, however, life was hard for the labourer and more especially for the womenfolk.

BEDFORDSHIRE POULTRY FARM

Feeding a flock of Rhode Island Red and Light Sussex hens on a Bedfordshire farm near Luton. In recent years most of the large flocks have been of specialized breeds. Both these strains are noted for their output of eggs.

Then came the collapse. The opening up of western North America to agricultural settlers led to a great increase in world production of wheat and meat; and the completion of the transport system put the products on British markets at prices with which the farmers could not compete. The final blow came in 1879 when an appallingly wet summer and autumn ruined corn crops and inflicted much disease on the animals, so that farmers had little to sell and they obtained only wretched prices.

Later seasons were better, but not the prices. Farmers struggled bravely on, but in the end they had to give up trying; some left the land, others stayed on and, by dint of great parsimony, survived. In the 1890s there was a bedraggled land-scape with hedges overgrown, becoming almost thickets; ditches and brooks untended, so that the banks caved in and the water overflowed; drains were blocked with the result that the fields long remained wet and boggy; much of the heavy arable land was left derelict, covering itself with wild vegetation; thorns and briars growing up. Cottages and farm-houses were neglected, and although the big house still stood, the owner was usually not interested in agriculture. Sport was now the chief use for the land, copses were planted to afford shelter for game, no wire fences were allowed in a hunting district, and those young men who wanted to remain usually had to become gardeners or gamekeepers.

Fortunately, during this time the soil remained, in spite of human neglect; it was sheltered by Nature's covering of wild vegetation and saved for the day of awakening which was soon to come.

The severe competition from North America could not continue indefinitely. Technically their method was hopelessly bad—it was simply that of medieval England, a fallow season followed by one or two grain crops, but, lacking the frequent English rainfall, the fallows remained bare with no vegetation cover. Matters were made worse by the disk cultivation which reduced the surface soil to a fine powder in the hope of conserving the moisture below. Soon the soil began to blow away, and the great Dust Bowl developed; the farmers who had ruined English agriculture were themselves ruined in the process; more completely, indeed, because they lost their soil, while in Britain it was still safe in Nature's keeping.

Meanwhile British townspeople were developing a taste for milk, eggs, meat, vegetables and fruit, some of which, especially the milk, best-quality meat, soft fruit, potatoes and other bulky vegetables, had to be home-produced. Livestock became the mainstay of farming, with fruit, vegetables and potatoes as subsidiaries of growing importance. Industry provided some useful by-products for animal food: oil cake, maize feeds and residues of the fermentation industry. Many farmers gave up arable crops and had only grass fields for their livestock and they purchased concentrated feeds.

From about 1900, prices improved and the system of agricultural education started in the 1890s began to tell. Agricultural colleges and experimental farms grew up, and Rothamsted, for long the only important experimental station in the country, took on a new lease of life, having begun its work in 1843. Agricultural science played an increasing part in practical agriculture, thanks to the devoted efforts of numbers of research workers, expert advisers and teachers. Farmers made more and better use of the artificial fertilizers introduced by John Bennett Lawes in 1842. For long they had relied chiefly on phosphates, but later nitrogenous and potassic fertilizers came into fuller use. Liming and chalking, neglected since the palmy days

POULTRY FARM NEAR MALVERN

Poultry farming is a comparatively recent rural industry. Before the turn of the century almost every farmer had a flock of poultry, but there were few who specialized. Their number increased rapidly after the First World War, especially in the Fylde district of Lancashire and in the western counties of England. Though their total has decreased since the peak of the 1920s, poultry farming on a scientific basis is now fully established.

of the 1860s, were again practised. Remunerative crops like potatoes, brussels sprouts, kale, mangolds and, later on, sugar beet, were more and more grown in place of the old costly swedes; these made excellent preparations for corn crops, and gradually the whole outlook for arable farming improved.

The framework of arable farming was still the four-course rotation, and even in 1944 about half the arable land of the country was in cereals, about one quarter in temporary grass and clover, and the other quarter in the cultivated crops such as those already mentioned. The grassland also was improved, first by means of basic slag, drainage and cultivation, afterwards by re-seeding with improved strains.

All branches of science have helped in these great developments. Animal diseases were studied, and steps taken to reduce them, though the work has not yet proceeded far. Plant diseases also were studied. The old Free Trade system and improved transport had permitted the introduction of American gooseberry mildew, wart disease of potatoes and other diseases and pests on which millions of pounds have since been spent in attempts at eradication.

RESULTS OF MECHANIZATION

The most important factor in the rehabilitation of agriculture has been the increased output per man per day, brought about by the more widespread use of machinery, in particular the small tractor. It works at double the speed of a horse and will pull a bigger load. A man with a tractor can plough several times as much per day as a man with a pair of horses. This additional speed is of great importance in the uncertain climate of Britain, for it means that a job which might otherwise have to be left half-done for weeks can be completely finished during a fine interval. The tractor fur-

ther has the psychological advantage that it appeals to the young mechanically minded countryman.

Electricity has also helped to increase the output per man per day by improved lighting of the farm buildings during the winter and by more efficient driving of grinders, chaff-cutters and other machinery. This increased output per day has enabled higher wages to be paid and so has helped to keep men on the land.

MORE ECONOMIC PRODUCTION

Throughout the years much has remained unchanged. Many of the fields still have the same boundaries as when they were enclosed in the sixteenth and seventeenth centuries, though some have since been subdivided. Even the boundaries of the medieval three fields still survive in many places and the numerous manor farms perpetuate the feudal lord's demesne. Many of the fields still bear the name of an early possessor.

The distribution of fields between the various farms, however, has often changed, and modern farms frequently have outlying fields and so lack the compact form which would make for most economical working. But the farms have remained small; a large part of the land of Britain is in holdings of fifty to three hundred acres. The number of farmers in England and Wales in the census of 1931 was almost identical with that of 1871; the amalgamations that so completely changed industry and commerce during those sixty years left farmers unaffected. Company farming is rare except as an adjunct to any activity such as processing or distribution.

Changes are, however, beginning. The tractor is more easily manœuvred in rectangular fields not too small, and for most arable purposes hedges, except when they are needed for shelter, are a nuisance, harbouring vermin and taking up space. Another factor that has led to greater economy in farm production has been a closer adaptation of the cropping system to the local conditions.

It is particularly interesting to note how the soil is used and particularly why it is so used. A good starting point is where the first agricultural settlers began—on the chalk of the southern counties, Wiltshire, Berkshire, Hampshire, Sussex, open rolling country with few hedges and fewer houses. Usually the soil is thin and very porous, so that, like sand, it dries quickly after rain, but otherwise it differs considerably from the sands: it is cooler, frequently free from acidity, rather more retentive of plant food and considerably more difficult to cultivate. Chalk soils need organic manure, potash and consolidation; then they will grow most crops.

In the old days sheep were the best cultivators and their use goes back to such remote times that they have become differentiated in the various chalk regions: Sussex, Hampshire, Oxford, for instance, all have their own breeds. The classical treatment was to grow a course of sheep feeds: swedes, kale, grass, clover, vetches, etc., turn sheep into the crop, enclosing them with hurdles so that their tramping consolidated the land and the manure enriched

MODERN FARM BUILDINGS

The replacement of old and tumbledown farm buildings has been greatly accelerated in every part of Britain since mechanization of the farm began. Like mechanization, it involves a heavy capital outlay but one which often repays the farmer with a high dividend. All too many old granaries were not proof against rats and damp, whilst unhygienic cowsheds lessened the yield of milk. This photograph shows a typical modern layout of farm buildings on a West Riding of Yorkshire farm in the foothills of the Pennine country.

PLOUGHING NEAR CUPAR, FIFE

Fifeshire is one of the richest agricultural areas of Scotland. Lying mainly between the Firth of Tay and the Firth of Forth, the whole area is under the shelter of the Scottish Highlands and enjoys a comparatively mild and dry climate. Oats, barley and roots are the principal crops but wheat grows well in sheltered localities. Here autumn ploughing is in progress, the plough drawn by a pair of horses, though many of the farms in the area are fully mechanized. Notice the seagulls which follow the plough in search of worms and grubs, and the trim line of stacks arranged in the traditional pattern of this district.

it. There then followed one or more, usually two, corn crops. Great ingenuity was shown in organizing the sheep crops so that there was an abundance of the right kind of food at each season of the year, especially at lambing time. Heavy wooden ploughs assisted in the consolidation of the soil, but great skill was needed to get a tilth as the soil is very apt to dry in hard, steely lumps.

The farms must be large so as to avoid overcrowding the sheep, for, as the shepherds say, the worst enemy of the sheep is another sheep. Considerable resources are required, and chalk-land farming is no occupation for a small man.

This sheep-folding system is, however, now uneconomic because of the large amount of labour involved and also there is a dearth of shepherds.

Cultivation is rapidly becoming mechanized, this being favoured by the freedom from hedges and the smooth, rounded contours of the land. It is quite common to see a whole chain of operations being done at once: ploughing, pressing, harrowing and sowing. The speed of working ensures that the seed is in before the tilth has dried out, while the rapid stubble-cleaning in autumn helps to get rid of weeds.

Passing eastwards, Sussex is well known for its small poultry farms, while English fruit-growing reaches its perfection in Kent. Here a race of highly skilled fruit- and hop-growers has developed which has fully earned for the county its title of "the Garden of England." The curious round oast houses in which the hops are dried, with the conical roofs surmounted by a vane, are a characteristic feature of the farm buildings. But the heavier soils of Kent are not suited for fruit; they are largely under grass, and the traveller to Dover by rail through the Weald of Kent, must often have wondered how it could accurately be termed a garden.

Passing northwards across the Thames, Essex epitomizes the agricultural history of England. On its heavy soils wheat and beans were long the common crops, but the cultivation was always troublesome and the farms were not large. When wheat became unprofitable in the 1880s and 1890s much of this land became derelict and tumbled down to very poor pasture.

Young men from south-west Scotland, reared on milk- and potato-farms and allured by the prospect of cheap farms

NORTHUMBERLAND FARMSTEAD

Northumberland is relatively poor farming country except near the east coast where the green plain is fruitful and most of the large mixed farms are situated. Inland, spurs of the Cheviot Hills stretch out long fingers of moorland where, as in the Yorkshire Pennines and the Border Country, only hardy breeds of moorland sheep find pasturage. Farm-houses in this district generally are small and scattered, many of them depending almost entirely on sheep rearing. This photograph was taken near Wooler, which is south of Berwick-on-Tweed.

near the rapidly expanding city of London, came down, bringing their farming system with them. By dint of hard work and considerable skill they succeeded. Essex has, however, some admirable brick earth and loams in the Rodings district and elsewhere, and on these crops are grown for seed, also vegetables, especially green peas.

Suffolk has always been a livestock county and its breeds of sheep, cattle and horses are amongst the best of the country besides being some of the most beautiful. There was always much artistry in Suffolk craftsmanship and it would be hard to find more attractive churches and towns than Lavenham and other Suffolk places. Its farms are of medium size and there is a wide range of

FARMING IN STAFFORDSHIRE

In the background is Hen Cloud; the distant line of moorlands is where the Pennine Chain merges into the Peak country of Derbyshire. The rolling countryside has a soil which is chiefly a mixture of limestone and clay; it is not unfertile, though most suitable for pasture. By the addition of lime good crops can be gathered. The field below is in the first stage of lime treatment.

cropping, with the vegetables on the lighter and sugar beet on the heavier land. Suffolk, however, has a considerable area of very light sand, the Breckland, which has been waste all through the years but has recently been reclaimed by liming and the growth of lucerne, cocksfoot and suchlike fed to dairy cattle, then ploughed and followed by sugar beet, barley or ley. Much, however, has been planted with conifers, the most economical treatment of this land.

Norfolk is the home of agricultural experiment and enterprise and an important centre of smallholdings. Its farms are generally of medium size; they are well managed and carry a wide range of arable crops of high quality. It has much more sugar beet than any other county and its malting barley is excellent. In recent years there has been a remarkable development of fruit-growing accompanied by the establishment of a cider industry formerly considered a preserve of the West Country.

Farmers and workers are both alert and ready to catch on to new ideas; Norfolk has always been the home of dissent and nonconformity in farming, politics and religion. But the Norfolk farmers have never been animal breeders and Norfolk is one of the few important agricultural counties that has no special breed of its own. It was for long famous for its beef fattened in yards during the winter; the store animals were usually purchased from the west or north. They were, however, kept as much for the sake of the manure as for meat. For the light arable soils of Norfolk need farmyard manure, although they respond to artificials; if the beef just paid for itself farmers were well content with the manure as profit.

In recent years, however, production in yards has been too costly, and dairying has tended to take its place. The old

WINTER HARROWING IN BUCKINGHAMSHIRE

Like the Berkshire Downs, shown on page 96, the Chiltern Hill country of Buckinghamshire is now much more productive of corn and root crops than previously. Its flinty soil is typical of all the ploughed land on the chalk in southern England. Though England is the most highly mechanized farming country in the world, a team of horses, as here, is still often used on many small farms, but use is increasing of machines which travel from farm to farm.

system required good farm buildings and ample bullock yards; to these have been added in many cases good cowsheds, dairies, piggeries and a silo. Swedes used to be the main animal food, and are still important but have been largely displaced by mangolds, sugar beet tops, either fed green or as silage, and by crops grown for silage. Pigs also are much produced in Norfolk.

In the eastern counties there is much more arable land than grass. Cambridgeshire, like the other eastern counties, is mostly arable and has chiefly general farms of medium size. The Black Fens

(including the Isle of Ely) are probably the richest soils in England; they produce great crops of wheat, potatoes, sugar beet and a few special crops like celery, and mustard for Norwich. Potatoes are not of high quality, and tend to blacken on boiling; barley is of malting quality only in dry seasons. Bedfordshire is much more specialized and has a most interesting market-garden region, rich, but with very unattractive villages.

The Holland division of Lincolnshire is perhaps the most specialized of all English counties. It has a superb silty

FORESTRY TODAY

At the Forestry Commission's school at Glentrees, Peebles, Scotland, students are cutting pit-props. The establishment of this school in 1946 was one more stage in the scientific re-afforestation of Britain through the agency of the Forestry Commission.

soil, it is mostly arable and nearly thirty per cent of this is in potatoes which are of high quality. It is usual to sprout them before planting, this gives earlier and larger yields; it is done in wooden trays in large glasshouses which form a distinctive feature of the farm buildings. In a few favoured regions, such as Leyston, potatoes come off so early that they can be followed direct by broccoli, making two profitable crops in one year. Green peas for canning are also largely grown in the Holland division. During recent years bulb-growing has been introduced and has been very successfully developed.

Lindsey is by far the largest division of the county; its farming is much more general than that of Holland and it has many more head of dairy cattle.

Yorkshire is one of the most varied counties of Britain; the Vale of York is highly fertile with many small arable farms; the Wolds are chalk and, as in the southern counties, the farms are large, mainly arable, dependent on corn, grass-fed sheep and cattle. The West Riding is wetter, has more grass and many more dairy cattle. It is also one of the chief beef-cattle regions of Britain, as is also the North Riding on a smaller scale. Yorkshire is well known for its white pigs.

Durham is famous as the cradle of the popular Shorthorn cattle and has a good agriculture with much potato cultivation and dairying on the coast. Much of the county, however, is spoilt by mining.

Northumberland is a land of sturdy independent farmers producing sheep on the hills and beef cattle in the valleys: it is second only to Yorkshire in numbers of sheep. Tweedside has some remarkable farms, some well mechanized. Few experiences are more stimulating than a discussion at "high tea" in a Tweedside farm-house with a group of local farmers comparing animals or yields and sizes of swedes. Northumberland and the hills to the north send many ewes to southern farms, where they are popular because they are such good mothers and commonly produce twins.

Scotland has some famous farming regions; its sheep are eagerly sought after.

The Lothians produce potatoes, vegetables, oats and barley; the Aberdeen region produces beef and seed potatoes free from virus disease because the aphis which carries it cannot tolerate the climate; Perthshire has an interesting raspberry area and the south-west produces potatoes and strawberries; there is also much dairying.

Returning to the west of England the region of grass is encountered. This is because of the high rainfall and, as sheep

V. VIEW OF DEDHAM: *Thomas Gainsborough*

VI. RICHMOND CASTLE: *P. Wilson Steer*

VII. SOMERIES CASTLE, BEDFORDSHIRE: *Paul Sandby*

VIII. THE HAY-WAIN: *John Consta...*

dislike rain, they are largely replaced by cattle. Cumberland and Westmorland, however, produce the strikingly handsome, very sturdy and somewhat pugnacious Herdwicks. Cumberland has some good tillage land in the Vale of Eden and around the Solway Firth, carrying a fair acreage of potatoes, much increased during the war.

Lancashire has a large population of dairy cattle and many pigs, turkeys and poultry. The Fylde is a very interesting agricultural region and around Orms-

kirk in a dry district large quantities of potatoes are grown.

Cheshire is the leading dairy county; much of the milk was formerly converted into cheese with pigs as a by-product; with improved transport much more of the milk is sold fresh. There is also a large area of potatoes. The Cheshire type of agriculture is suitable to the small man and there are many good small-holders there.

Shropshire, especially the northern plain, has good mixed farming with

TIMBER FELLING IN WORCESTERSHIRE

Two world wars, during which import of timber from overseas was of necessity restricted, have sadly depleted stocks of mature timber, especially the oak and beech, in the woodlands of Great Britain. The policy now is to conserve what remains and to plant especially conifers. This photograph shows oaks felled on the Shrawney estate in Worcestershire, which has supplied much of the timber required for the new House of Commons.

much dairying and sugar beet. The hills to the south are not too wet and in consequence carry many sheep.

Worcestershire has much specialized production, particularly of plums and vegetables. The Vale of Evesham, an undulating tract, is one of the richest in England, where owing to the good climate a body of small farmers is raising an astonishing amount of produce from the land. An important industry in fruit and vegetable preserving has developed. Outside the Vale can be seen some interesting and highly developed mechanized farming which attracts many agricultural pilgrims.

Warwickshire, Leicestershire and Rutland are all grass counties on the heavy limestone clay much used for bullock fattening—an industry that goes well with fox hunting; much of the land is still laid up in the old ridges made when it was arable. The famous fattening pastures of Leicestershire and Rutland are very productive but form only a small proportion of the whole grass.

Herefordshire produces the wonderful beef breed, the Hereford cattle, which have found their way into many other countries. It is also a fruit and hop country, though its orchards lack the distinction of those of Kent and Norfolk.

Passing from Herefordshire into Wales, the pattern of agriculture is set by the environment, the hills and the high rainfall in the west diminishing as one goes eastwards towards England. Small family farms are the almost invariable rule; till recently the farming was mainly for subsistence, now it is for market. The products are cattle, sheep and, where practicable, milk. The country life has many distinctive and interesting features, but it involves hard work with often no great recompense.

Returning to England, Gloucestershire is a grass county. It has a good deal of fruit and produces a special breed of pigs, the "Gloucester Old Spots." The Cotswold section has conditions and types of farming like those of the chalk.

Somerset also is mainly grass and has much dairy and beef production.

Devon, also largely grass, is the leading beef-cattle county of Britain and much dairy farming is carried on there. It produces two famous breeds of cattle, the North and South Devons. On its fertile red soils there is good mixed farming, and in many places fruit.

This bird's-eye view of British agriculture does far from justice to the subject because it misses so much of the finer points and special features. Every county can show something of distinctive interest, the result of the great diversity of soils and climatic conditions

THE OLD MARKET, WYMONDHAM

Markets grew up towards the close of feudal days in England. In some cases a cross marked the site. In others, there was a small covered market like this one at Wymondham, Norfolk, which was built in 1618.

BULFORD MILL, ESSEX

The rural mill is one of the few features from the earliest village communities which have survived. Many mills retain their original sites, though the power to drive them is no longer derived from the water wheel. Apart from water, the chief source of power was formerly the wind, and it is only within the last few years that windmills in Britain have ceased to be operated on a commercial basis. Today most mills are driven by either electricity or steam.

and of the enterprise and independence of mind and persistence of British farmers. Repeatedly a man has initiated some new method, developed it in spite of opposition or even ridicule and in the end made it part and parcel of the local farming practice.

Britain's farmers have a special flair for livestock, and their breeds, evolved over long years of patient and laborious work, are widely used in many parts of the world. The country's arable farming at its best will stand comparison with any and has the great advantage that when economic conditions have made it unremunerative the land could always

be put down to grass, still offering a living to a reduced number of men while it lay safe awaiting the day when it could profitably be broken up again.

This change from arable to grass and from grass to arable is a regular feature of the agricultural history of Britain, but farming never returns to quite the same position; the artistry of the 1860s has gone, but there is a steady increase in yields per acre of all arable crops ever since 1886, when statistics were first taken, and the value of output per man per day has steadily risen so that it has become possible to pay the worker a much better wage than formerly.

ROCKY COAST OF NORTH DEVON

The Valley of Rocks near Lynton is one of the most beautiful parts of a coastline which is justly famous for the grandeur of its scenery. The cliffs, deeply eroded by sea and weather, rise almost sheer to a height of three hundred feet or more. In the many small bays which break up the coastline there are beautiful stretches of golden sand hemmed in by craggy promontories.

The Heritage
of Scenery

THE keynote of the scenic heritage is intimate beauty allied with great diversity. Great Britain, by comparison with many other countries, is a relatively small area, yet within its confines it contains samples of almost every scenic type, from rugged mountains to quiet pastoral landscapes.

Travellers from the New World are always amazed at the changes which they see in the face of the landscape over a journey of a mere hundred miles or so, accustomed as they are to the limitless vistas of the Canadian prairies or of the great plains of the United States, where a traveller can journey for hundreds of miles without finding any appreciable change in the scenery. They find it well-nigh unbelievable that a journey of four hundred miles from south-east to north-west through England reveals something of almost every type of country.

Something akin even to the arid wastes of the deserts, far-fetched as it seems, is represented in the rich heritage of Britain. There certainly are no great deserts, but on a tiny scale the Braunton Burrows of Devonshire, the Culbin Sands of Scotland, and a few square miles of the sandy tract known as Breckland on the borders of Norfolk and Suffolk reproduce in miniature some of the qualities of the world's deserts.

The county of Kent is often called the Garden of England. It is equally true that three-quarters of England is like a garden on a vast scale, in which the beauties of Nature are enhanced by the handiwork of man and in which almost every square mile is cultivated and yields its proper harvest, whether it be grass on the hills or corn crops and roots in the valleys. There are trees and wild flowers in every county; even where main roads have despoiled limited strips of beautiful countryside the lanes and by-ways remain narrow and winding, ablaze in spring and summer with the varied colouring of wild flowers flanked by hedges or stone walls, and often overhung with a canopy of trees.

By contrast, there is little of the quality of a landscape garden in the rougher, more austere countryside of the north and west. Only a little of Wales and about a third of Scotland is reminiscent of the traditional English landscape. Perhaps it is this transition from the bountiful and fertile lowlands to the inhospitable and unproductive highlands that most amazes the visitor from overseas; for the transition is abrupt, startling in its suddenness and the two worlds of the uplands and the lowlands are so sharply distinguished, so opposed to each other, that they scarcely seem to belong to the same country.

Landscape, which changes so swiftly

at times, so gradually at others, and is never the same for many miles on end, is difficult to divide into scenic types except in broad outline. In southern England alone there are scores of rock layers, all of them exposed at different places, often very close to each other. Since each of these underlying rocks produces its own individual scenery and determines as it were the pattern of the rural scene, a complete description of the scenic heritage would involve a breaking down of the landscape into a hundred or more types, each different from the other in some small degree, yet many of them so similar that to the ordinary observer without specialized knowledge of plant life they would be indistinguishable.

So in order to appreciate the more contrasting types represented by the whole range of the heritage, it is necessary to pick out some of the most outstanding types of landscape associated with particular parts of the country. Reference has already been made to the few meagre tracts of land which are in appearance akin to desert country. These are the starting point; even they have a beauty which is all their own, a beauty which does not belong to the real deserts of the world, if only because the dunes of Braunton or Culbin are so limited that there is no chance of mono-

RIVER STOUR AT SUDBURY

The Stour Valley provided the inspiration for many of Constable's most famous paintings. Running down from the East Anglian heights, the river flows through Sudbury and Bures and forms the boundary between Suffolk and Essex. Its banks, as this photograph taken from the bridge at Sudbury shows, are well wooded; the stream in most parts is wide and sluggish.

ELM COUNTRY

The elm is one of the traditional trees of the English countryside. Many of the finest examples occur in the alluvial soil bordering the great river estuaries and the lowlands near the sea coast. Disease is now denuding all parts of the countryside of the finest elms. This photograph, typical of the district, is of the level Essex landscape near Upminster, looking toward the Thames.

tony in the scene since always there are fertile fields at no great distance in the background.

From that unpromising start the traveller proceeds, still in a quiet vein, to the countryside which is nearly entirely level, again only a tiny part of the country's scenic heritage and confined almost entirely to small parts of southern and eastern England. First there are the Fens, the only stretch of countryside which is truly level for several miles in every direction. Most of the Fens are, in fact, below sea-level and their most distinguishing feature is the black earth of the fields, black earth which is wonderfully fertile.

Almost everything grows well in the

Fen country. There are rich corn crops and thousands of acres under roots, which include the sugar beet, the latest of all the major crops to be introduced into Britain and one which is grown in such proportions that it ensures the domestic sugar supply of the whole country, without the need to import from abroad.

Where the Fens extend into Lincolnshire there is a native industry in the growing of tulips for flowers and for bulbs. Around Spalding a landscape, which all over the area is strangely reminiscent of the flat lands of Holland, takes on in spring the vivid colouring and unforgettable appearance of the tulip fields and reminds the traveller still more forcefully of the Dutch scene.

There is real beauty in the Fens, but it is a beauty for the connoisseur rather than the casual wayfarer. It is the beauty that goes hand in hand with the wealth of growing things, a beauty that is linked with the productive processes of Nature. To the inhabitants of the towns and villages near the Fens who see this landscape at every season of the year it has a fascination which grows and grows until the grandeur of mountain scenery or the rolling vistas of the downland country seem uninteresting by comparison. There is, too, a sense of limitless vistas, especially towards sunset on clear summer evenings, when looking across the Fens is like looking over the expanse of the ocean, with a line of trees or maybe a farm-house just showing above the western horizon.

There is no other countryside in Britain comparable with the Fens. Nowhere else are there level landscapes of such extent and such fertility. The closest approach to them is the alluvial plain which fringes the south coast between the whale-back ridges of the South Downs and the Sussex shore. But here there are hedges in the place of the Fenland dykes, with hedgerow timber and occasional coppices to break up the scene. The land is almost as fertile as that of the Fens, but its variety is greater and there is fine grazing land for cattle as well as ploughed fields. The

RIVER SCENERY OF EASTERN ENGLAND

This photograph of the River Waveney near Diss in Norfolk shows many of the features which are repeated again and again in the scenery of the low-lying country of eastern England. This river, which for part of its course forms the boundary between Norfolk and Suffolk, flows lazily across a countryside which is almost level. On either bank, rich pasture fields which are liable to be flooded in winter extend towards more wooded country on the slightly higher ground. This view also shows the willow trees which grow near the banks of many of the streams of Essex and East Anglia. Willows from these areas provide most of the wood which is used for making English cricket bats.

FAIRFORD, GLOUCESTERSHIRE

Tributary of the Thames, the Coln, a swift shallow stream, with lush meadows beside it and fine willow trees along its banks, gives added colour to this view of Fairford, in which the magnificent late Gothic church, famous for the medieval stained glass of its windows, dominates the village. This is a place the name of which has not changed much through the ages. It means a clear or smooth ford, a natural place for primitive people to build a settlement. A bridge now spans the stream near the site of the ancient ford.

villages, too, are older, for in the Fens, except in the medieval islands like the Isle of Ely, the villages were built not more than one hundred and fifty years ago, when the draining of the Fens was completed. But the village homes of the Sussex Plain often date back three or four hundred years, while the village church is generally much older and, in a few instances, belongs to the time when this area was first colonized by the Anglo-Saxons.

Then there are the Romney Marshes in Kent. They certainly are level enough, but the landscape is entirely different, for this is today, as it has been for hundreds of years, a great sheep-grazing country. Ploughed fields are few and far between; where they occur they mostly produce root crops. Much hay to feed cattle during the winter also is grown. But here, as in the Fens, there is a sense of great distances where the marshes stretch away from the foot of low hills towards the Kentish coast. Perhaps it is the lack of timber that helps to give the

THE AVON GORGE, SOMERSET

From the chalk country of Wiltshire the River Avon flows through Somerset and in its lower reaches forms the boundary between Gloucestershire and Somerset. On its banks lie Bradford-on-Avon, Bath and Bristol and at its mouth is Bristol's port, Avonmouth. All along its course it passes through pleasant and often dramatic scenery, first where it has scooped a deep valley out of the chalk and later after crossing the Somerset plain, where it has cut a way between the Cotswold Hills and their extension, the Mendips. It is here between Bath and the sea, and particularly near Bristol, that the Avon Gorge attains its most magnificent scenery. The limestone hills rise abruptly from both banks in the foreground of the photograph. The natural steep slope of the hills is accentuated by a quarry. Hanging woods cloak the hillsides as far as eye can reach. As in most of the great valleys of Britain, road and railway closely follow the course of the river. On the left the railway to Avonmouth can be seen winding under the hillside. On the right is the new road which closely follows the river.

sense of great distances when really the marshes are only twenty miles long and half that distance broad. For here trees are confined to the clumps which have been planted as break-winds around some of the villages and larger farmhouses.

The marshes which fringe the coasts of Essex and Lincolnshire are in the same tradition, but these are on a smaller scale, less distinctive in colouring, and less outstanding in their character. Some of the land defies cultivation and in summer the waving grass rises waist-high and rare species of wild flowers flourish almost unseen, for visitors are few and local inhabitants even fewer. There are bird sanctuaries, too, appropriately since this is surely the loneliest part of the English lowlands.

The story of Britain's lowlands is completed by the plain of East Anglia, the valleys of the great rivers which flow slowly from west to east, especially those of the Thames, the Ouse, and the Humber, the eastern coastal plain of Scotland and the wide belt of lowlands which link the Firth of Forth with the Firth of Clyde.

The Thames Valley and the great Midland Plain vie in prosperity and fame with the Vale of York and the lowlands of Scotland. For sheer richness of land there is little to choose between them. But to many observers it seems that the harsher climate of Scotland has produced, if possible, a more energetic and more hard-working race of husbandmen who draw to the uttermost limits upon the wealth of the land and unstintingly upon the labour of their own hands.

In the east and south, including the gently undulating plain of East Anglia, it is cornfields, cornfields all the way, for East Anglia is the granary of Britain. There is never a dull mile in these fertile vistas. By contrast with the Fens and the marshes, they are never entirely flat, except in the lowest reaches of the great rivers where a narrow strip of meadowland forms the flood plain of the rivers and is inundated when the streams carry down a more than ordi-

THE VALE OF EVESHAM, WORCESTERSHIRE

For many miles on either side of the River Avon from Evesham down stream to its confluence with the Severn there are extensive orchards of plum, apple and pear. Apple and plum trees even grow in the hedges of the winding lanes which link village with village in the rich valley. The photograph was taken from Broadway Hill, which rises to a height of over a thousand feet, looking across the Vale toward distant Bredon Hill.

SCENERY OF THE HAMPSHIRE DOWNS

This view of St. Catherine's Hill, near Winchester, shows the Hampshire Downs countryside in its most attractive light. As everywhere in the downland country there is a fine contrast between the trees and meadows in the valley, where the oak, the sycamore and the poplar stand out clearly, and the barer slopes of the chalk hills with only an occasional clump of trees on the skyline to mark some famous viewpoint or ancient encampment.

nary volume of water from the hills in which they rise.

For the rest, the land always rises more or less steeply from the river's banks and gives a pleasing impression of low hills concealing within their folds charming places and well-wooded hollows, a promise which is always fulfilled for the wayfarer who wanders away from the river. This is true of every river, whether in England, Scotland or Wales. The rivers that flow into the North Sea are longer, wider and more leisurely than those of the west, but that is the only difference between them. There is nothing austere or unkind about the valley of the greatest of the rivers of the west, the Severn, with its tributaries, the Wye and Avon.

The villages which lie near the banks of England's great rivers are an integral part of the heritage of landscape; nor is this surprising when it is remembered that so many English villages were founded by the Saxons and it was by river or by seashore that the Saxons chose to build their settlements.

But lovely though the villages along the Thames and Severn may be, there is no river which can vie in this respect with the Ouse. Rising above Buckingham it flows by Newport Pagnell and Olney to Newton Blossomville and Turvey before it reaches Bedford. There is no district in England where such grace of architecture, such loveliness of setting are combined as in this string of villages.

Lower down the same stream there are Godmanchester, Hemingford Abbots, Hemingford Grey and St. Ives; the two medieval bridges at Godmanchester and

St. Ives, as it were, enclosing a reach of the river in which the villages are like gems in a setting of incredible perfection. The wide lush meadows are carpeted in spring with an unbroken expanse of yellow, pink and white flowers, willows overhanging the stream, and rows of tall poplars breaking the skyline. That is England at its finest— perhaps the finest landscape of its kind in the whole world.

So much for the heritage of the lowlands. This brief survey reveals them as always interesting, nearly always fertile, often beautiful. But it is the hills which give the lowlands their very character, the lines of hills which are laid across the southern half of England and which

THE NORTH DOWNS AND THE PILGRIMS' WAY

The North Downs extend from the chalk plateau of Salisbury Plain through Surrey and Kent to the sea at Dover. The Pilgrims' Way, which is here seen approaching the Medway gap by Holly Hill, hugs the southern slopes of the Downs from Winchester to the cliffs of Dover. First blazed by prehistoric man five thousand years ago, the Pilgrims' Way has had continuous use through the ages; many miles of it today are country lanes or hedge-girt paths. Among the many romantic legends surrounding it is the tradition that thousands of pilgrims came along it on foot from Winchester and the west of England to the shrine of St. Thomas in the ancient cathedral at Canterbury.

with their variety and charm make it, as already pointed out, like a garden on a vast scale.

First there are the chalk downs, the most significant of all the southern hills, including the South Downs of Sussex, Salisbury Plain, the North Downs of Surrey and Kent, the Berkshire Downs, the Chiltern Hills and the Dorsetshire Downs. What a catalogue of inviting country, ranging from the blunt bare ridges of the Sussex Downs to the dense beech-covered slopes of the Chilterns.

The downs in fact are bare of trees where the chalk comes near the surface, but trees grow in profusion where there are pockets of clay above the chalk, and of the downland trees the beech is the most characteristic. So beeches form the clumps of the South Downs, like Chanctonbury Ring, far-seen landmark for the traveller who journeys across the Weald. Beeches, too, give the Chiltern Hills their intimate loveliness, and it is still mostly beeches when we come to the thickets of Cranborne Chase, away across the hills which reach into Dorset.

Though the high ground is often unwooded there is compensation in the springy turf which covers the barest ridges, turf which has been cropped from time immemorial by the great flocks of sheep which find pasture in the downland sheep-walks. Often, though the long ridges are bare, there are woods and streams in the quiet valleys that intersect them, whether it be where the Mole cuts through the North Downs or the Cuckmere through the South, or in the long Vale of Pewsey which divides Salisbury Plain into two.

Near the summit of many of the chalk ridges there are long trackways, ancient roads which may first have been blazed by prehistoric man. Along them are the relics of an age when Salisbury Plain was the centre of a Stone Age civilization which flourished more than four thousand years ago.

Apart from the hilltop trackways, with their nearby stone circles, fortified villages and prehistoric burial chambers, there are other ancient roads which served as links connecting one end of the chalk country with the other. Two of these stand out from the rest. One is the Pilgrims' Way, which extends along the southern slopes of the North Downs from Hampshire through Surrey to the Shakespeare Cliff by Dover; the other is the Icknield Way, which follows the line of the Chiltern Hills and the East Anglian Heights, almost unbroken from the Marlborough Downs as far as the Wash.

These two are bound up with the scenic heritage, if only because the beauty of the countryside is so well seen

CHANCTONBURY RING

One of the great landmarks of the South Downs, situated near Steyning in Sussex, the clump of beech trees marks an ancient camp which dates from the Iron Age or earlier. It marks, too, one of the highest points on the Sussex Downs—814 feet—and can be seen from the North Downs.

HENGISTBURY HEAD, HAMPSHIRE

The Hampshire coast is a fine mixture of golden sands and sandstone cliffs. Here at Hengistbury Head the cliffs are broken in a ravine half covered in drifting sand dunes. The characteristic rank grass of the sand dunes grows from the cliff top and the soft rock is broken off in steps and ledges. The headland owes its name to the tradition that it was here that Hengist and Horsa, the Jute heroes of legend, landed with their forces to found a new kingdom.

from the narrow footpaths and hedge-girt lanes which today follow the course of the ancient tracks. Always there are the downs on the one hand and the fertile expanse of the valley on the other, whether it is the Weald of Kent or the Midland Plain, stretching away as far as the eye can reach. In summer there is brilliant colouring in this no-man's-land between the chalk of the hills and the clay of the valleys, when the rich tint of poppies growing on the edge of the ploughed fields, in the hedges and on the downs themselves brings a splash of scarlet to set off the green of the hills and the yellow gold of the ripening corn-fields.

The sandstone hills are less dominant than the chalk downs, but they, too, form a significant part of the scenic heritage of the south. Mostly they run in ridges parallel with the downs and it is in Kent, Surrey and Sussex that they reach their greatest beauty. The pine-clad slopes of Hindhead, the bare beauty of Blackdown, the hanging woods that

SURREY WOODLANDS IN WINTER

Of all the Home Counties, Surrey is the least fertile. Much of it falls within the area of sandstone country which includes Leith Hill, Holmbury Hill and the wide belt of heathland to the south of the Tillingbourne Valley. Elsewhere the landscape is mainly dominated by the chalk hills. This photograph was taken on the slopes of the Hackhurst Downs which extend to the Hampshire boundary.

BEECH-WOODS OF THE NORTH

Although the Chiltern Hills contain the most magnificent groves of beech trees in Britain, the beech is common in many other parts of the countryside. This view taken near Hovingham in Yorkshire could just as well have been taken almost anywhere in the south country. It shows beech trees coming into their spring-time glory, the bright sunshine penetrating the new foliage, and sheep with their spring lambs grazing on the pastures beneath the trees.

cloak Toys Hill in Kent, and the heather- and bracken-covered commons of Ashdown Forest—these are all sandstone country. The pine woods and rhododendron plantations are the glories of the sandstone, in just the same way as the beech woods are the glory of the chalk. Deciduous trees grow only where there is clay above the sandstone, for the sandstone country is very dry and porous and relatively unfertile.

The sandstone is the country of the park lands, for where man could not grow crops easily he wisely chose the land to lay out fine estates for hunting and pleasure. Many of these estates have survived from the later Middle Ages right up to the present day and contain some of the most dramatic man-made scenery in all England. Knole Park by Sevenoaks and Paddockhurst Park in the forest ridge are typical of dozens of others. They stand out in the memory largely because of their size and the richness of their mature timber.

Much of the sandstone country is bare heath-land, good neither for man nor beast. Thousands of acres of the Surrey countryside grow nothing but thin heather and stunted bracken, with a little furze and here and there a clump of pine trees. It is in autumn here that the scene takes on its grandest colours; the heather blooms in a riot of purple and turns whole hillsides into a panorama which resembles on a small scale the

IN ARUNDEL PARK, SUSSEX

This photograph was taken on the path which leads toward the summit of the downs from the lake in the park of Arundel Castle, Sussex, home of the Duke of Norfolk. It is one of the largest and loveliest parks in Britain.

IN THE UPLANDS OF LANARKSHIRE

Tinto Hill forms the background of this view across one of the valleys of Scotland's southern uplands. In the valley there is a village grouped about the large farmstead, almost surrounded by noble trees. The land rises gradually to the vast unfenced sheep-walks of the hills, famous for their springy turf and extensive views. Much of the scenery of southern Scotland is like this, from the eastern coastal plain almost as far as the Atlantic seaboard and from the moorlands of the border country northward as far as the lofty, rugged peaks which overlook the lowland belt of the Firth of Clyde.

autumn glory of the Scottish moors.

There is another kind of sandstone country, even more outstanding in its colouring. This is the country of the old red sandstone of Devonshire, which once seen is immediately recognized, for the ruddy hue of the underlying rock appears in the colouring of the ploughed fields, in the red cliffs that stand out in startling contrast with the whiteness of the sands of the seashore and in the building stone which has been used in village and town and is best seen in noble buildings like Exeter Cathedral.

To the south of Dartmoor, as far as the sea, most of the landscape belongs to this rock formation. Its uncommon colouring is the chief quality which has made the scenery of South Devon world-famous. The land is never flat, but undulates gently. On high ground and low there are fertile fields and a

EXMOOR PONIES

Exmoor is one of the last surviving homes of many species of wild life. The red deer which once roamed freely over all the moorlands of Somerset and North Devon are almost extinct. But, as in Hampshire's New Forest, a few wild ponies survive. They are entirely untended and find food, winter and summer, on the wooded slopes of Exmoor, and even foal in the open.

rich growth of wild flowers and ferns in the lanes, the Devonshire lanes which poet and novelist alike have praised.

The old red sandstone of South Devon is only one part, though a magnificent one, of the complexity of scenic types which together make the Devon and Cornwall landscape conspicuously lovely in colour and composition. In the north of Devon the finest hill and cliff scenery of England is where Exmoor breaks off at the sea. Along the coast westward from Ilfracombe the cliffs themselves are often wooded. At other times they rise sheer for close on five hundred feet.

Inland Exmoor alternates between heather-clad slopes reminiscent of the sandstone country of the south-east and densely wooded combes and valleys like the valley of the Badgeworthy Water, the Lorna Doone country. Here is one of the traditional homes of the red deer and a great hunting country. Exmoor is now first and foremost a holiday district. But it has not lost its intimate beauty or its sequestered ways. Its area is too great for that and the towns which surround it where holiday-makers can find accommodation are too few and too small.

Entirely different is the granite country of the south-west, a landscape type which includes Dartmoor, Bodmin Moor and the rocky promontory of Land's End. Dartmoor is bleak and windswept and wet, its almost uncharted boglands matching the high rainfall on the hills and the long days when the clouds touch the ground and their misty darkness covers the countryside in a grey unbroken pall. Yet there is brightness when the sun shines and the valley scene is spread out before the wayfarer who ascends to the peaks, but the highlands even under the blue sky and the warm sun remain lonely and desolate, for they grow nothing but rank grass and thin heather and over thousands of acres not even the hardy mountain sheep can find pasture.

The bedrock granite is exposed in the tors of Dartmoor and granite fragments are strewn down the steep hillside. At Land's End, too, the granite is exposed and this is one of the wildest and rockiest headlands in the whole world, certainly the most impressive in Britain. Unlike its northern counterpart, John o' Groats, Land's End does give the impression of being the end of the land. As one looks out across the seething cauldron of the Atlantic, whipped and torn by the rapid currents that rush round the Cornish coast, it is as though one were standing on the deck of a ship out at sea, an impression heightened by the roar of the waves as they break against the hard granite and the whistling of the wind as it sweeps round the crevices and chimneys of the deeply eroded rock face.

The granite, then, represents what is wildest and most lonely in the south. By contrast the limestone stands for everything that is pleasant and quiet and charming. Limestone is the rock which underlies the long chain of hills that reaches from Somerset across central England into Yorkshire. Whether the hills are known as the Mendips or the Cotswolds or the Leicestershire Wold, or the Lincolnshire Cliff or the North York Moors, the scenery clearly belongs to the same family type. The escarpment, with its wide views and the steep drop to the plain, faces to the north and west. South and east of the high ridge the land falls away in a tumbled mass of hill and dale, watered by many streams beside whose banks are the stone-built villages which have made the wold a byword for beauty of cottage architecture.

The magnificence of the Cheddar Gorge in Somerset, where the limestone cliff has been worn away and rises sheer from the pass road for hundreds of feet, is matched by the quieter but none the less dramatic beauty of the Windrush Valley in Gloucestershire and by the steep hill country on the borders of Leicestershire and Rutland which is the epitome of all the country of the hunting shires.

One element binds together this vast tract of country—that is the Cotswold

VALES AND HILLS OF EXMOOR

From Grabbist Hill, near Dunster, Somerset, the view extends across the fertile valley toward the uplands of North Devon. On the high slopes nearest the camera only heather and bracken and the hardy pine tree flourish. By contrast on the lower ground rich grass fields bounded by trim hedges with generous hedgerow timber alternate with coppices and an occasional ploughed field. In this one view are all the elements which go to make up the rural scene in most of the hill country of the south and west of England, where the climatic conditions make intensive cultivation of the land impossible.

HEATHLAND ON HANKLEY

Between the valley of the Wey and the heights of Hindhead, hundreds of square miles of Surrey are open heathland, unsuitable for cultivation owing to the thin soil and the porous sand composing it. In parts, where the soil has an admixture of clay, there are

building stone, which is used from end to end of the wold, a warm grey limestone which weathers beautifully and tones with the prevailing hues of the landscape. It is found in cottage and manor-house, in farmstead and church, in medieval building and in modern town. It is the most splendid building stone of rural England, more significant, if only because more widespread, than the granite of Aberdeen, the cobblestones of North Norfolk or the rubble and flint of the chalk country. Its fame has spread beyond the region of the Cotswold; Peterborough Cathedral is built throughout of Barnack stone,

COMMON, SURREY

clumps of trees, evergreen as well as deciduous. Otherwise the vegetation con-
sists almost entirely of heather and bracken. In this picture, beyond the silver birches
is the dip known as the Lion's Mouth, which lies between Thursley and Tilford.

which is a local form of Cotswold stone; and towns like Oundle, which lie many miles from the wold proper, still somehow are united with it by virtue of the stone from which they are built.

Apart from its buildings, the Cotswold and the hills which belong to the same limestone have many other claims to rank high in the order of English landscape beauty. Except on the very highest ground, the land is fertile. Though the wych elm, which gave its name to several Cotswold villages, has nearly disappeared, there is still a wealth of timber to give added beauty to the scene, and even on the upper slopes of the Cotswold itself corn crops are grown and yield a good harvest. There is nothing in the Cotswold that fails to delight the eye; there are magnificent manor-houses like Compton Wynyates, exquisite villages like Lower Slaughter or Bibury, exhilarating commons like Cleve Common, the hanging woods which cloak the valley sides round Stroud, and even heather-covered moors in north Yorkshire. They are all part and parcel of the heritage of beauty and they are all derived from the properties of the limestone soil.

Another great ridge in which limestone predominates forms the backbone of England. The Pennine Chain stretches southward from the Border country and the highland that falls away from the Cumberland mountains as far as the Peak in Derbyshire. This is a very different countryside from that of the Cotswold, much greyer, much bleaker, yet often revealing unsuspected beauty and in its beauty and in its hundreds of miles of unfenced hills giving to the moorland trampers of Yorkshire and Lancashire an ideal countryside in which to roam for miles without reaching village or town.

The Pennine Chain is the watershed of England. In the boggy morasses of its high places most of the rivers which flow into the North Sea and into the Irish Sea have their origin. In Yorkshire they have carved out long and tortuous

A KENTISH FARM-HOUSE

This panorama of orchard-land at Newington, near Sittingbourne, shows a modest farm-house entirely surrounded by hundreds of acres of apple trees. The farm-house is characteristic of the homesteads of the "yeomen of Kent," the small freehold farmers who won a reputation for good farming and substantial wealth. Behind the farm-house are the conical-capped oast houses in which hops are dried. There are still hundreds of acres of hop gardens in the Weald of Kent, but elsewhere hops have been replaced by fruit trees or pasture.

SCOTTISH BORDER COUNTRY

A little-known part of Scotland, the country which lies to the north of the Solway Firth has much lovely scenery and a wide belt of good agricultural land. This photograph taken near Dumfries shows harvest time in the plain near the Solway Firth against the background of the rolling grass-covered hills. All the central part of the Scottish Border country is high fell and moorland where the Cheviot Hills reach their highest points. But near the east end of the boundary between the two countries there is another belt of flat green country-side called the Merse, which is the most southerly division of Berwickshire and is very similar in appearance to these lowlands of Dumfries.

valleys deep-set in the moorland massif. These are the Yorkshire dales, among them Wharfedale, Nidderdale and Wensleydale. The beauty of these dales is derived partly from the grandeur of the surrounding scenery, the contrast between the green fields and woods of the valley and the naked moors which are never far away and partly, too, from the man-made beauties of riverside villages and the ruins of the many abbeys which the Benedictine and Cistercian orders founded in Norman times as oases of culture in these wild places.

The contrast between the serried streets of Rochdale and the open breezy moorland that begins a bare two miles from the centre of the town is as startling as it is effective. To drive or walk on any of the roads that lead from the cotton towns on the west of the Pennines or the woollen towns on their eastern slopes and come suddenly upon the grassy slopes of the hills where an occasional stone wall and the scattered farm-houses are the only signs of human habitation is like entering a new world. As the traveller mounts higher, even these links with civilization disappear and there is nothing but grass and sky and views without apparent limit.

CHEDDAR GORGE, SOMERSET

The most remarkable rocky pass in England, the Cheddar Gorge, carries the road from Cheddar northward to the summit of the Mendip Hills. The sheer rock face, eroded into pinnacles and ledges, is composed of the limestone which makes up the whole long line of hills. The rock is soft and porous. Underground rivers have worn away huge caverns, several of which lie at the southern foot of the gorge between Cheddar and Wookey.

Equalling the loveliness of the Yorkshire dales are the valleys where the Pennines break up to the south of the Peak. Here the Dove has eroded for itself a deep chasm in the limestone hills, which are fantastically shaped and equally fantastically named—the Twelve Apostles, or, as it may be, the Lion Rock or Tissington Spires. Here is beauty of scenery which combines the austerity of rocky canyons with the calm serenity of wooded valleys and quiet pastoral country.

The Pennines are the link between the lowlands and the highlands. They partake of the nature of both. Just as at their northern end they merge into the Cumbrian mountains, so at their southern extremity they end as a ridge of high ground overlooking the Midland Plain.

The only real mountain scenery of England is that contained in the Lake District, a small area of mountain and lake so well known, so often described and visited that it seems to have lost something at least of its true character. For if there is one thing that makes the highlands the most magnificent part of the scenic heritage it is their loneliness and vast expanses. These the Lake District of England lacks, though on a small scale it reproduces much of the majesty of the Scottish Highlands. But the distances are so small that the area has something of the quality of a peep show, with Nature, as it were, conspiring to show a sample of her every glory with the greatest possible economy of space. Granted this limitation, the Lake District yields pride of place to nothing in England or Wales. The upstanding peaks of Scafell Pike, the placid beauty of Windermere, the sheer cliffs of Wastwater and the high pass that climbs from Wasdale Head over and around Scafell—those are a few of the beauties of the Lake District which

RIVER LYD, DEVONSHIRE

The River Lyd flows westward from the heights of Dartmoor into the Tamar. Throughout the greater part of its short course it is a rushing stream which tumbles and cascades over a rocky bed in which are several small waterfalls. As it approaches more level ground it passes through these dense woodlands which are situated to the west of Lydford, a village nearly seven miles to the north of Tavistock, the foliage of the trees in summer making a solid arch of greenery through which the sunlight only rarely penetrates. Near the village of Lydford is a cascade said to be one of the finest in the country.

evoke memories of loveliness and splendour without flaw, scenes more noble and splendid than even the genius of Wordsworth could portray.

The fells and grey-green hills extend eastward from the Lake District and form part of the country of the Roman Wall, that great monument to the engineering skill of the Romans nearly two thousand years ago. This in turn forms the southern confine of the Border country and the southern uplands of Scotland. So all this upland mass of northern England and southern Scotland is interrelated in its various parts. Between the Cheviot Hills on the very borders of England and Scotland and the Lammermuir and Moorfoot Hills, which are an outstanding part of the scenic heritage of Scotland, there is a difference of degree only and not of kind.

There is something in these southern uplands of Scotland which is akin to the

The English mountains reproduce on a small scale many of the majestic features of the Welsh and Scottish Highlands. This view of Ennerdale in the Lake District shows the Steeple and Pillar mountains to the left, with the deeply shadowed Kirkfell crags in front of them. There is an interesting comparison between this view and

140

THE LAKE DISTRICT
the photographs of the Scottish Highlands shown on page 144. There is the same barren harshness of the high ground, the same magnificent sculpture of the rocks, and the same sense of vast distances which dwarf every minor feature of the beautiful but rugged and lonely landscape dominated as it is by the mountains.

IN THE MANIFOLD VALLEY

The Pennine Chain ends in the peaks of Derbyshire. Southward a tumbled mass of hill and deep cleft valley stretches out toward the Midland Plain. Here Dovedale and the Manifold Valley throw the limestone crags into bold relief. Wetton Mill Farm, pictured in this photograph, lies at the foot of the scarred moorlands and is the centre of a narrow strip of farming country where cattle find good pasturage in the meadows which fringe the swift-flowing river. The abrupt rock faces and the exposed crags are a feature of this countryside.

South Downs of Sussex. Had he written of them, Kipling must have used the same sort of phrase as he did of the South Downs—"blunt bow-headed whale-backed" green grassy slopes rising to a long treeless skyline, with river valleys intersecting them which in their richness and graceful contours are not unlike even though they are far greater than their Sussex counterparts.

The valleys of Teviot and Tweed and, farther north, of the Clyde, set off the beauty of the hills and like so many of the hill valleys of Britain are exceptionally rich in timber. Because of the relatively high rainfall they are also exceptionally green, with something of the colouring traditional to Ireland, at every season of the year. This is the Scott country; from Melrose to Peebles, from Jedburgh to Selkirk, the countryside is the background against which the great novelist wrote his romantic tales.

Enthralled by the greater magnificence of the highlands there are many who scarcely spare a thought for the south-western peninsula of Scotland, for the counties of Ayr, Wigtown and Kirkcudbright. All three fall within the complex of the southern uplands, with many hills exceeding two thousand feet in height and hundreds of swift streams flowing into the Solway Firth or the Firth of Clyde. It is a country which is all the better for being so little known and includes a coast road which winds round the cliffs from Ayr to the Solway Firth and is as varied, and colourful, as any coast road of Britain.

For very many country-lovers the western and northern highlands of Scotland represent the high spots of the British countryside. It is here and here alone that Nature is untamed, that the works of Nature can be seen without the addition of human trimmings, for the land of western and northern Scotland is mostly intractable, the population scanty, villages are few, and towns fewer; distances are great and the country people live a life which is apart from the life of the rural peoples of the rest of Britain. Deep long inlets bite into the coastline, stretching for scores of miles inland, with lochs taking a long winding course so that sea and river are confused. At one point the Caledonian Canal, which is a canal in name only because it consists of three great lochs joined by only the shortest of man-made watercourses, cuts right through the country from the Irish Sea to the North Sea.

In many ways these western districts

WROXTON, OXFORDSHIRE

Situated about three miles to the north-west of Banbury, not far from the Gloucestershire boundary, Wroxton is in appearance and tradition a true Cotswold village, even though well removed from the wold proper. Every house and cottage in the picture is of Cotswold stone, as is the wall bounding the cottage garden. The roofs almost without exception are thatched and the picture is completed by the village pond, complete with the old pump, which was once the only source of water supply for the people who dwelt there. The termination "ton" shows that the settlement was founded by Anglo-Saxons.

seems to emanate from the quality of their beauty. In summer and autumn the moors are heather-clad purple, glowing, impressive beyond comparison, the true sporting country of Victorian tradition, in which salmon really do leap in the swift-flowing rivers and grouse wing their way across the moors and wild deer roam across the highlands.

The days of the hunting "lodge" are nearly over, but there are still "sportsmen" to hire the grouse moors and here and there notices which prohibit the chance wayfarer from walking unhindered across the moors. But in general, human presence is not often discernible. Argyllshire admittedly is the playground of Glasgow, Oban a flourishing health resort, the Trossachs and Loch Lomond

THROUGH THE TROSSACHS

The Trossachs rise abruptly from the central plain of Scotland and look southward across the Vale of Forth. In their midst is Loch Katrine and the towering slopes of Ben Venue and Ben Ledi, the latter rising to almost three thousand feet. This photograph shows well the pleasant country which lies amid the foothills of the mountains.

PASS OF GLENCOE

Through the heart of the highlands the road from Loch Leven leads towards the high peaks of the Grampians, passing along this rocky gorge. Famous alike for its scenic grandeur and its historic past, the Pass of Glencoe is the most inspiring gorge in all Britain.

of Scotland resemble the fiord country of Norway. There is the same sense of unscalable precipices, deep unfathomable lochs, wild desolate glens. A village may be but ten miles from its neighbour, but the only way from one to the other is by sea or by a course through highland passes and over heather-clad moors, which takes the traveller forty or fifty miles to reach his objective.

In most of the western highlands there is colour, and a vivid life which

IX. COTTAGE IN A CORNFIELD: *John Constable*

X. BLACKMOOR VALE: *Gilbert Spencer*

XI. KESWICK MOUNTAINS: *Sir Charles J. Holmes*

XII. JUNCTION OF THE LLUGWY AND CONWAY: *Davia*

VALE OF EWYAS, SOUTH WALES

Amid the Black Mountains of South Wales on the borders of Monmouthshire and Breconshire the valleys are broader and infinitely more fertile than in the mountain country of the north. In this quiet valley a prosperous farm-house lies in the midst of a broad strip of fertile fields. Wooded slopes rise gently from the valley. It is only on the high ground, seen in the background, that the land is not worked by farmers. Even there the face of the mountain is grass-covered.

thronged in their season with holiday-makers. Farther north and in the great central massif of the Cairngorm mountains the wayfarer will not meet another traveller in a day's walk. The roads are narrow and passing is possible for motor cars only at rare intervals. Highland country is as magnificent, as lonely, as inspiring as ever it was.

In the extreme north, where the climate is inhospitable, the land is still more barren, and bright colour is lack-

ing. Greyness takes the place of the lighter tints of the hills farther south. In Sutherland there are many inland lakes high-set, surrounded by hundreds of acres of bogland, adding to a general scenic effect which falls little short of desolation. For a few connoisseurs of the beauty of loneliness this is the grandest part of Britain and indeed of all Europe, but for most there is a point at which a barren land seems useless instead of magnificent and loneliness palls. In the fastnesses of central Sutherland this sense of loneliness and barrenness is expressed with a certainty and bluntness that few parts of the temperate regions can approach.

The mountains of North Wales stand out in contrast with the Highlands of Scotland, because there is never the same expanse of moorlands nor the same absolute divorce from human workmanship or labour. The highest peaks, like Snowdon and Cader Idris, lack nothing of the grandeur and the majesty of Scottish mountains, nor on some of their slopes is there any sense of human nearness. Yet these mountains are more obviously a holiday district than Scotland, or rather the thousands of holiday-makers who visit them make their presence felt more keenly, whether it be on the summit of Snowdon, with its ill-placed tea room, or by the romantic falls of Bettws-y-Coed, or by the shores of Lake Bala.

WELSH MOUNTAINS

The valleys are more thickly wooded than the corresponding valleys of the Scottish Highlands, where most of the timber is pine and spruce and deciduous trees occur only in the south, while in the far north the country is entirely treeless. In North Wales, by contrast, there are fertile valleys between the screes and narrow strips of pastureland fringed by woodland, all helping to give an impression of a beauty which is almost self-conscious in comparison with the untrammelled freedom of the Scottish Highlands. Even so, the mountains of North Wales are as impressive as could be desired and a very real part of the British scenic heritage, especially where the mountains approach the coast round the shores of Carnarvon and Merioneth, and the vast landscapes unfolded from the hilltops include vistas across the sea to the island of Anglesey and the more distant outline of the Irish Coast.

South Wales, too, has mountains but they are of a very different kind. The Brecon Beacon in the Black Mountains is only a few hundred feet less high than Snowdon, but whereas Snowdon has rocky sides and great expanses of exposed rock, the mountains of South Wales are almost entirely grass-covered and give pasture to flocks of sheep which range far and wide from the high slopes towards the river valleys. In some ways there is here more resemblance to the hills of southern England. This is especially true where the mountains fall away on the one hand to the hills of Shropshire which belong to the watershed of the Severn and on the other to the rolling country of Carmarthen and Pembroke. Pembrokeshire has been well named "Little England beyond Wales," for the hinterland is gentle rolling country, the villages are like English hamlets and although nearby is some of the loneliest cliff scenery in the whole country, even in this region are exquisite landscapes.

FOREST-LAND

No account of the scenic heritage of Britain is complete without a brief mention of the forests, now much less extensive than when they were first set aside by the Norman kings to be hunting preserves. To most country-lovers the terms forest and woodland are synonymous, yet many of the medieval forests have not a single tree, such as the forest of the High Peak. The primeval woodlands such as the forest of Anderida, which once covered the weald of Kent and Sussex, have disappeared, but there are still in existence fine woodlands in at least two of the medieval forests, the New Forest and the Forest of Dean, in both of which the commoners still preserve some of their original rights.

146

CARDINGMILL VALLEY

Shropshire is one of the most beautiful of the English counties and probably one of the least known. Most of the countryside of the Welsh Marcher counties, of which Shropshire is one, is hilly and the hills are at their most magnificent near Church Stretton. In this photograph of the Cardingmill Valley the two hills seen in the background are Caer Caradoc on the left and Hope Bowdler Hill on the right. A striking contrast is made between the rough open pastures of the hills and the well-tended hedged fields of the sheltered valley.

The term scenic heritage is generally meant to imply the heritage of natural beauty. But enough has been said in this review of British scenery to prove that it is only in the highlands that natural beauty has not been at least modified by the work of man. Nature certainly constructs the bold outlines of the countryside, but it is man who has changed its face beyond all recognition wherever the land is cultivated.

If he had lived two thousand years ago the traveller would have seen a very different sight from that which greets him today in any part of the lowlands. It was the Romans who brought with them new skills and new ways of working the land. Before that there had been cultivation only on the downlands because the valleys were undrained. Vast areas of bog covered in a mass of undergrowth prevented the earliest inhabitants from making a living out of it. They had no tools with which to clear the undergrowth and no means of draining the land. But because they had to live, even our prehistoric ancestors cultivated strips of land on the southern slopes of the downs.

As the centuries went by the downs were no longer ploughed. All traces of those earliest farmers of Britain disappeared except for the outline shapes of the ploughed strips. In some places these strips, which run like steps down the slopes of the hills, can still be seen and are a reminder of this first effort of man to modify the scenery.

The Roman colonizers, who came to Britain as an outpost of empire in just the same way as British people went out to the new lands of Australia and Canada, transformed what was almost a barren country into a fruitful landscape. The forests were cleared, much of the land was drained, and new corn crops were introduced. Though the Romans were in Britain for only about four hundred years, their work continued, and the Anglo-Saxons, from

GOATHLAND, NORTH RIDING OF YORKSHIRE

This attractive stone-built village, situated nearly ten miles to the south-west of Whitby, looks across a fertile valley to the promise of the Yorkshire moors on the skyline. It is one of the many English villages built round a green. In this case the green is a long strip of pasture on which sheep are put out to graze in the tradition of the true feudal village. Something of its story appears in its name, which means the land of the Goda, an Anglo-Saxon name which shows the influence of the Danish occupation by the substitution of "th" for "d." Thus it belongs to that large group of villages most of whose names end in "thorpe" or "by," the villages of eastern England which owe their name and in many cases their foundation to the Scandinavian invaders.

THE YORKSHIRE DALES

Wharfedale, which includes the romantic ruins of Bolton Abbey and Bolton Bridge, is one of the loveliest of the Yorkshire Dales, running eastward from the high ridge of the Pennines into the fertile Vale of York. It is watered by the River Wharfe. Near the head of the valley, only a few miles from the moorland springs which feed the river, the village of Kettlewell nestles among the sparse woodlands of the valley under the frowning peaks of the Pennine moors.

whose sturdy stock the British people are descended, carried on the cultivation of the valleys.

Since then British agriculture has never looked back. Even so, the countryside in the Middle Ages was very different from what it is now. In medie-

val times Britain was under the Feudal System. One of the features of this system was that the land was not enclosed as it is today and this single fact is the key to the whole of the difference.

Imagine the English landscape without its hedges or its walls. Imagine a small village near a river-side grouped about its church and manor farm with the land ploughed in long narrow strips near the village, and open grazing ground beyond. That will give some idea of southern England in the twelfth or thirteenth century. Of course, not the whole of the land was cultivated. There were not enough people living in the country to do the work.

The feudal villages were almost as numerous as modern villages but much smaller, while the scattered farm-houses between villages which are such a feature of rural Britain in the twentieth century were entirely absent and there were still large areas of uncleared under-growth and tangled forest-land.

Many of the familiar features of the countryside came much later, after the land had been enclosed and the era of great estates had begun. Between then and now all the parklands have been

CUB HUNTING IN HAMPSHIRE

Here in the Hursley Wood near Romsey is the very spirit of traditional England. In the bright morning sunshine the huntsman crosses a glade in what was originally part of the great "New Forest" set aside by the Norman kings for their own sport and that of their followers. Not all the New Forest is wooded; in fact it never was, for the word forest implies hunting country rather than woodland, and the word has gained its present meaning because many of the great forests are densely wooded as well as having tracts of open country.

LINK BETWEEN NORTH SEA AND ATLANTIC OCEAN

Made up of long sea lochs and a stretch of river which has been confined within artificial banks, the Caledonian Canal links the North Sea with the Atlantic Ocean. It cuts straight through the western and central highlands of Scotland from Fort William to Inverness. Along its banks is some of the most magnificent scenery in Britain. Here it is seen at its southernmost end where it joins Loch Linnhe. Three east-coast fishing boats have just passed through the loch at Banavie on their way to the west-coast fishing grounds. The Grampian Mountains, wild and rugged in the north, but in the south affording good pastures, are seen rising to a considerable height in the background.

laid out and almost all the farmhouses have been built. Roads have taken the place of primitive trackways and that, too, has made a big difference to the scene. Reservoirs have been built in remote country districts to provide water for the millions who came to live in big towns during the last century. The railways and the lines of electric pylons are two of the most recent additions to the landscape which are taken for granted. Many people regard these things as ugly, but it must be remembered that when things are familiar they are accepted as part and parcel of the landscape and the fact that they were once thought unsightly is forgotten.

Though by building big industrial towns in open country mankind has ruined hundreds of square miles of beautiful scenery, man must also have the credit of bringing fresh beauty to the countryside, for bringing the blossom of the fruit trees to the Weald of Kent and the Vale of Evesham, or for causing green crops to grow in the fields of East Anglia. There are few more beautiful sights than the waving corn in late summer, at the time when it is just beginning to turn colour and gold takes the place of green.

It is only when the handiwork of man strikes a discordant note that notice is taken of it. Necessary things are unfortunately not always beautiful. Many of the new houses in the country spoil the charm of quiet villages and take away from the beauty of well-loved landscapes. But that is not always because they are ugly in themselves (in fact, many are well designed by famous architects). It is because of their very newness, the glaring new colours of red bricks and tiles, which prevent them toning with the more subdued colouring of the country scene. When they are a hundred years old people who see them for the first time will probably accept them as part of the scene—if they notice them at all.

So it is true to say that Nature is at work all the time transforming what man has built into something more beautiful, and assimilating things that are new or ugly into her own scheme of beauty. There is another difference, too, between most new buildings in the countryside and the old ones. The new houses are usually built from bricks and mortar with roofs of tile or slate. But the older

PASS OF LENY, PERTHSHIRE

This photograph was taken between Callander and Strathyre, below the point where the River Leny issues from Loch Lubnaig. It shows a typical highland glen with the bare rocky mountains rising to a height of more than two thousand feet in contrast with the green fields and pleasant woodlands of the high valley. Here as in all the highland country of north and west Scotland, communications follow the course of the valleys. Railway and road can be seen closely following the curves of the river from one end of the glen to the other.

GLEN OF ARRAN, WALES

Local stone has been used to build these houses which nestle near the foot of Cader Idris. Fitting harmoniously into the scene they show that the handiwork of man can blend with the beauty of even the wilder parts of the landscape.

houses in the country are often built of other materials, including timber and stone. And that makes all the difference to the effect they have on the landscape. If locally quarried stone is used, the colour of the building, whether it is church, mansion or the humblest cottage, never clashes with the prevailing colour of the surrounding fields. The modern brick industry allows a greater number of houses to be built more cheaply, but it has had the effect of robbing many a pleasant landscape of a beauty which it need not have lost if local stone could have been used instead.

In the Cotswolds building stone is so plentiful and so easy to quarry that it is still being used for new dwellings. The result is that towns and villages are uniformly gracious to look at and tone perfectly with the natural beauty of the countryside. That, indeed, epitomizes the spirit of the scenic heritage—the blending of man-made vistas with Nature's bounty in perfect harmony.

THE MARKET CART, BY THOMAS GAINSBOROUGH

*Painted in 1786 this canvas, which can be seen in the National Gallery, is at
once a symbol of Gainsborough's mastery of the English landscape and an
interesting commentary on changes in rural life. Then, as now, market day
was a red-letter day in the farmer's life, an occasion to combine business
with pleasure and a journey to the nearest town with his family.*

Britain as seen by
the Artists

ART in some form or other is as old as the mammoth hunters, but landscape painting is surprisingly modern. In China, it is true, an impressive tradition existed a thousand years ago, but, in the West, landscapes remained for centuries merely a background against which the artist depicted biblical and saintly personages. Landscape painting arose early in Chinese history but late in the history of Europe and it is curious to reflect that even one who lived as recently as Shakespeare did not know landscape painting as an independent form of art, and had no pictures of the English countryside hanging on his walls. In Shakespeare's time this countryside differed in many ways from that known today, and it would be of great interest if it were possible to see it through the eyes of a contemporary landscape painter. But one cannot get more than occasional tantalizing glimpses; Elizabethan printmakers were not as a rule interested in the subject and are usually less informative about the appearance of contemporary England than were the medieval illuminators.

But some twenty years after Shakespeare's death a foreign traveller from distant Prague arrived in England. He was a careful and thorough artist named Wenceslas Hollar and the London which he drew and etched with such remarkable neatness and accuracy was the medieval London which perished in the fire of 1666. The huge, dilapidated Gothic cathedral of St. Paul's—old St. Paul's—towered up from the crowded roofs of the ancient timber-framed houses. An almost incredible number of lesser churches raised towers and spires above the chimney pots. On the south side of the river were a few houses and the bear pits and the round theatres of the time. Hollar's drawings have enormous historical value and it is well to remember with gratitude this "ingenious Bohemian gent" (to quote his memorial tablet), for another reason: he began the topographical tradition which has been of such value to British art.

But we must leave Hollar patiently at work in a London we would consider very small, picturesque and probably rather rowdy, and pass on some seventy years. The eighteenth century was thirty years old. London's medieval houses, crazy but picturesque, had mostly disappeared in the flames of those terrible September days of 1666; Sir Christopher Wren and his assistants had been busy; and now, instead of Hollar's half-derelict Gothic pile, rose the dome as it is today; but the river was as it had been in the days of Hollar with its ships and boats, and Old London Bridge still crossed it, bearing its fantastic load of

WOOD-SCENE, CORNARD, SUFFOLK, BY THOMAS GAINSBOROUGH

Gainsborough was a native of Sudbury, and many of his finest paintings derive their inspiration from the charming Suffolk scenery in which he spent his youth. The Sudbury country is essentially in the tradition of characteristically English landscapes, a quiet mixture of peaceful river valley flanked by green meadows and low, partly wooded hills. This woodland scene, now in the National Gallery, was painted near Cornard, about two miles from Sudbury.

top-heavy houses—the strangest bridge in Europe.

In this new London that had risen from the ashes of the old there were some English landscape painters at work. The eldest was Peter Monamy. His *East India Wharf* (now at the Victoria and Albert Museum) is clearly the work of an accomplished and experienced artist. In 1730 Monamy was about sixty, but Samuel Scott was only beginning his career; he also was a painter of London River and, with the short-lived, obscure Charles Brooking, painted the lower Thames and portrayed

the shipping that must have made it a scene of great liveliness and fascination.

Leaving London River for the present and travelling to the very different landscape of the Welsh border, we come to a village in Montgomeryshire where the first of the great landscape painters of Britain was born. Richard Wilson was the son of a parson who, like John Constable sixty years later, made a false start as a portrait painter before he discovered where his real gifts lay. It was a visit to Italy that is said to have opened his eyes to the possibilities of landscape painting and after he returned home he

THE PORINGLAND OAK, BY JOHN CROME

*One of the founders of the Norwich Society, at which he exhibited frequently,
Crome specialized in landscape painting, his work being influenced mainly by
the Dutch painters. The above painting, from the National Gallery collection,
is an example of his late style and was painted in 1818 or 1820. Poringland
is a village about five miles to the south-east of Norwich.*

began to paint English—and, more particularly, Welsh—scenery with some of the same luminosity and grandeur he had observed in the pictures of Claude.

His pictures were appreciated by only a very few. At that time landscapes were regarded as things imported from abroad, souvenirs of the grand tour, and English paintings of English scenery were regarded rather as cowslip-wine might be by those who could afford vintage port. Wilson painted landscapes, in the classical manner, of the country round Rome, and also a few views of the Thames at Richmond and Kew, but perhaps his finest pictures are the Welsh ones: Carnarvon Castle and Pembroke Castle and the grim stony tarn at the summit of Cader Idris. Snowdon he painted superbly and it was to Llanberis, at the foot of Snowdon, that he retired when at last a legacy rescued him from poverty; for, though Wilson painted Wales superbly, few came to buy. Even today his landscapes are perhaps more appreciated by artists than by the general public, yet his grandeur of design and subtlety of colour have been equalled by very few landscape painters in any country.

Wilson loved Wales. He once said that Welsh scenery provided him with everything he could require and these green hills and wooded valleys, these lakes and stony mountain-tops have never been painted with more knowledge, intimacy or understanding.

PAINTERS OF SUFFOLK

The scene now changes and we leave the Welsh hills and travel east to the little market town of Sudbury standing on the River Stour which divides Suffolk from Essex. If we had been there round about 1750 we might have seen a tall youth sketching in a small oak wood. He has a pencil and a small sketch-book and he is studying with great care the shapes of the trunks and branches and of the banks of the rutted little lane. Between the tree trunks Thomas Gainsborough can see the valley of the Stour with the small river winding among pollard willows, and in the distance a village church and the roofs of cottages among the trees. It is a quiet scene, not—like many of Wilson's Welsh haunts—one that would attract a passing tourist. Yet young Gainsborough seems quite content with this mild county of Suffolk, he is busy sketching and memorizing, and, when he gets home, some of the results of his study will appear in the ambitious oil painting on which he is engaged—a painting which today hangs in the National Gallery; it is called Wood-Scene, Cornard, Suffolk.

GAINSBOROUGH'S CHANGING STYLE

The young Gainsborough who worked on this picture was already a portrait painter with a considerable reputation among the local squires, and it was not long before he left Suffolk and went first to Bath and then to London where wealth and fashion flocked to him to have their likenesses taken. Deprived of his constant study in the fields and woods round Sudbury, his landscapes change in character; they cease to be pictures of places and become paintings of moods. His trees cease to be the sturdy and recognizable oaks of Great Cornard Wood and become poetical trees of indeterminate species. His later landscapes are charming but his early ones show clearly that a magnificent interpreter of the ordinary agricultural England—of which Suffolk is a type—might have arisen nearly a century before Constable, if only fashion and fortune had not called him to Bath and London.

It is perhaps a coincidence that East Anglia enters so much into any account of British landscape painting. Gains-

EDINBURGH CASTLE, BY PAUL SANDBY

The capital city of Scotland has changed its appearance very considerably since Sandby created this impression of the castle rock. It conveys admirably the almost invincible strength of the .rock which was first occupied by King Edwin of Northumbria in the seventh century. The painting is in the Tate Gallery.

borough's feeling for the Stour Valley was not like Constable's and the little wood of oak trees at Great Cornard possessed nothing that might not have been matched in a thousand oak woods in other parts of the country. Nevertheless, coincidence or no, our next change of scene necessitates no more than a journey to another part of East Anglia, from Suffolk to Norfolk, where, round about 1800, anyone wandering in the neighbourhood of Norwich, might have passed another small oak wood where another young artist was sketching in a note-book. This was John Crome, whose father, like Gainsborough's, was connected with the cloth trade; but whereas Gainsborough's father had been a reasonably prosperous clothier, Crome's

was a mere journeyman weaver, a "working man," and Crome started, at the age of thirteen, to work as a doctor's errand boy.

Few English artists have been so completely identified with one place as John Crome. He lived in Norwich all his life and travelled little. His town had been, in the Middle Ages, the second city of England and in the eighteenth century was still one of the largest and wealthiest in the country. The great cathedral spire soared above the roofs, and from every street rose the towers and spires of lesser churches, built from the profits of the wool trade. Round Norwich stretches mild, unexciting agricultural country. Jane Austen's *Emma* describes this kind of scenery perfectly when she declares that she knows "every field, hedge, pond and pollard" along the road.

This was Crome's country, and one might have supposed that this provincial artist, whose output was small and who so seldom left his native town, would show a certain monotony in treatment and choice of subject. This, however, is far from being so. In London today, for example, one can see four great works by him, all of which are strikingly different. There is the Water Frolic in the Kenwood Collection, where a fine design is made from the big brown sails of wherries in a way that might be mistaken—that has been mistaken—for the work of the Dutchman Cuyp; there is Mousehold Heath, Norwich, in the National Gallery, which shows a great sunlit expanse of common land and an immensely spacious sky; there is The Poringland Oak (also in the National Gallery), perhaps the most faithful as well as the most poetic portrait of a tree ever painted; and there is that other National Gallery picture where, for once, Crome painted mountains and painted them with sombre impressiveness. This last picture stands almost alone in British art; there is nothing else quite like it. No one knows exactly where these mountains were but the probability is that they were somewhere in Cumberland; if so, this picture is the finest ever painted of the Lake District, a countryside which has been less fortunate in its artists than Wales.

NEW WATER-COLOUR TECHNIQUE

Before leaving Norwich in the year 1800 let us remember that two years earlier a talented boy of sixteen called John Sell Cotman had left the city to go to London and learn the trade of an artist. We shall meet him again.

Returning to London, it is appropriate first to take an old man who at this time lived in the suburban neighbourhood of Bayswater—Paul Sandby. Born in Nottingham as long ago as 1725, and thus Gainsborough's senior by two years, he had visited the highlands of Scotland after the Young Pretender's rebellion of 1745, as a topographical draughtsman attached to the army. He had evolved a water-colour technique based on the tinting of drawings previously completed in monochrome with Indian ink; and incidentally he had greatly improved the paints available for water-colourists.

TOPOGRAPHICAL ARTISTS

Sandby's drawings of Windsor are perhaps his best-known works but he was an indefatigable traveller; he made his pleasant drawings in all parts of Great Britain; he even visited Ireland, a country until then quite unknown to landscape painters. There were many other artists who followed Paul Sandby, adopting his simple but expressive technique and travelling to all parts of the country and to the continent of Europe, working up their sketches into finished drawings during the winter months. It is hardly necessary here to consider these artists separately, though each one of them has his own importance in the history of landscape painting. Their subjects included mountains and picturesque scenery of all kinds; views of the coast and harbours with all the variety of sails shown by the fishing fleets—now entirely a thing of the past; views of the fine dignified Georgian streets of London, Dublin, Bath and Edinburgh; and views of "the country seats of peers and gentlemen." It was, of course, these last subjects which provided the most important part of the topographical artist's livelihood, for in the days before photography the man who wanted a picture of his country house had to hire a topographical artist to take its likeness as he would hire

HAWES, YORKSHIRE, BY THOMAS GIRTIN

*Near the head of Wensleydale, Hawes is still a quiet and secluded town (more
an overgrown village than a modern town) with all the spirit of the Yorkshire
moors and dales. Almost entirely stone-built, it is in perfect harmony with
the grand but austere beauty of the moorland scenery. The river flows down
swiftly from the uplands, seething and cascading over a score of rapids and
waterfalls with the magnificent sense of power suggested in the painting.
Hardraw Force, a mile or so upstream from Hawes, is a famous waterfall
where the drop is more than one hundred feet. The painting, which was executed
in 1800, is now in the Birmingham City Art Gallery.*

a portrait painter to take his own. In 1800 there were several of these artists working in London besides old Paul Sandby. First comes Thomas Girtin, a Londoner born. In 1800 Girtin was twenty-five and already well known as a water-colour painter. Perhaps his finest pictures are those he painted in Yorkshire, such as that of Kirkstall Abbey by its river—not so grimy then as now—and the pictures of the wide valleys and bare, flat-topped hills of Wharfedale, Airedale and Nidderdale. But Girtin was also a painter of his native London and his free and spontaneous sketches of panoramic views across chimney pots to Westminster or the City have a place of their own in the pictorial records of the world's largest town.

TWO LONDONERS

With the name of Girtin the newspapers of the day used to couple the name of Joseph Mallord William Turner. Like Girtin, he was a Londoner; his father was a barber in the City. But he was in many ways a striking contrast. Girtin was universally popular, gay and amusing; Turner was inarticulate, reserved, rather mean and intensely ambitious. By the time he was twenty-five Girtin had had considerable success, but Turner had shown extraordinary early brilliance and had been elected to an associateship of the Royal Academy at the very early age of twenty-four (he became a full member at twenty-six). There was another difference between these two young men, though their contemporaries could not know it. Turner had fifty-one years more to live; Girtin had only two.

In 1800 John Constable was admitted as a student at the Royal Academy schools. Girtin and Turner were already masters at twenty-five but Constable, only a year younger, was still a student,

impressing his teachers with his patience and persistence rather than with his talent. Turner was extraordinarily quick off the mark; Constable very slow.

Finally, before leaving 1800, reference should be made to the weakly son of a Birmingham blacksmith to whom someone gave a box of paints to amuse him when he was ill, and the son of a doctor in the Potteries who had a Dutch name. David Cox was seventeen and Peter de Wint one year younger.

There were many landscape painters in 1800. There were even more in 1830. John Crome was dead and so was Sandby. Girtin was dead—a tragic loss —and the years between 1800 and 1830 saw both the birth and death of another short-lived genius—Richard Parkes Bonington, whose achievement is so extraordinary in its extent and in its precocious accomplishment. His landscapes are, however, more often of French scenes than English ones, for when Richard was a schoolboy his father got into trouble of some sort and decided that he had better take himself and his family across the Channel.

JOHN SELL COTMAN

The two great masters who dominate nineteenth-century landscape painting (in modern eyes, not those of their contemporaries) are, of course, Turner and Constable; before returning to them, however, take another glance at Cotman, whom we last saw leaving Norwich—where John Crome dominated the horizon—and coming up to London to learn his trade. There are some things about Cotman even yet not fully understood. It is strange to see him making a very promising beginning in London as a sort of junior to Girtin and Turner and then in 1806 throwing all this up, retiring to Norwich and practically ceasing to send any pictures to the Royal Academy (then the

162

OLD HOUSES IN GORLESTON, BY J. S. COTMAN

These ancient houses dating from before the seventeenth century have disappeared, but there are still thousands of cottages and farm-houses in East Anglia built in lath and plaster like the crumbling fabric of the houses in the painting, which is in the Norwich Castle Museum and Art Gallery.

only place where a young artist could exhibit his work). However, back to Norwich he went and there, or at Great Yarmouth, he lived nearly all the rest of his life, only to return to London in 1834 when (owing chiefly to Turner, who had always admired his work) he obtained the post of drawing master at King's College.

THE NORWICH SCHOOL

Cotman and Crome are the two great artists of the Norwich school. Cotman, however, was less exclusively a Norwich artist than was Crome. He travelled a good deal in Great Britain and some of his best-known water-colours are of Durham and the Yorkshire dales. He made many elaborate architectural drawings of cathedrals and abbeys in France and illustrated books on antiquities. He was at times a very second-rate artist, but everyone has a right to be judged by his best work and Cotman's best is impressive. In his famous water-colours of Greta Bridge (Yorkshire), of the great towers of Durham with the wooded ravine of the River Wear below, and perhaps most of all in that remarkable picture where a cloud shadow sweeps across a ploughed field and a yokel stands among the scarecrows, is to be found a really novel and original interpretation of British landscape. The audacity of pattern is oddly like that of the great Japanese masters and yet no one could ever doubt that these are English scenes painted by an Englishman.

But it is time to return to the later history of Turner and Constable. In the thirty years that elapsed after the beginning of the nineteenth century, Turner's production was sensational in its range and variety. He painted the sea, in calm and storm and in a hundred effects of light. He painted The Shipwreck, Fishing Boats Attempting to Rescue the

Crew, where the sea boils like a pot; he painted Spithead: Boat's Crew recovering an Anchor, where a moderate breeze is raising a lop on the water; and he painted The Sun rising through Vapour, where the ship's sails hang limp in a flat calm. He painted equally varied pictures of the land. There was A Frosty Morning; Sunrise, where farm workers gather beside a cart and blow on their fingers. In striking contrast to this homely realism is The Garden of the Hesperides, and other landscapes of a mythological kind, where crag is piled on crag, and idealized lakes and trees and nymphs gracefully fill the foreground. The last and possibly the most remarkable period of Turner's work came after 1830, but even by this date he seemed to have painted almost every kind of landscape that was possible to paint and his works ranged from a farmyard realism as earthy as that of any Dutchman to ideal scenes more visionary than Claude's. In 1830 it must have been difficult for anyone to think of any kind of landscape painting at which this queer, silent man with the big nose did not excel.

INFLUENCE OF TRAVEL

Turner resembled a one-man band. Merely to glance through his *Liber Studiorum* engravings reveals something of his variety of subject and mood. Flint Castle shows a wide sandy bay with ships unloading; Holy Island Cathedral shows a solid Romanesque ruin filling the entire picture: Pembury Mill, Kent, is rural peace; The Yorkshire Coast, near Whitby, is tempest; Martello Towers, near Bexhill, Sussex, is dramatic and a little theatrical; St. Catherine's Hill, Guildford, is quiet and straightforward description (a very fine picture); East Gate, Winchelsea, is calmly sunlit; Ben Arthur, Scotland, and Solway Moss show threatening gloom

164

THE BLACKSMITH'S SHOP, BY J. M. W. TURNER

The heritage of craftsmanship passed almost unnoticed by the early painters of the English scene. That was mainly because the rural crafts were accepted as an essential part of country life a century or so ago. The craft of the smith is one of the few that have survived, for the horse retains a place in work on the modern farm. This painting is in the Tate Gallery.

over mountain tops and over flat marshland respectively. Crowborough, Sussex, is a snow scene; Sheep-washing, Windsor, takes place in midsummer. Norham Castle on the Tweed shows sunrise, but in Isleworth the sun is setting. The titles indicate something of Turner's continual restless travelling.

John Constable, on the other hand, travelled little. Like Crome, nearly all his famous pictures are of the fields he had known as a boy. As has been already said, it may be a mere coincidence, but it is striking nevertheless, that the countryside of Constable's youth was practically the same as that of Gainsborough's, for Flatford Mill, which Constable made so famous, is only a few miles down the little River Stour on which stands Gainsborough's Sudbury. Here Constable painted, making no attempt to rival Turner's encyclopædic energy, but with an unobtrusive determination to express the atmosphere and character of these familiar scenes with the utmost possible truth, subtlety and vividness. In this he succeeded surprisingly. Gainsborough had endowed this unsensational East Anglian landscape with romantic charm and Crome had endowed it with a sort of rustic dignity; in Constable's pictures it appears with a lively brilliance. The weather has become in some respects the

VIEW ON CLAPHAM COMMON, BY J. M. W. TURNER

*One of the most famous landscape artists of any country and of any period,
Turner is famed for his sunsets. He painted a prodigious number of works
both in England and abroad, a large proportion of which he bequeathed to
the British nation. This picture, painted in 1802 and now in the Tate Gallery,
shows a portion of Clapham Common, one of London's many open spaces.*

most important thing in the scene, not weather of thunder and eclipse like that which Turner delighted in, but the chequered sunshine of an ordinary summer day with white clouds against the blue sky and a breeze tossing the tree tops; weather as ordinary and as beautiful as the East Anglian landscape was ordinary and beautiful. It was the extraordinary truth of Constable's painting, the remarkable vividness of his sunlight and cloud shadows, which created such a sensation when his Hay Wain was shown in Paris in 1824; and it was this picture which had such a remarkable influence on the theories and practice of the French Impressionists.

Constable's great pictures of the Stour Valley are perhaps his finest achievement, but his pictures of Salisbury run them close. He painted the spire of the cathedral many times, in sunshine and shadow, framed in trees, or appearing across the water meadows. He also made exquisitely clear and limpid sketches of Hampstead Heath where he settled for a while, and he was fond of the little Dorset village of Osmington which was close to the wide shores of Weymouth Bay.

Turner made a fortune from painting landscapes. Few other artists succeeded in doing this. David Cox certainly did not. He was a Birmingham man and most of his life he lived either in or near Birmingham or at Hereford. He would

TWO LANDSCAPES, BY JOHN CONSTABLE

Best known to lovers of the British countryside as an interpreter of the beautiful landscapes of the Stour Valley on the borders of Suffolk and Essex, Constable also painted many famous scenes far from what has become known as the "Constable country." Malvern Hall, Warwickshire (above), is situated on a tributary of the River Leam near Long Itchington. The view of the Salt Box, Hampstead Heath (below), shows how little in many ways, yet how much in others, a century of changing conditions has affected London's own countryside. Both paintings are in the National Gallery collection.

RHAYADER, RADNORSHIRE, BY DAVID COX

This little town nestles on the banks of the Wye under the rounded spurs of the Radnorshire hills, seen in the background of this painting, now in the Birmingham Art Gallery. For several miles the bed of the river is strewn with rocks which the river itself has carried down from the heights of the Plinlimmon range in which it has its source. Rhayader is the English form of the Welsh word "rhaiadr" which means waterfall.

set off each summer on a sketching expedition, to the South Coast, to the Lakes, to France, to the Peak District, but more often than any of these to the Royal Oak at Bettws-y-Coed. For twelve years (from 1844 to 1856) he visited this romantic Welsh valley without missing a year and there exist a remarkable number of paintings which bear testimony to Cox's affection for the place. It was, and is, a valley of great charm, but Cox was not always inspired when sketching there and some of his best works show quite different places. His famous Vale of Clwyd, it is true, was painted not so very far away from Bettws, but his equally famous War and

Peace shows the coast scenery of Lympne, near Hythe in Kent.

It is interesting to see how different is Cox's North Wales from that painted by Richard Wilson nearly a hundred years earlier. Wilson's Wales is a place of serene and impressive calm: Cox's is a place of broken and dancing light and shade and hurrying clouds. When, as sometimes happened, they painted almost the same subjects, the difference between the results is interesting and instructive and both are very like Wales.

Had Cox been another Constable, those twelve summers at Bettws-y-Coed might have produced results more memorable than in fact they did.

Unfortunately, though there was a resemblance between the two artists, and Cox's achievement often has great charm, he was no Constable. Had the son of a Suffolk miller not taken to landscape painting, more might have been thought of this son of a Birmingham blacksmith.

Peter de Wint was another Midlander. In 1800 he was a schoolboy. In 1830 he was an established artist. The countryside with which he is particularly associated is that of Lincolnshire and many of his best paintings are of the ancient city of Lincoln. It is interesting that this man of Dutch ancestry should have taken to painting the part of England which most recalls Holland in its great levels, its wide skies and its red-tiled houses.

De Wint was a serious, sober type of artist and Lincolnshire, as he painted it, was a serious, sober sort of place. The red roofs of the houses and the grey skies above make in his pictures a quiet harmony and the huge, level fens stretch away to the horizon in a fashion all the more impressive for not being obviously picturesque. This odd and exceptional part of England found a recorder who was by no means unworthy.

Before plunging into the jungle of Victorian art, perhaps the writer may be allowed one inclusion which can hardly be justified by the importance of the artist. The mention of this picture may bring to mind a number of admirable landscapes which were painted in

A WARWICKSHIRE LANE, BY PETER DE WINT

The countryside of the Avon Valley is distinguished above all else by the bountiful and mature timber of the hedgerows and the long, narrow greens which fringe main roads and rural lanes alike. Both features are suggested in this painting, which is now in the Tate Gallery. This scene, entirely in keeping with the highest traditions of Midland countryside, is one which the wayfarer might find today anywhere between the foot of the Cotswold Hills and the fringe of Birmingham's "black country."

Britain between 1750 and 1850 by artists almost unknown, or known for other kinds of painting. The work referred to is in the Tate Gallery and is by a minor portrait painter named George Robert Lewis. He was about the same age as Cox and Cotman. The picture is a sound, sensible, convincing sort of picture of a group of labourers in a harvest field; beyond stretches the Herefordshire countryside and in the distance is the profile of the Malvern Hills.

INFERIOR PAINTINGS

Now for the dark period, for a dark one it is. Vast landscapes were being painted throughout the reign of Queen Victoria, great sums were paid for them and they were proudly hung in enormous gold frames in public galleries. It would be a mistake to suppose that all of these were bad, but certainly most of them were. When one does come on a good one it has very often been painted by some young man whose early promise faded away, spoilt by success even more surely than some of the eighteenth-century painters were spoilt by failure. There were cases of artists renowned for quite another kind of picture who continued to paint landscapes for their own amusement and pleasure. These small pictures are today sometimes regarded with far more respect than are the same man's ambitious academy works. James Sant is a striking instance. Perhaps the reproductions of his famous works, The Soul's Awakening, She Never Told Her Love, and Napoleon, the Last Phase, are today banished from even cottage bedrooms but there are two small pictures in the Tate Gallery which show with fresh naturalness the charm of an English garden, a subject which has led so many astray into mere prettiness and sentimentality.

One artist is worth mentioning because of the fantastic prices fetched by his pictures in sale-rooms today. Birket Foster's popularity is undeniable, indeed his biographer may have said nothing more than the truth when he wrote that no other artist had given so much pleasure to the people of Britain. This tells us little about Foster's merits but it says a great deal about the standard of taste. Foster lived in Surrey among the sandy heaths and commons of the Forest Ridge, and painted, with a sweetness that soon becomes unendurable, village children playing on them or gathering flowers, labourers walking home at evening, or market carts crossing Surrey streams.

Peter Graham went in for the dramatic and grand. At least he did so in his big picture in the Manchester Art Gallery. A Spate in the Highlands has been aptly described as a "*tour-de-force*, dingy, but impressive." Later he painted woolly highland cattle in the mist. Henry Moore and Colin Hunter painted the sea. Inchbold painted moorlands, particularly Dartmoor, carefully drawing every heather bell.

PRE-RAPHAELITE INFLUENCE

Pre-Raphaelite influence was responsible for producing two landscapes of some importance: Dyce's Pegwell Bay, Kent, and Brett's astonishing picture called The Stonebreaker, which represents with unbelievably minute accuracy the pile of flints by the roadside and distant Box Hill. There is also the interesting case of William MacTaggart, the son of an Argyllshire crofter, who developed independently a style strangely like that of the French Impressionists, in which he painted the white sands and tumbling seas of Machrihanish Bay near Campbeltown, only a mile or so from the croft where he was born.

There were, no doubt, other worthy

STRATFORD-ON-AVON CHURCH AND LOCK, BY B. W. LEADER

Now in the Manchester City Art Gallery, this painting shows the church in the chancel of which is Shakespeare's tomb.

171

landscape painters in the second half of the nineteenth century but it is a pleasure to come to that provocative American named James McNeill Whistler, who arrived in England from Paris in 1859 and settled in Chelsea. His landscapes are only a minor part of his work as an artist, but they have their importance for they show us for the first time another aspect of London River, the twilight and mist of evening and autumn when the first light appears, and the sentiment never becomes sentimentality. Whistler learnt from the great Japanese, Hiroshige; but this American, working under Japanese inspiration, produced pictures that even to those who have known it all their lives, are completely satisfying representations of the Thames at Chelsea.

Toward the end of Queen Victoria's reign some new and interesting talents began to appear. The Royal Academy at that time combined financial prosperity and artistic bankruptcy, so it was decided to form an independent society —the New English Art Club. Its first exhibition was held in 1886. At least four of the early members are important in the history of British landscape painting: P. Wilson Steer, W. R. Sickert, C. J. Holmes and Muirhead Bone.

Steer, in his youth, was influenced by many other painters including Constable. This influence on British landscape painters has usually been a bad one, for, like many other great men, Constable led where few could follow, tempting lesser talents to efforts at brilliant painting before they had fully grasped Constable's great powers as a designer. But Steer was an artist who apparently could see through the brilliant execution to the qualities that were less obvious and some of his big oil paintings of the pastures and woods of the Severn Valley, of Shropshire and Gloucestershire are most impressive. There are, of course, pictures of other scenes as well—seashores in Suffolk with paddling children, pictures of London River and the Medway—but it is with

CHELSEA REGATTA, BY WALTER GREAVES

Walter Greaves (1846-1931) was the son of a famous boatman and skiff-builder, hence his interest in river scenes. This painting, from the Manchester Art Gallery, shows the view from Old Battersea Bridge to which the pier and gangway on the right are attached. On the left is the tower of Chelsea Old Church, and in the distance Chelsea Bridge. The Adam and Eve Inn, headquarters of the regatta, disappeared when Chelsea Embankment was built in 1874.

PLYMOUTH HARBOUR, BY J. W. B. KNIGHT

Painted in 1891, this canvas, now in the Tate Gallery, is also called The Wooden Walls of England. Under sail, steam and oil, famous ships have berthed in Plymouth Harbour ever since Britain became a mercantile and naval power, and in earlier centuries many seafaring pioneers sailed from this port to seek new lands and wealth beyond the ocean or to do battle with the Spanish Armada. In modern times transatlantic liners and the battleships of the Royal Navy sail to and from Plymouth and the neighbouring dockyard of Devonport.

the West Country and the wide Severn that Steer is usually associated. Bridgnorth was one of Steer's favourite sketching grounds and the Tate Gallery has a superb picture of Chepstow Castle, near the mouth of this great river. Steer liked castle ruins. He painted the huge square keeps of Richmond (Yorkshire), and of Rochester and certainly found it no drawback that hundreds of other artists had done so before him.

Steer was a water-colourist as well as an oil painter and his water-colours are remarkably original. The complex hues and tones and shapes of the English landscape have never been stated so completely with such slight means.

A few subtle washes of colour and some simple and rapid drawing with the brush were enough, in Steer's hands, to suggest with remarkable completeness, some view across an estuary, a wide tree-dotted expanse, or even a subject such as a line of farmers' carts parked in Thame High Street on market day.

Steer was a landscape painter who produced a few fine portraits and interiors. Sickert was a painter of interiors, or, to use a somewhat obsolete word, of genre, who painted a few very interesting landscapes. The subjects are usually street scenes—French street scenes in many cases, but sometimes Brighton streets or Bath ones. Sickert's

PULTENEY BRIDGE, BY WALTER SICKERT

Born in 1860 in Munich, Walter Sickert is descended from a family of painters and studied for a time under Whistler in Chelsea. He has produced many first-class paintings of the British scene such as this one of the River Avon at Bath, flowing under Pulteney Bridge which was built in 1770.

pictures have often queer, harsh, original colour, stimulating and unexpected, and yet—when one has had time to get used to it—completely convincing.

Another artist who was an early supporter of the New English Art Club was Sir Charles J. Holmes, who will be chiefly remembered for his pictures of industrial Lancashire. It is amusing to compare the titles of some of his pictures with earlier fashions in titles. Gainsborough and Constable both had the habit, maddening to posterity, of exhibiting their pictures as "Landscapes" and nothing else. In Victorian times the works of Royal Academicians received elaborate and allusive titles:

Old December's Bareness Everywhere, or Their Only Harvest. The bluntness and particularity of Holmes's titles are in quaint contrast: The Wigan Coal Company's Yard may serve as an example for both title and picture—a sensible title and a fine, dignified picture which shows clearly that beauty and prettiness are not the same thing. Besides painting the industrial north, Holmes painted the Pennines; bleak but spacious pictures which have an austerity that matches the countryside.

The fourth of the early members of the New English Art Club is Muirhead Bone, who is mainly known as a landscape draughtsman whose quantity and variety are extraordinary. Perhaps the range of his subjects is best shown by the statement that he has done few pictures in Ireland and none in Eastern Europe. His drawings and engravings of London are probably among his best-known work, but this is perhaps chiefly due to the fact that they are some of his earliest work and have "got a start," so to speak, in popular esteem. He has done a great deal of work abroad. In his own country his subjects vary from the Orkneys to Kent and Cornwall, and from industrial Glasgow and the slums of Leeds to the ancient cathedrals of Wells and Canterbury. The old topographical tradition has appeared again, but the scope of this artist's work has no real precedent.

It would be of little interest to continue with a long list of landscape painters, but a few names may recall to

WHERNSIDE, BY SIR CHARLES J. HOLMES

One of the loftiest peaks of the Pennine Chain, Whernside is 2,400 feet above sea-level. This inspiring canvas, now in the Tate Gallery, brings out the contrasting masses and the interplay of light and shade which, together, make up much of the beauty of these stern hills, a beauty which owes nothing to the work of man. From the green valley with its hardy plantations straggling up the hillside, the land rises to the bare craggy outlines of the long, dark ridge.

the reader something of the variety of contemporary work. The late Paul Nash and his brother John have produced pictures of English scenery which are "modern," and yet, in some odd way, traditional as well. Paul Nash studied the beechwoods and chalk downs of Buckinghamshire and anatomized them—particularly in their winter aspect—with great skill and knowledge. John Nash is perhaps not so profound but has a lyrical charm. Another "Home County" artist is Stanley Spencer, whose enthusiasm for the Thames-side village of Cookham became a joke among his fellow students. But Stanley Spencer's enthusiasm has been justified by results. Whereas Richard Wilson found all he wanted in Wales, Stanley Spencer seems to find it in Cookham, and his brother, Gilbert, in another part of Berkshire.

London is much painted by contemporary artists. Victor Pasmore has painted autumnal mists on the Thames, and an older artist, C. R. W. Nevinson, has painted the smoky glitter of the river and the city's innumerable roofs. Sussex and Essex have appeared in the work of the gifted Eric Ravilious, who was lost at sea during the Second World War. Ravilious's pre-war pictures show-

BALLANTRAE, AYRSHIRE, BY SIR MUIRHEAD BONE

Muirhead Bone, born in Glasgow in 1876, was the first British official artist to go to France during the First World War and much of the work he did there can now be seen in the Imperial War Museum. He is best known for his architectural drawings and etchings but has done many fine landscapes. This view of Ballantrae, below, is a typical example of his work.

XIII.   ON THE WYE: *Richard Wilson*

XIV. DURHAM CASTLE AND CATHEDRAL: *Thomas Girtin*

XV. ST. BENET'S ABBEY: *John Sell Co*

I. OLD HOUSES ON THE HIGH BRIDGE, LINCOLN: *Peter de Wint*

XVII. CHEYNE WALK, CHELSEA: *R. P. Bonington*

XVIII. BEHIND THE INN: *Paul Nash*

WEST BAY, BRIDPORT, DORSET, BY C. R. W. NEVINSON

Nevinson (1889-1946) was also an official artist in the First World War and painted many canvases in a modified cubist style, which was very effective in conveying the drama of warfare and its inevitable destruction. This quality almost disappeared from his later paintings.

ed a delightful wit which, without losing any of its point, became deeper and more serious when he was employed as a war artist. Edward Bawden at one time produced drawings of a rather similar kind but his style seems to have developed in a different direction since he was sent as a war artist to Mesopotamia, Abyssinia and Syria.

Four other war artists deserve mention. Richard Eurich has painted ships and harbours with careful concentration; John Piper has painted dark and romantic landscapes of buildings ruined by war or merely decayed by time; and

Evelyn Dunbar has produced pictures of an agricultural England where tractors have replaced the horse. Graham Sutherland—not influenced by Picasso— paints fantasies firmly based on the British landscape.

The British countryside has changed considerably since the days of Shakespeare—even since the days of Constable and Turner—and the towns have changed out of all knowledge. Artists are still at work recording the appearance of the landscape, and there. may be some among them whose names, unknown to their contemporaries, will

THE GATHERING OF THE FLOCKS, BY DAVID COX

The son of a blacksmith, David Cox studied painting under various masters, and worked both as a scene-painter and a drawing master. In 1805 he visited North Wales, and many of his pictures were painted there, including the one shown above, which is now in the Manchester City Art Gallery.

be familiar to those who live a hundred years hence.

It is pleasant to speculate on the possibility that British landscape painting may have some of its greatest achievements to come; certainly there are a thousand potentialities which have never been developed by any artist. So many varieties of British scenery exist and only a few of them have ever been adequately painted; some have never been painted at all, in spite of our long and illustrious muster of landscape painters. The topographical water-colour painters, it is true, penetrated to almost every part of the British Isles, but in spite of their many merits, they often spent too much time wandering about to seize the exact and subtle differences which exist between one place and another, superficially similar. The topographers applied a sound and well-tried method to one kind of scenery after another and it is not perhaps surprising that the results sometimes suggest mass production. There were times when even Turner seems to have failed to find the true traditional atmosphere of a place and concealed this with huge firework displays of his astonishing technical skill.

It would be of interest to see what sort of pictures could be made of any of the mountain limestone districts of Britain—Derbyshire, the Mendips and the Yorkshire Dales—by some artist of the stature of Constable, or even Crome, and with the same attachment to his native place. Girtin showed something of the pictorial possibilities of

Yorkshire limestone, and there have been recent artists, but the real master of the limestone country has not yet appeared. The Lakes have produced poets rather than painters; the artists who have attempted to work there have not usually been the sons of the place either in fact or in spirit.

PAINTING SCOTLAND

What can one say of Scotland? There have been a few native painters in the past, of agreeable but modest achievement, and some fine melodramatic pictures of bens and glens have been painted by Turner and other visitors, but there is surely room for a great master here. Perhaps he will appear in the hill-foot country of Angus and the Mearns, or in Tweedale and Clydesdale, or far north where the grey farms stand among the pale Caithness fields.

But it is not in this fashion that great landscape painters appear. East Anglia has already been painted by three great men. The next great landscape painter is just as likely to appear there as anywhere else. Even in the Stour Valley, which was studied so intensely by perhaps the greatest of them all, it is possible for an artist to catch glimpses—if he has an eye for such things—of beauties of light and shade, tree shapes and cloud shapes, quite unlike those that John Constable discovered.

It sometimes seems, when one considers British landscape painting as a whole, that the strikingly picturesque scenery has interested artists less than the ordinary agricultural scenes of East Anglia or the Midlands, the ordinary countryside where men earned their living by growing crops and tending beasts and which one could see in all its beauty round almost any village in the land. It is true that Turner appears once more to be a striking exception, for he travelled indefatigably to paint ancient abbeys and castles and places of romantic grandeur, but Turner's pictures of such subjects are often concerned less with these tourist attractions themselves than with dawn and sunset, cloud and storm and sudden sunlight and the infinitely various sea. Throughout his long and active life Turner painted the weather, absorbed and delighted with our meteorological pageant that many of his countrymen find so exasperating. Many of Turner's finest pictures do not represent places of romantic associations or appearance and Crome and Constable drew their inspiration almost entirely from the ordinary agricultural England that one can see from any field gate in any English lane.

DECLINE IN SCENIC BEAUTY

It seems extremely likely that the countryside of Britain reached its supreme beauty at the beginning of the nineteenth century. The fine trees, planted in such numbers fifty or a hundred years earlier, had reached maturity; squalid industrial towns had hardly begun to encroach upon the country; rural villages and farms may have been less sanitary than they are today, but they were workmanlike, full of character, and suited their surroundings.

Since then there has been a general decline. Nevertheless the ordinary agricultural countryside is still beautiful and this beauty of the ordinary is an immensely valuable inheritance. Britain is not one of those countries where a few well-known scenic attractions are separated from each other by miles of dreary monotony. The unique fame of British scenery rests—or used to rest—on the idea that *every* view was beautiful.

THE MARBLE HALL, HATFIELD HOUSE, HERTFORDSHIRE

This is a Jacobean adaptation of the medieval Great Hall. Covering almost the whole width of the house its remains much as when it was built. The carving on the screen and minstrels' gallery shown here is the original; the ceiling is also original though the painting on it dates from 1878.

Heritage
of the Home

MANY beautiful examples of the domestic building of the past are still to be found in Britain, both in town and country, and, as far as architecture is concerned, it is probably in this tradition that Britain excels among nations.

Whether large or small, such buildings still make their appeal as homes, and it is a remarkable thing that so many are serviceable even today, not only the dignified houses of the eighteenth century, but the timbered cottages of the late medieval and Tudor periods.

The development of this rich and varied tradition goes far back in history and the story begins in Saxon times. The Saxon and Danish invaders no doubt used timber and thatch in a way that was more fully developed during the Middle Ages. The Saxon chief built his "hall" from the trees which he cleared by the labour of his bond peasants.

This prototype of the manor-house was in the nature of a large barn, thatched with reeds or straw. During the day the "houseplace" formed the living-room of the family and the servants; at night it provided shelter for human beings and cattle. Logs were burnt on a hearth in the centre of the hall, the smoke finding its way out through an opening in the roof. The fireplace was used for cooking during the day and for the comfort of the master and his festive companions at night. Town houses must also have been built of framed timber, with infillings of clay, and thatch for the roofs.

Passing to the eleventh century, we find the changes effected by the Normans were chiefly connected with the erection of castles at strategic points, as at Dover, Rochester, and the Tower on the east side of London. Then followed the building of cathedrals and churches, often far larger than those in Normandy. Timber-framed buildings with mud-clay filling were built in towns of the importance of Winchester and London. In this way the Saxon tradition was continued side by side with the new methods of the Norman masons.

It was the rich alone who could afford the expense of a stone dwelling. The famous Mill House at Christchurch, in Hampshire, and the building at Lincoln, known as the Jew's House, should be regarded as exceptional. The more ambitious aspects of Norman domestic architecture and prowess can be seen in the design of the hospital at Huntingdon, or the buildings connected with the monastery at Ely.

Examples of domestic architecture in

the twelfth century are scanty, but it is still possible to form certain conclusions. In southern England houses other than the hovels of the villeins, or serfs, were built to an almost similar plan. There was the hall, or main apartment, sometimes raised over an undercroft partly sunk in the ground; two sleeping chambers generally adjoined the hall. In addition there was a kitchen and a larder. Towards the end of the twelfth century the roofs of stone-built halls were vaulted, thus necessitating the erection of one or more rows of columns from whence the roof vaults sprang.

The town dwellings of the twelfth century were built of wood, the roofs being covered with straw or reed thatch. Destruction by fire was so frequent as to cause some citizens to build stone houses and to protect the roof timbers by tiling the slopes. Another change was the introduction, by agreement, of walls of stone between individual houses. This marks the beginning of "party walls."

In general the character of town houses at the time of the Normans was similar in all towns. Certain differences

THE JEW'S HOUSE, LINCOLN

Norman times are recalled mostly by the ruins of castles and abbeys and by the great cathedrals and village churches. This ancient house at Lincoln (like a similar one at Bury St. Edmunds, by a curious coincidence called by the same name) is exceptional in that it is a private residence dating from Norman times and is therefore one of the two most ancient private dwelling houses in Britain. Notice the round-headed arch of the doorway and the round-headed windows, also the great strength of the stone building, as massive in its own way as the masonry of the Norman castles.

CARNARVON CASTLE

Many of the great Welsh castles, of which this is one of the largest and most magnificent, are later than the majority of English castles. Carnarvon was built in the reign of Edward I, but the last stones were not laid until Edward II had been crowned king. In contrast with the Norman castles, which depended on a central fortress as a last line of defence, the whole strength of Carnarvon rests in the outer walls and the turrets which protected them and enabled a cross-fire to be kept up on attackers from any direction. Yet in spite of this, Carnarvon was overcome by the Welsh within a few years of being built.

existed according to locality: for example, the ease with which materials could be obtained and also the particular local requirements of individuals. In London we have to imagine the effect of narrow streets and alleys, with houses built of varying size but of uniform pattern. The irregular sites, the winding streets, the accidental contrasts of buildings large and small, no doubt made up a scene far from monotonous and one which can only be imagined.

The principal cities and towns after London were Winchester, York and Lincoln. The seaports included the Cinque Ports and Southampton on the south coast, as well as Harwich, Lynn and Boston on the east. Yarmouth was the staple market of the herring industry,

and from Rye came every sort of fish.

The outward appearance of the streets was that of narrow winding thoroughfares, broken at irregular intervals by churchyards, or by market-places where stalls could be set up. The houses themselves were of unequal size and approximate siting, the majority were timber-framed; as yet, the innovation of projecting the different storeys, one in advance of the other, was unknown. All the façades, whether of stone or timber, were lime whitened. In some cases the white lime-wash was slurried over the reed thatching as a protection against fire. Every parish church owned a thatch-hook pole which was available for willing hands to use when thatched roofs were ablaze. At this period inns where people could lodge for the night were few; on the other hand small taverns were plentiful. Travellers were given hospitality within the numerous monasteries established in the towns, or scattered about the countryside.

By the close of the thirteenth century, castles began to adopt features of domestic character such as lancet windows, worked-stone fireplaces, framed-timber roofs for the halls, and external stone stairways in the courtyards. There

CARISBROOKE CASTLE

One of the few medieval castles still used as a residence, Carisbrooke is the traditional home of the Governor of the Isle of Wight. In its long and eventful history it has been in turn Norman stronghold, a state residence of Queen Elizabeth, and the prison house of Charles I in 1648. The embattled gatehouse shown below dates from the thirteenth century.

was little difference between the details of churches, castles and palaces, during the period known as Early English. The Liberate Rolls of Henry III contain minute records of building works undertaken at the command of the king.

The Plantagenet dynasty rose to its zenith in the fourteenth century; many advances had by this time been made in all the crafts. The manufacture of linen had been introduced by the Flemings; leaden water-pipes were in use, wax and tallow candles were available and coal was introduced as fuel for Londoners.

Under the first, second and third of the Edwards architecture became richer in form and detail. This was due in no small measure to increased prosperity. The richer citizens could now afford to found almshouses, as well as hospitals, for the support and care of the needy and sick.

The London taverns had become famous as meeting places for all classes of citizens, many found entertainment at the Mermaid, Cornhill, or within the Three Tuns of Newgate. Equally renowned was the Salutation Tavern, Billingsgate, or the Boar's Head of London Stone. The great inns for travellers arriving from the south were in the Borough; for those from the east, in Whitechapel; for those from the north, there were the inns of Smithfield. Travellers from the West Country frequented the inns near Warwick Lane.

Early in the fifteenth century changes took place in the planning of small castles, or manor-houses, with little or no attempt at fortification; the moat, however, was continued as a form of outer defence. At Chesterton, near Cambridge, stands the old rectory house, a building typical of the changes then taking place. For town houses timber was the chief material for construction and many examples still exist. Among the famous inns of the fourteenth cen-

HURSTMONCEUX CASTLE, SUSSEX

All the grandeur of later medieval castles and manor-houses is epitomized in this moated mansion. It was built as a residence and the battlements were for show rather than for use, but the gatehouse is as embattled as are those of any of the early castles. The drawbridge has been replaced by the many-arched bridge on the left, but otherwise the exterior is much as it was in the fifteenth century, though the interior is modern. Hurstmonceux is the new home of the Royal Observatory formerly housed at Greenwich.

tury are the Angel at Grantham, the George at Glastonbury and the George at Norton St. Philip, Somersetshire.

In remote parts of the country, the peasants still lived in hovels, the latter clustered in the form of hamlets and villages. Very slowly th:ngs began to improve. There are, for example, the timber houses of Kent, some little bigger than cottages; there are the more pretentious town houses of Saffron Walden and there are the timber mansions of Chester and Shrewsbury. Yet it is along the great highways of East Anglia, through Essex to Colchester and Ipswich, and through Bishop's Stortford to Cambridge and Norwich, that some of the best examples can still be seen: for instance, the house of Thomas Paycocke at Coggeshall. The improvements in the style of these houses can be attributed to the wealth gained from the manufacture

of cloth in rural areas of the country.

In the principal streets of London there were a few shops for the display of goods, but shops in the modern sense were unknown. The majority were "locks" or store-rooms. Retail trade was mostly confined to markets and fairs. Following ancient custom the stores or locks were generally partly below ground, as at Stamford and Chester.

Every shop and store had its own particular projecting sign, just as the tavern keepers put out ale stakes and bushes. Merchants and shopkeepers lived over their trade premises. The room on the first floor was called the solar and this was in constant use by the family as the chief dwelling-room in the house. The space in the roof above the bedrooms on the second floor provided additional storage for goods. Kitchens were on the ground level, or slightly

PENSHURST PLACE, KENT

*Penshurst Place is one of the oldest
ancestral homes of England. It was
founded in the fourteenth century, and
the later medieval and modern parts
of the mansion are built round the
original hall. This corner of the hall
shows the mullioned window and part
of the oaken roof, as well as the open
hearth in the centre; the smoke from
the burning logs escaped through a
vent hole in the lofty roof.*

lower, at the back facing a small court.
The solar was sometimes approached by
means of an external staircase of wood
or stone in the courtyard.

It is thought that the famous Rows at
Chester were evolved, after a fire, by
building the shops above the vaulted
cellars and placing the solars at a higher
level still. In the late fifteenth century
the practice of projecting successive
storeys outwards, one over the other,
was begun. At the same time the introduction of angle posts, elaborately panel-

led and sometimes carved, allowed the
carpenter to show his skill.

The guild system was now the chief
binding organization of the crafts and
trades. It was laid down in the rules that
all following the trade should first have
served as apprentices. Thus the working
of materials used for building accorded
with a system which was general in
different parts of the country. The prosperity of towns, however, depended very
largely on local conditions of wealth and
trade, hence the need to take account of
local history in every case, and to
recognize regional characteristics as
expressed in the planning and external
appearance of houses.

Among many facts the perfecting of
wrought-timber work is very striking.
The framed-oak roofs of the halls and
solars, even in houses of lesser importance, evidenced the skill of carpenters
whose names have vanished. The bed-
chambers with their moulded beams and
joists, stone fireplaces and painted plas-
terwork, were equally fine. The halls of
great houses were noted for the elaboration of hammer-beam roofs, for wall
panelling and screens. Winter parlours
displayed linen-fold wall panelling from
floor to ceiling. In some houses the
boarding, and also the heavy joists,
were painted and gilded, a fashion
deriving from the Continent. Such
rooms were becoming popular in the
time of Richard III and Henry VII.
Some explanation is necessary regarding
the distinctive style of house which
today is known as Tudor: the reason
lies in the changed conditions of social
life.

Above everything else was the phenomenal expansion of the cloth trade which
aimed at increased exportation of fine
cloth to the Continent. This was the
main factor which gave new impetus to
domestic architecture. Flemish weavers
had long been settled in England, they

186

had intermarried and had imparted the secrets of their craft to many. The most progressive of the crafts, therefore, was weaving which could be followed in town and countryside. The centres of the cloth trade were East Anglia, the Cotswolds, parts of Somerset, Westmorland and Yorkshire. It is not surprising to find some of the finest examples of late fifteenth- and early sixteenth-century building in these regions.

The decline of feudalism made land a marketable commodity, thus the rich merchant could become a landowner with the result that thrifty commoners formed the beginnings of a new aristocracy. The increase of wealth meant a more even distribution of money among the middle classes, including the body of yeomen who later became the squirearchy.

Improvement in domestic architecture had been initiated earlier in the century: there were now to be fresh advances in planning, especially towards symmetry of treatment; Queen's

RUFFORD HALL, LANCASHIRE

This is one of the medieval manor-houses which have passed for safe keeping into the management of the National Trust, to whom it was presented by Baron Hesketh of Hesketh. Founded nearly five hundred years ago, Rufford Hall became one of the richest houses of Lancashire and was enlarged and embellished again and again. The banqueting hall seen below retains many ancient beams decorated with lovely carvings and much oak panelling of the greatest artistry. The photograph shows also some of the collection of medieval armour and weapons which is now deposited in Rufford Hall.

College, Cambridge, and the Bishop of Lincoln's Palace at Buckden, the latter representative of the fifteenth century, show regard for brickwork in emulation of the buildings of Flanders.

Manor-houses such as South Wingfield in Derbyshire, 1435 to 1440, gave ideas for groups of collegiate buildings, later the form of the great house suggested smaller types: the use of local materials determined certain regional characteristics in style.

MORE ELABORATE BUILDING

The choice of brickwork for domestic buildings in the Home Counties and East Anglia accords with the spirit of the time. When houses were built of timber, the brick chimney-stack, finished with tuns or shafts, remained as a dominant feature. Great wealth as well as middle-class prosperity was expressed in the variety of mansions, manor-houses, farms and town dwellings, which were erected during the reign of Henry VIII. Fortunately, they still survive in numbers although many town dwellings of the period have been refaced in later times.

The streets of cathedral cities became picturesque in an accidental yet seemly way, while rural settings were enriched with buildings which appear to grow out of the soil. Tudor architecture in all its bearings was eminently English in character. The crafts, such as smithery, glazing and leadwork, had attained a status which has never since been equalled. All that followed from the sixteenth to the end of the eighteenth centuries in this connexion owes something to the continuity of traditional craftsmanship.

Fresh changes were, however, already in motion. It was not until the accession of Queen Elizabeth that the outward appearance of houses differed from those characteristic of the reigns of King Edward VI and Mary Tudor.

Apart from the buildings where actual details can be studied, there is the authority of the deserving William Harrison, expert on Britain as he was, for a description of contemporary systems of construction. He writes: "the greatest parte of our buylding in the cities and good townes of Englande consisted only of timber, for as yet fewe of the houses of the community (except here and there in the West Country townes), are made of stone, although they may in my opinion in divers other places be builded so good cheape of the one as the other. In olde tyme the houses of the Brytons were slitely set uppe with a few postes and many radles, the like whereof almost is to be seene in the fenny countries into this day, where for lacke of wood they are inforced to continue this ancient method of buylding." He goes on to describe the distinction between building methods in "Playne and woodye country," and he stresses the use of local material, particularly stone, tiles, slate, reeds and lime. The custom of finishing the outside of houses with plaster is referred to as being general. Harrison describes this to be common in England and different from foreign methods. "Many of our greatest houses," he points out, "have outwardly been very simple and plaine to sight which inwardly have been able to receyve a Duke with his whole trayne and lodge them at their ease!"

DESIRE FOR COMFORT

By the middle of the sixteenth century, many improvements had been introduced. For example, horn was replaced by glass set in lead frames for windows; brick or worked stone was preferred to timber; living-rooms became more stately and the place of convenience was moved into a secluded spot away from the living quarters.

STRANGER'S HALL, NORWICH

A feature of the medieval hall was the minstrels' gallery. A few of these, including one at Penshurst Place and this elaborate one in the Stranger's Hall, at Norwich, have survived the ravages of time. The Stranger's Hall is later than that at Penshurst Place, for the records show that it was built in the fifteenth century. It is now an English Folk museum.

Greater comfort was now desired in cold weather and this led to the building of fireplaces in almost every room. Harrison mentions "from the hearsay the multitude of chimnies lately erected in all parts of the kingdom." At the same time attention was given to improving bedding.

It was not until Queen Elizabeth had reigned for ten years that the style of architecture finally changed from Tudor to what is now called Elizabethan. Certain diversions had begun in the early days of Henry VIII, but the products of the periods which intervened were far from striking. The Elizabethan

WEAVERS' HOUSES, CANTERBURY

In the later Middle Ages Britain became the adopted home of Walloon and Flemish weavers many of whom settled in Canterbury. These beautifully restored old houses overlooking the River Stour are among the oldest of the houses in which these welcome refugees plied their craft.

designers now approached the Renaissance by imitating first French and then German versions. Later on, Englishmen of different rank were to travel to Italy and gain first-hand knowledge of the arts and sciences.

The building of the first Royal Exchange in London, due to the enterprise of Sir Thomas Gresham, was the main factor which heralded the new style in its entirety. At Cambridge Dr. Caius was remodelling his college, subsequently called Gonville and Caius. College building in progress at Oxford and Cambridge gave scope for craftsmen, who were generally recruited from neighbouring counties. Thus every new building of importance within these academic spheres influenced taste in other parts of the country.

It was inevitable that a new type of domestic architecture should succeed the style related to church buildings which the Reformation had checked. The part enacted by the universities in providing colleges, therefore, should not be overlooked. The majority of those who became undergraduates were the sons of landowners, who in turn would be fascinated by the desire to build. That these collegians were impressed by their college buildings is not to be doubted. The mysteries of architecture had perforce to be left to the taste of surveyors to whom the task of drawing up plots and elevations was assigned, but the initiation of a project began with the patron.

In the late sixteenth century one of the leading designers was John Thorpe; there were also highly competent master builders and stonemasons in London who contrived to find access to foreign books on architecture and decoration. All such men were employed by colleges and societies or by wealthy patrons in town and country.

The Elizabethan designer eschewed

MEDIEVAL TIMBER-WORK

In the counties that border on Wales and in East Anglia, many of the manor-houses and farms dating from medieval days are built of timber or are timber framed because there was a lack of local building stone. This elaborate building is in the Maldon district of Essex. It is typical of many others in that county and in Suffolk. Notice the steep pitch of the eaves and the way in which part of the building has fallen out of truth, yet remains in perfect condition, a tribute to the skill of medieval craftsmen and builders.

haphazard planning, yet he respected certain traditional arrangements; for example, he retained the hall and the screens. John Thorpe apparently had recourse to Andronnet du Cerceau's *Les Plus Excellens Bastiments de France* for the basic ideas of some of his designs. In this regard the great house at Houghton Conquest, Ampthill, in plan closely resembles Ancy le Franc. Open planning was also coming in with plans of E and H formation. Bay windows were introduced to suit the fancy of both architect and client. Among the great houses, Longleat, in Wiltshire, 1550 to 1580, is remarkable for the horizontal characteristics of the elevations and the contrast afforded by a number of towers and turrets.

One of the finest examples is Kirby Hall, Northamptonshire, 1575, which is renowned for purity of detail. In country districts, the Cotswold houses represent a tradition in stone extending from Chipping Norton to Stamford. In East Anglia the brick mansions of Norfolk and Suffolk form the basis of the later Elizabethan style; for example, Long Melford Hall, 1599. Nearer London, Hatfield House, 1612, forms a link between late Elizabethan and Jacobean. It is, however, in the rich grazing country of Northamptonshire that the smaller stone houses of the squirearchy can be seen almost untouched.

No finer example of an Elizabethan bayed front exists than Sir Paul Pindar's house, now in the Victoria and Albert Museum at South Kensington. Preference must, however, be given to the smaller houses which are comparatively unknown. Among these are Pilton

SAFFRON WALDEN, ESSEX

The Cromwellian house at the corner of Market Hill, seen in the left foreground, is now vested in the National Trust. The timber-work of the lower storey is in keeping with the best tradition of domestic architecture from Jacobean times onwards. The design in plaster which decorates the upper storey is a craft known as pargeting, and is a form of embellishment which was brought to special perfection in Essex and the East Anglian counties. The appearance of this corner of Saffron Walden, which is the market town for the surrounding farms, has changed little in the last two hundred years.

CHIMNEYS OF FRAMLINGHAM CASTLE

One of the main decorative features of the home in the sixteenth and seventeenth centuries was the chimney. In early medieval times there was no chimney, the smoke from the open wood fire escaping through a hole in the roof. From the fifteenth century onwards fireplaces with chimneys were usual in large houses. These chimneys from Framlingham Castle in Suffolk are characteristic of two periods; on the left is one dating from Tudor times, on the right one typical of Elizabethan architecture. In 1636 Sir Robert Hitcham gave Framlingham to the Master and Fellows of Pembroke Hall, Cambridge.

Manor-house, Northampton, or in Devonshire, Chevithorne Barton, Bradninch Manor and Sydenham House. The spread of the picturesque style in the succeeding reign engendered fresh regional characteristics. For instance, Derwent Hall, Derbyshire, has gables of slighter pitch than similar buildings farther south. Felbrigge Hall, Norfolk, a great house in miniature, stresses exact balance of features. In Cheshire, Worcestershire and other counties, timber was the chief material for building, and this practice was continued well into the seventeenth century. Manton Hall, Cheshire, and Shell Farm, Droit-wich, are representative examples of traditional continuity in this regard. The Home Counties of Kent, Surrey and Sussex show a variety of small houses which are unrivalled for their proportions and apposite use of materials.

In the universities where colleges were being built the classical influence was accepted at once: but the main centre for the change of manner was London; and here it was possible to purchase illustrated books on architecture.

Built by Inigo Jones, the Banqueting Hall, Whitehall, which was completed in 1699, was acclaimed for novelty of design. The effect on the minds of the London builders and craftsmen was remarkable. Squires came up from the country to see the wonder for themselves; the nobility who contemplated adding to their houses consulted the King's Surveyor, Inigo Jones, for advice. Foremost among the clients was the Earl of Bedford, who agreed to the formation of Covent Garden with its noble church and handsome piazzas. It is somewhat remarkable that such town planning concepts as the layout of Lincoln's Inn Fields and Covent Garden should have received approval at a time when buildings similar to Sparrowe's

House, Ipswich, and the picturesque buildings in the High Street, at Oxford, reached the height of recorded taste in the provinces and were typical of the contemporary outlook in London itself.

It was a customary practice to obtain details from the Flemish pattern-books, and these were then interpreted by carpenters and masons as they thought fit. Inigo Jones, on the other hand, aimed at scholarship in architecture which would enable him to rival the masterpieces he had studied in Italy. How the leaven worked can be seen in the design of Cromwell House, Highgate, 1630, where

SYNYARDS, OTHAM, KENT

The yeomen of Kent, the chief group of yeoman farmers in medieval Britain, established a reputation for substantial prosperity and the progressive working of the land. The homes they built for themselves were in keeping with the vigorous life of their farms, and many of the finest houses in mid and east Kent were originally built by these yeomen. This one near Otham was built in 1480 and enlarged in 1663. It is one of the best preserved hall houses of England, in which there is a central hall or living-room, with a number of other rooms subsidiary to it and ranged round it.

ALNWICK CASTLE, NORTHUMBERLAND

There is something typically English about the sight across an ornamental park of a feudal castle. This view of Alnwick, one of the historic castles of northern England, takes tone from the well-wooded parklands and the artificial watercourse, an example of landscape gardening on the grand scale. Alnwick has long been the seat of the dukes of Northumberland. Once a Norman castle, it was rebuilt in the fourteenth century and has since been much restored.

the façade by Gerbier resembles the work of Inigo Jones.

Strict formality was now the keynote for house planning; the dining parlour and the withdrawing room, together with a spacious staircase, formed the main features. All the living-rooms were panelled, the fireplaces were of stone with overmantels of wood. This was the period when plaster ceilings were enriched with elaborate geometrical patterns, foliations and pendants. A draw-

ing showing a party at the Duke of Newcastle's house gives an accurate idea of the austerity of the furnishing.

The small farm-house at Woolsthorpe, near Grantham, the birthplace of Isaac Newton, can be regarded as typical of many similar buildings. Here the exterior echoes the local traditions of Stamford and Grantham; the internal construction being remarkable for its ingenuity. Certain floors are formed of reeds floated with cement, an early form of reinforced flooring. Individual pieces of furniture were both strong and elaborately decorated, the ornamental parts deriving from Flemish and French prototypes.

In the farm-houses of Westmorland, oak dressers were built in as partitions to divide the "eating parlour" from the sitting-room. The scale of the smaller farms and cottages can be best understood by observing the lowness of the ceilings compared with the floor area of the living-rooms. In all houses the fireplace was considered to be the focal point of an apartment, a fact which explains the beauty of irons and firebacks.

OLD HOUSES AT METHWOLD

The sixteenth-century brick gable-end and the crow-stepping of the gable itself are in the tradition of Dutch architecture of a slightly earlier date. The windows in the top storey are original; before reconstruction all the windows were of this type.

AT THORINGTON, ESSEX

These seventeenth-century cottages illustrate the use of weather-boarding. This is one of the later developments in the small house in England: it acts as a chute for rain-water and so prevents moisture seeping into the walls. Often the wall behind the weatherboarding is of lath and plaster.

Life was both strenuous and difficult for ordinary folk at a time when the prosperity of London was increasing. It was to be made more exacting by the upheaval of the Civil War and rigours of Puritan control. Under these circumstances architecture practically ceased and the crafts languished under the strain of political despotism.

The reactions which followed the return of Charles II, therefore, had wide implications, for, in a sense, society began to form on a modern basis. It was the revival of social and cultural distinctions more than anything else which encouraged people to build once again. At this juncture the character of domestic architecture became formal; founding a new tradition which continued through the eighteenth century. The pioneer labours of Inigo Jones had been obscured by narrow views which aimed at the repression of art. There were few architects confident enough to gather up the threads of Jones's individual manner of design. On the other hand many who had spent years of exile in Holland and France were now at liberty to cross the Channel, bringing with them memories of the bias for Dutch methods of building in brick, and of the taste for French display in works of civic stamp.

The building of the great Palace of Versailles with its innumerable treasures of art focused the attention of all Europe on France at a time when London was still a picturesque medieval city. But this sharp contrast between the matured arts of France and the backward state of art in England was soon to be changed, strangely enough by a disaster which struck dismay in the minds of the citizens. The Great Fire, following closely on the year of the Plague, destroyed more than a hundred and thirty thousand dwelling houses as well as the greater number of the parish churches and left St. Paul's Cathedral a shell of tottering walls. Plans for rebuilding were forthcoming while the ashes were still hot; but the city was destined to rise piecemeal on the lines of the ancient streets. It was at least apposite that advice was taken regarding the grading of the houses, and the observance of rules for their erection. If Wren was denied the opportunity of planning the City as an entity, he at least had the satisfaction of encouraging taste for proportion and seemliness.

From all accounts Londoners took pride in seeing their city rise on the old lines, but it was a slow process. Gresham College served as the Exchange, the Excise Office was removed to Bloomsbury, the General Post Office to Covent Garden, the Customs House to Mark Lane and Doctors' Commons was moved to Exeter House, Strand. There were improvisations on every side.

There was also feverish activity to regain foreign trade which it was feared might pass to the Dutch. The analogy between this period and the present is very striking.

In this emergency the master builders and speculators organized thousands of craftsmen who came from the Home Counties to offer their skill. The new orientation of taste, even in the design of simple buildings, must be ascribed to the omniscience of Wren and his collaborators.

There was also close contact between

IN SHERINGHAM, NORFOLK

Often it is the material rather than the architecture which gives a building character. In north Norfolk, from Sheringham eastward along the coast, there is a "stone belt" in which many of the dwelling places are built from the local cobblestones. These cottages at Sheringham are in the best traditions of this curious style.

the Court and the City, an intenseness of interest maintained by the personal efforts of the king. From close study of the period emerges the fact that the rebuilding of London was of the greatest importance to the nation as a whole. The novel style of the houses with their façades of brick and windows rhythmically spaced, horizontally and vertically, made an appeal which was soon imitated in all parts of the kingdom. The London manner for houses was to be imposed with variations on rural England as well. For such reasons English domestic architecture developed a character distinct from that of either France or

NEAR ELSTEAD, SURREY

Between Farnham and Godalming, along the banks of the River Wey, there are a number of fine Georgian homes. This water-mill near Elstead is a graceful example of the design characteristic of all Georgian architecture combined with severe utility. It is built throughout in red brick.

Holland. It was in fact the spontaneity of the effort, together with the confidence shown in the regulations for construction, which assured success. By some strange chance, the houses of the period link quite naturally with the style initiated by Inigo Jones and his kinsman John Webb. There is continuity of interest and no great departure from the pure classicality which had been the aim of Inigo Jones before the Civil War.

The lessons which formal grouping offered by the layout of Covent Garden and Lincoln's Inn Fields were not ignored when Wren rebuilt the precincts of the Temple. They were followed by other Inns of Court, and led in turn to the dignity of the houses in Bedford Row and the lesser streets off the Strand.

The new building vernacular had something in common with the brick architecture of the Tudor period. The plasticity of the style was demonstrated in rows of small houses as well as in isolated family mansions. Later, the London merchant built his four-square house at Tottenham, Enfield and Snaresbrook ; Church Row, Hampstead, attracted another type of resident. Similar houses can be seen today surrounding the Close at Salisbury, or standing in proximity to most cathedrals. It was beyond doubt the speedy recovery of London after the Great Fire, together with the increase of foreign trade, which resulted in the rapid expansion of the capital towards the surrounding villages.

By the end of the seventeenth century the planning of houses in towns followed definite lines. For example those in Queen Anne's Gate, London, have the spaciousness of country houses. This was effected by combining the entrance hall and staircase. The large rooms on each floor were arranged in pairs. A secondary staircase from the basement gave access to the second-floor bedrooms and the

COWDRAY CASTLE, SUSSEX

These picturesque ruins, set in a charming situation on the edge of Cowdray Park, near Midhurst, Sussex, give an idea of the magnificence of the English home in late Tudor and Elizabethan times. In the sixteenth century Cowdray was the seat of Sir Anthony Browne and one of the finest of the unfortified manor-houses of the south country. There is a tradition associated with the castle that Sir Anthony, who was presented with Battle Abbey by the king, ejected the monks of Battle and was visited with the curse of fire and water. Two hundred years later the buildings were burnt out and the owner, a direct descendant of Sir Anthony, was drowned in an attempt to shoot the rapids of the Rhine in 1793 at the very time that Cowdray was burning. The ruins of the castle are now being preserved; over the gateway to Cowdray Park the Browne arms can still be seen.

attics. Small dressing-rooms, or powdering closets, were contrived at each level. The plan of the smaller town houses consisted of a passage with a staircase facing the front door: the rooms above were arranged in pairs back and front. In most cases the kitchens and sculleries were below ground. In some of the smaller country houses the basement was reserved for cellarage, and the kitchen, scullery and other offices were placed in a low wing, as at Eggington Manor, Leighton Buzzard, and Aspley House, near Bletchley. A very distinctive plan is that of Fenton House, Hampstead.

The practice of giving importance to the staircase and the living-rooms, initiated by architects of the Wren school, was continued down to the

Victorian period. The value of studied proportion for rectangular windows was first recognized when London was rebuilt. For many years tradition had favoured the mullioned and transomed type, but the advantage of double-hung sashed frames was now grasped and towards the end of the century sashed windows were widely adopted. Windows framed into rectangular divisions set within marginal boxings became part of the treatment of ordinary elevations. Window openings with quoins and arches of gauged Dutch bricks formed a fine contrast with the field of surface brickwork. This treatment was reserved for mansions of the first importance.

Another sign of the desire for comfort was the demand for panelled walls. The earlier method of covering walls with wainscot oak, framed into small panels, was looked upon as old-fashioned; as a result, larger surfaces of wood were introduced. Projecting, moulded panelling, known as bolection, of deal or pine, with skirtings, chair rails and wooden cornices, now became the mode for the principal rooms of houses large and small. In the better-class houses a similar treatment was carried to the walls of the hall and staircase. It is not difficult to picture the comfort of a living-room of the late seventeenth century. There is the background of the painted panelling. There are the sashed windows with the shutters folded back into their recesses; the inviting window seats and the panelled doors with brass rim-locks. The fireplace with its open hearth, marble surround and shining dogs formed the chief focal point. One can view these effects in the state apartments of Hampton Court, but it is interesting to know that the houses of middle-class people were appointed in similar fashion.

The most fascinating period of English domestic architecture begins with the reign of Queen Anne and ter-

minates with the period of the Regency. We now enter upon an epoch of stability, far different from the preceding age and one in which fresh comforts were shared by a greater number of people.

London, as ever, was the centre of activity and the emporium for the luxury trades. In the capital, fashions were originated and spread outwards to satisfy the taste of the new country families, who for the most part were recruited from the trading class.

When George I became king, the nation was entering upon an era of commercial expansion, which developed and eventually provided the means to fight Napoleon at the close of the century. Defoe's England flourished and gave way to scenes familiar to Johnson

IN HAMPTON COURT PALACE

Hampton Court Palace is unique in that it combines supreme examples of the craftsmanship of Tudor times with some of the most superb work of the Renaissance. The early part of the palace was built by Cardinal Wolsey for his own use, but the whole of the wing which lies towards the gardens, including the famous Fountains Court, was constructed to the design of Sir Christopher Wren nearly two hundred years later. Both in the external fabric and in the interior decoration of the rooms no trouble or expense was spared to obtain the most perfect results. How magnificent these results were is shown by the two photographs. That on the left demonstrates the perfection of linenfold panelling before the art of panelling began to deteriorate. Notice also the severe but graceful lines of the Tudor doorway. The photograph above is of a room in the part of the palace designed by Sir Christopher Wren. Here there is a wealth of ornament and decoration in striking contrast with the severity of Wolsey's room, yet the decoration is not over-elaborated. It represents truly the progress in man's ideas of beauty and comfort over two hundred years.

and Reynolds; in due course came the Industrial Revolution which brought into being new social problems. As the century advanced towards the middle period, dress became simpler, taste more diffuse; and although class distinctions were sharply defined the process of levelling up was on the whole beneficial. Through all this amazing activity the arts flourished, slightly dulled, it is true, by the parsimony of the first two Georges, but rising to brilliancy during the long reign of George III.

The success of the eighteenth century in these islands was due to the skill of individuals who were free to develop their ideas. Viewed in retrospect the period has many attractions. It was a time of gradual change during which the apprenticeship system survived and the rural industries maintained a measure of sturdy independence.

There remains to be explained why the smaller houses bear a family resemblance to the mansions of the wealthy and why the technique of construction was so consistent. This was due in no small measure to the influence of the upper classes who acted as patrons to architects and builders. Because the bias of taste was in a classical direction, the plastic arts were bound to reflect contemporary moods. The outward form of objects for use and beauty mattered most, a fact which accounts for the universal character of both furniture and domestic appointments. This, too, is why there is no essential difference of

COTTAGES NEAR ABERYSTWYTH

It is not only the districts in which stone is quarried locally that produce dwellings of a characteristic nature. In many areas there are traditional styles of decoration or embellishment. Conspicuous among these are local styles of colour washing or whitewashing. In this respect Wales shares with parts of East Anglia the distinction of leading the way in the tradition of whitewashing outer walls.

form between silver articles and those made of Sheffield plate or pewter. It was not a coincidence that the social gradings found their counterpart in the choice of metal for teapots, spoons and tankards.

Notwithstanding influences from France and Italy English architecture flourished in sedate austerity, finding exponents among artificers as well as professional architects. The high level of design in detail can be attributed to the small illustrated copy-books which were published from 1730 onwards. Thus carpenters and masons were able to produce doors, windows and fireplaces, to exact rules, thereby adding to the beauty of small houses in every town and village in the kingdom. The general participation of artificers in the visual crafts connected with architecture could have only one result, namely a real understanding of elegance of form.

Innumerable examples of small houses, all of which are equally attractive, come to mind. These include the Vicarage, Chesham; the bay-windowed houses of Saffron Walden; the houses in St. Peter's Street, St. Albans; and Robert Mylne's house at Amwell in Hertfordshire. Among the later examples are the Old Warden Rectory, Bedfordshire, which has a gambrel roof; the brick cottages of Southill, Bedfordshire, built on the Whitbread estate, and many others at Wallingford, Abingdon and Newbury. Hampshire can boast many small houses of distinction, as, for instance, at Southampton, Lymington and Netley. Similar types can be found in Devon and Cornwall, in Lincolnshire and in Norfolk. Nearer to London, Wick House, Richmond, built in 1775 by Mylne, is regarded as outstanding.

For originality of composition the two houses in the market-square, Buckingham, built in 1776, should be noted. Here can be seen the beginnings

RHUG HALL, CORWEN, MERIONETHSHIRE

Amid the romantic scenery of Merionethshire, Rhug Hall is one of a number of large mansions which lie along the tributaries of the Dee and Severn. In Wales the classical style of architecture came later than it did to most of England, for the Renaissance, like almost every other movement which has affected Britain, spread its culture in the far west and north more slowly than it did in the lowlands. Even so, this mansion is a finely developed example of the Romano-Greek style of building, with its symmetrical windows, its classical columns and round-headed arches, and the pediment (a triangular structure similar to the portico of a Greek building) over the oldest part.

of a style which later became identified with the modern semi-detached villa. But how infinitely superior in detail is the Buckinghamshire prototype.

Once the quest is begun the pursuit of the small houses seems never-ending. All are well proportioned, yet few are exactly the same. Whether they are chanced upon in Arundel, Sussex, discovered at Epping or Harlow, or admired in the villages surrounding Cambridge or Ely, they are recognized at once for their simplicity and charm. Not less alluring are those weather-boarded examples in the Essex peninsula and throughout the Home Counties. Here can be seen numerous examples of small houses which are related to that great tradition of timber-framed buildings which enriched colonial America.

BLICKLING HALL, NORFOLK

*Now the property of the National
Trust, Blickling Hall was built at
the beginning of the seventeenth century on an estate which had been the
property of the Boleyn family and
where Henry VIII is reputed to have
gone courting Anne. The architect of
Blickling was the same Robert Lyminge
who built Hatfield House, shown on
page 180. This detail of the main
entrance shows well the growing
elaboration of the Jacobean style as
compared with the Tudor and Elizabethan styles of domestic architecture.*

English domestic architecture in all
its branches attained to the heights of
formal elegance towards the close of the
century. Many features such as doors,
windows, fire-grates and ironmongery
had become standardized. This, however, did not restrict variety of composition. Hence the diminutive terrace
formations and the sequence observed
in street architecture. The keynote is
proportion; ornament is reduced to a
minimum, or reserved for salient
features. It was, in fact, the perfection of
the simplest forms of building construction that caused such convincing results.

The majority of the houses erected in
London between 1774 and 1800 were
the result of private enterprise. Even
architects of the status of the Adam
brothers entered upon the treacherous
ground of building speculation and they
had innumerable imitators. When the
great landlords came into the lists,
London was extended in a westerly
direction to Paddington; the vacant
lands of Bloomsbury were built over
and Camden Town was started. William
Cowper was prophetic when he described the encroachment of the growing
streets. Peeping back into the vanished
age of George III, it is not difficult to
reconstruct everyday life or to recognize
the familiarity of surroundings which to
a great extent are our own.

The England of Jane Austen and
William Cobbett was far different from
what it has since become. London, apart
from its East End slums and the mean
dwellings which lined the main roads
leading out of town, was famous for its
squares and residential streets. The
spirit of eighteenth-century Palladianism
on heavy classical architecture was in
process of translation in terms of stuccoed brick to Regent's Park. The great
London estates were being developed
under the direction of architects; open
spaces were railed in and gardens were
laid out for the benefit of the surrounding tenants. In the Midlands and the
distant North the Industrial Revolution
had already created grim centres which
segregated whole populations from the
enjoyment of beauty.

Rural England was much as it had
been for centuries, as can be seen from
the contemporary water-colour sketches
of Turner and Buckler. A new order of

GRANTHAM, LINCOLNSHIRE

Almost every old town in England and Wales, and many of the smaller villages, has a little group of Georgian houses, like the one seen on the left in this photograph, which show the severe but pleasant lines of classical architecture. The front door retains something of the appearance of the medieval gatehouse which it superseded. Georgian houses are spacious and have large windows.

205

society was forming in which class distinctions multiplied with ever-increasing complexity. At the close of the Napoleonic Wars reactions set in which led to the further disruption of old English life. The social structure was becoming unbalanced by the influx of the rural population to the industrial centres and by the attraction of London and its promise of employment to the unskilled.

CHANGES AND DEVELOPMENTS

It was a world of transition, creating scenes viewed with mild interest by the passengers who travelled on the outside of stage coaches. It was a time of general change scarcely realized by leisured folk who dwelt in turn in town and country. Architecture expressed the new aspirations, particularly the divergence from the taste of former generations. The traditions of the eighteenth century were still strong when Queen Victoria came to the throne in 1837. The new villas of Cheltenham and Tunbridge Wells had their exact doubles at St. John's Wood, Brixton and Dulwich. Stuccoed terraces on the great scale were the pride of Belgravia and Tyburnia. Residential London was now going out of town with a vengeance, especially towards Shepherd's Bush, Stamford Hill and Streatham.

The greatest change came when the railway system was developed between 1837 and 1848. Then compartmented coaches were placed on iron tracks, distances were reduced and the mail routes with their picturesque inns and associations were soon forgotten. The reaction against the eighteenth-century house was almost as remarkable. There was complete revulsion shown for the bricklayers' "packing-cases," and in its place there arose a desire for pretty transcripts in the pseudo-Gothic, Swiss, or Grecian styles. This in turn gave place to a craze for the Elizabethan, encouraged by drawings of mansions of the olden time.

By 1875, the railways had carried some of the population to new residential points well beyond the London area. Snaresbrook, Walthamstow and Loughton each had a quota of pretentious villas; Wimbledon, Acton, Ealing and Richmond received new families·as fast as houses could be built. On the northern heights and in the neighbourhood of the Crystal Palace building activity was on the increase. In Hertfordshire the newer parts of Watford reflected the character of Highbury. Harpenden at this period was advertised as a residential area well served by the newly opened Midland line.

During the last decades of Victoria's reign the outward expansion of London was limited only by the capacity of the railways to deal with suburban traffic. General prosperity seemed assured, large houses and large families were the rule, involving the services of domestics whose labours were made difficult by four flights of stairs.

THREATS TO THE COUNTRYSIDE

The turn of the century saw even wider movements which threatened the whole countryside. Not only were pleasant houses built to meet the whims of the newly rich but whole villages were disfigured by accretions of semi-detached villas run up by local speculators. No architect intervened in the design of these strange interlopers: legislation could do little but enforce the rulings of the London Building Act in the guise of local by-laws.

With the coming of motor transport the future of rural England seemed destined to become a vast ribbon development, thinning out between great centres of population.

That matters could be altered for the better was being proved by the wisdom

206

PARK CRESCENT, LONDON

To many lovers of the architectural heritage of Britain the beginning of the nineteenth century appears as the end of the golden era of building. Certainly this crescent, which formed part of the town planning scheme in the early 1800s and which transformed the area between Regent Street and the Marylebone Road, is as much in keeping with modern taste as it was with that of nearly one hundred and fifty years ago. There is a symmetry and a dignity about the conception which has never been surpassed. It is one of the most attractive parts of Georgian London, which, together with Georgian Bath, stands for the supreme development of the English home before the Industrial Revolution.

of private enterprise which engaged in the development of Port Sunlight and Bournville. Here the skill of accomplished architects introduced groups of houses which are well planned and a delight to the eye. Later the vaster projects at Hampstead and Letchworth were taken as models in Europe and America. Neither should the Herculean labours of the architectural department of the London County Council be overlooked.

It was shown that small houses could be sited graciously and could, moreover, be beautiful in themselves. It is necessary to name only the estates at Tottenham, at Edgware and Old Oak to substantiate the truism that beauty matters.

SALISBURY, WILTSHIRE

The only city of England founded and designed to be a cathedral city, Salisbury has no history earlier than its cathedral. The cathedral is built throughout in the Gothic style; its spire, dating from about 1330 and over 400 feet high, is the highest of any cathedral or church in England.

The Heritage of the Town

MANY of the oldest and most historic towns of Britain date from the time when most of England was a province of Rome.

To make a list of certain of the Roman sites that have been classified as towns is not easy when it is remembered that a great number of prominent military stations cannot be so considered and that, judged by modern standards, quite a number of Roman names would today stand only for villages. Perhaps the following will suffice, though Bath should have a paragraph to itself if only for its healing springs, gushing uninterrupted for unnumbered centuries, that the Romans discovered and developed with fine architectural adornments, relics of which remain. Anderida (Pevensey with Westham), Aquae Sulis (Bath), Calleva Atrebatum (Silchester), Camulodunum (Colchester), Corinium (Cirencester), Corstopitum (Corbridge), Deva (Chester), Portus Dubris (Dover), Durnovaria (Dorchester), Durovernum (Canterbury), Eboracum (York), Glevum (Gloucester), Isca Augusta (Caerleon upon Usk), Isca Dumnoniorum (Exeter), Isurium (Aldborough), Lindum Colonia (Lincoln), Londinium (London), Luguvallium (Carlisle), Magna (Kenchester), Ratae (Leicester), Regnum (Chichester), Sorbiodunum (Old Sarum, Modern Salisbury), Venta Belgarum (Winchester), Venta Icenorum (Norwich), Venta Silurum (Caerwent), Verulamium (St. Albans), Uriconium (Wroxeter).

Taking first the many towns of which the names end in -chester (*castra*), these always imply an original encampment, sometimes renamed by the Normans, such as the three Newcastles, implying a new fortress in or near an older military site. When the Roman occupation ceased the land must have been full of these waste -chesters. The one which bears this name most prominently today, medieval Chester (the Roman Deva), was deserted for three centuries. Bede speaks of the camps in and near Cambridge as being similarly abandoned. Verulamium was deserted when Saxon St. Albans sprang up and would have been abandoned had not the bricks and stones, particularly the bricks, of the older city formed a valuable quarry for the new. Silchester must have been forgotten by the Rædingas, in their new town of Reading on the Thames. Roman Anderida and Roman Uriconium are waste places to this day. London affords a curious piece of evidence as to its abandoned site. Gracechurch Street lies athwart the remains of a building of considerable size. When the Saxon tribes re-entered Londinium and the smallest of their "kingdoms" arose, that

209

CHESTER, THE ROWS

The Rows at Chester are a unique feature in English towns, a covered way between the ground floor and second floor of the buildings that line the main streets. First built as part of the late medieval city, they have been reconstructed in modern times. Chester was one of the chief Roman towns of Britain, a military as well as a commercial centre, and the present town, so far as its four main streets are concerned, is based on the plan of the Roman city. Modern Chester is a cathedral city and the county town of Cheshire.

of the Middle Saxons, the streets of the new London did not always, it appears, coincide with the old. Ancient alignments were forgotten, probably implying desertion for some decades at least.

This question has therefore to be answered: can any single Romano-British city claim to have possessed a continuous history all through the ages? Yes, for that may be said of Exeter and possibly of Lincoln. Exeter is the one important city which survived the Teutonic conquest and with institutions that possessed unbroken descent to the present day. The reason lies in its situation. Hengist, Horsa, Cissa and the successive hordes of heathen freebooters stopped short of Dumnonia, that lovely land of contrasting red and green which is today called Devonshire. Before their descendants arrived at the Exe, some generations had elapsed. Though the date of this retarded Saxon occupation is unknown, historians assume that no longer were the inhabitants massacred or dispersed. Indeed, there is evidence that Britons and Saxons, or, as they may now be called, Welsh and English, lived side by side in different quarters of the town. Exeter, too, seems to have retained its ancient Roman walls, repaired by its new Saxon owners, as a defence against the Danes.

Lincoln's claim to continuous, unbroken history is slender. Perhaps it is better to take a middle course and suggest that even if it were left desolate its abandonment was of short duration. Certain it is that Lincoln has kept its name and that of its northern gateway, the Newport. The former is very remarkable, Lindum Colonia, a colony

even as Cologne was. The great city of the Rhineland, however, has lost the prefix of the unknown tribe of savages whose centre it was; Lincoln has not. Of York, where the Emperor Hadrian lived, where the Emperor Severus died, and where the Emperor Constantine was hailed Imperator, nothing is known after the Romans left it. The darkness of two centuries descends upon it.

Carlisle perhaps, because of its exceptional history, claims attention next. Less important civically than Lincoln or York it was a frontier fortress of the first rank, its inhabitants always on the alert against attacks which did not cease until modern times, as its ruined cathe-

BY THE COLNE, COLCHESTER

The story of Colchester is bound up with its river, the Colne, which is navigable by sea-going craft as far as the Colchester docks. Along its tideway were brought the materials to build the Roman town of Camulodunum and to rebuild the ruins of the Roman town in Norman times. Through the centuries Colchester has traded by water with the Continent and other parts of Britain. Even today coastal barges and shipping from overseas, including oil tankers, use the port. This photograph shows a coasting barge berthed beside a mill.

dral nave still bears witness. It has lost its Roman name and retained its Celtic one, for its life seems to have gone on after the Romans left. Its troubles did not come from Saxon invaders but from Scots and Norsemen. The strangest scene of all in its eventful history was when William Rufus re-settled the city not with Normans but with Saxons. Some Roman towns (but not London, as indicated) have retained the alignment of their principal streets, four meeting at a central point as at Chichester and Gloucester, or two at right-angles as at Chester. It may be noted that though Gloucester has retained the names of its gates and Chichester has not, in both towns, save for a few fragments, all the gates or fortified entrances have gone.

ROMAN BRITAIN

Is it safe to infer, then, here as elsewhere, from the preservation of this ancient alignment of their respective towns, that there has been continuous occupation since Roman times? It is doubtful, for the evidence is lacking. Consider the case of the three towns of Roman Sussex—Anderida, Portus Adurni and Regnum. Of Anderida nothing is known save the record of a dreadful massacre. Of Portus Adurni even the site cannot be located; possibly had it survived it would today have formed part of the modern borough of Hove. Regnum was probably the largest town of the three and became the capital, Cissa's Ceaster, after that successful Saxon commander had dealt with Anderida. A march of three days would have brought him to Regnum, where news of the slaughter must have preceded him. Probably the inhabitants fled. Admitting the utmost speed in Cissa's settling down, there was probably an interregnum of some years.

Roman Britain's greatest monument —and if its posts were added up, its largest town—has yet to be mentioned, the seventy-mile-long wall from the Solway to the North Sea. Antiquaries are now agreed that it began as a rampart of earthwork and turf like the Antonine Wall between the Firths of Clyde and Forth; and that it was replaced by one of stone under the Emperor Hadrian, a great construction, and renewed under Severus. Kipling in *Puck of Pook's Hill* has provided a vivid picture of this thin, variegated line, which had additional towns or military stations at either end with several intermediate places such as Corstopitum (Corbridge), where the wall was crossed by Watling Street, Cilurnum (Chollerford), Borcovicium (Housesteads), and others. Here in this wild outpost of the Roman Empire amidst the clamour of every tongue and the practice of every cult the legions were gathered together for training, sometimes to meet the foe on the other side in friendly chaffering, sometimes in deadly strife.

COUNTRY HOUSES

There is one important fact in the history of the Roman occupation perhaps not stressed sufficiently, though the buildings themselves have generally been well examined, and that is, the wide *rural* settlement of at least the southern half of Britain. The very striking, indeed imposing, fragments of Roman walls still remaining, as at Leicester and in London itself, should not obscure the fact that by far the greater part of the inhabitants did not dwell in cities at all. They lived in the country which, not far off as often now, lay at the very doors of the few towns, if such they can be called, so small were they. Southern England must have abounded in country houses not unlike a two-storied timber-built house of to-day, but on stone or flint foundations and with an amazing range of outbuildings, bath-houses, together with rooms for alternate use in summer and winter, often adorned with mosaic floors of both home and imported marbles. All were served, needless to say, with adequate slave labour.

Bath-houses have been mentioned; and strange to say it is in London itself that the best-preserved example of a Roman bath is to be found. All Londoners should know the ancient Roman bath off the Strand, with a spring of excellent water which no doubt ensured its preservation through the ages. This relic, bigger than an ordinary "slipper" bath but not quite big enough for a swim, must once have stood in a little garden-house in a London suburb, well outside the walls. The existence of this one and others such as that in the Charterhouse are perhaps the best proof that the land enjoyed a measure of peace and security for centuries that it never knew again until the nineteenth century.

What were the houses like in Roman London and other cities? They were small, one- or two-storied dwellings, not greatly differing from those of medieval

ELY, CAMBRIDGESHIRE

For a thousand years or more Ely has been a centre of culture and religion. It was the capital of the Isle of Ely when this area was the only district to rise above the morass of the Fens before they were drained. An abbey was founded here by the king of Northumbria in the seventh century and the town flourished afterwards under the protection of the abbots, who worked hard to extend the area of cultivation on the dry lands above the intractable marshlands. In the interval between the time of legend and recorded history Ely won added fame as the last stronghold of Hereward the Wake in 1070. The battlemented tower which is at the west end of the cathedral is of Norman workmanship with some later additions: it suggests a fortress rather than a church.

CARDIFF, THE

One of the largest seaports in the world, Cardiff has had a continuous history since
Roman times. The keep of the Norman castle built at the end of the eleventh century can
be clearly seen. Part of the walls and the great west gate have been reconstructed, but the
general appearance of the castle has not changed much since 1404 when it was besieged

214

CHIEF CITY OF WALES

and taken by storm by the Welsh hero chieftain Owen Glendower. The castle and grounds have now been presented by the Marquess of Bute to the people of Cardiff. To the right in the picture are the civic buildings of Cathays Park, including the City Hall, the National Museum of Wales and the University College of South Wales.

England. Sometimes, as at Silchester, there were rows of detached houses, each with its little garden, with narrow pavements and roadways. Everything and everybody would probably have seemed very small; and when the Anglo-Saxons visited Rome it was the bigness of everything, churches and houses as well as the Colosseum, that impressed them above all else.

MONASTIC FOUNDATIONS

Civilization's debt to the monastery cannot be measured. Before it created towns the monastery had planted fields and gardens in waste places; had provided schools, hospitals and infirmaries; had organized water supplies and efficient systems of drainage and that at a time when such were unknown, even in kings' palaces. Those wonderful agriculturalists, the Cistercians, carried their improved methods as far as Scandinavia. To this day there exist in the archives of the Vatican, records of their religious houses in Greenland, wiped out by the Black Death, so it is supposed, in the fourteenth century, together with the towns they had made and the people who lived in them.

It is well to begin with a few simple definitions. It may be asked what is the difference between an abbey and a priory. Actually none, it is merely a question of classification, not always constant. Thus, if self-contained as to its administration, a Benedictine or Cistercian house was called an abbey; if dependent upon another, a priory. A small "branch establishment," so to speak, was called a "cell."

Cluniac houses were called priories, being dependent on the mother house, Cluny Abbey in Burgundy. Houses of the canons regular, mainly Augustinians, and of the Carthusians were usually called priories. Yet again it is customary to speak of cathedral priories where the bishop's see houses a monastery as well and of which the bishop was the titular abbot, the prior the business manager. Thirteen of Britain's cathedrals were of the old foundation, that is, they were served not by monks but by secular canons, each of whom lived in his own house as the members of cathedral chapters do today. By a coincidence the cathedrals of the new foundation after the Reformation were thirteen in number, too. Of these, seven were attached to Benedictine monasteries, so called because at the Reformation though they ceased to be served by monks or canons regular, they received a new constitution with a dean taking the place of prior. These seven were Canterbury, Durham, Ely, Norwich, Rochester, Winchester and Worcester. Carlisle, a house of Augustinian canons, Chester, Gloucester and Peterborough of the Benedictines and two Augustinian churches, Bristol and Oxford, were started afresh as cathedral sees by Henry VIII. All these developed and in some cases actually created towns. The lovely ruined abbeys, however, mainly Cistercian, which still adorn the Yorkshire valleys did not. They were agricultural communities; model farms in fact. An exception is, however, the church of St. Mary Graces, near the Tower of London, on the site of what is now the Royal Mint.

SAXON WESTMINSTER

Of the towns thus created, Westminster, a bishop's see for a few fleeting years, easily takes pre-eminence. Here, however, as with so many English sites, it is essential to go back to Roman and pre-Roman times. The legend of the great abbey's foundation by King Sebert of the East Saxons, and the story of the divine origin and dedication of Westminster, is well told by Matthew Arnold. Monastery and king's palace grew up together, their very proximity

DURHAM, FORTRESS TOWN OF THE NORTH

Built on a rocky promontory, almost surrounded by the River Wear, Durham is at once a cathedral city, a medieval stronghold and a market and county town. Like the bishops of Ely, the bishops of Durham in the Middle Ages wielded something that approached royal powers. The cathedral on the right in the picture is on the site of a church which, tradition records, was completed in 999, where the remains of St. Cuthbert were finally buried. Much of the present building is Norman. The castle, seen to the left of the cathedral, was for many centuries the palace of the bishops. Originally a Norman stronghold, it has been restored again and again until little of the original remains. It at present forms a part of Durham University.

suggesting royal burials within the choir. A town developed and, though aware as one treads the streets of the West End how great a thing the City of Westminster has become, one hardly realizes of how long standing is that greatness nor how utterly it has changed, perhaps more than any other city, save for its one great building.

During the reigns of the Stuarts, Westminster had become the second largest town in Great Britain, succeeding Norwich and York. Its greatest change has taken place almost within living memory, yet few can now realize what it looked like before the extensive opening-up of Victoria Street cut through scores of medieval gabled dwellings.

It is difficult to assign the next important town after Westminster that was clearly the offspring of a religious house, for the towns to be found clustered around monastic churches were not necessarily created by them. Canterbury and Rochester were not. Both were capitals of petty Saxon kingdoms and so was Winchester, but more important, and Worcester less so. All were of Roman origin and all were greatly helped in their development by the big cathedral-monastery in their midst. Canterbury, Winchester and York had additional Benedictine houses, so well provided with religious buildings were these ancient cities. Canterbury became the ecclesiastical capital of the English-

217

speaking world and is so still. Winchester remained the political capital of Anglo-Saxon England until after the Conquest.

Not always, however, did the monastery come first. It was the domain of a feudal lord that often decided the status of the county town, as at Lewes or Stafford and as at the cathedral cities of Chichester, Lichfield and Coventry, but Coventry comes in again in another category. Where Saxon bishops had chosen small places with little chance of development for their sees it was a Norman policy to remove them to larger towns, as from Crediton to Exeter, Selsey to Chichester, Thetford to Norwich and elsewhere. It is therefore sometimes a mistaken assumption that modern railway and business enterprise have created a town, say, like Reading. To such enterprise, of course, its great modern development is due, but Reading was a town in Anglo-Saxon times and before that the meeting place of the tribal clan of the Rædingas, its Benedictine abbey being one of the greater monasteries with a royal sepulchre. Some of its medieval churches still remain, and, indeed, Reading was one of a chain of beautiful abbeys on the banks of the Thames. Besides Westminster there were, from east to west, Barking, Bermondsey, Chertsey, Dorchester, Abingdon and Oxford.

MONASTIC ORIGIN OF OXFORD

Oxford, scarcely of Roman origin beyond the inevitable Roman use of its fords and tracks, possessed two great religious houses, both of Augustinian canons, Oseney and St. Frideswide's, the latter named after a Saxon princess of the eighth century, who first founded a nunnery there which later changed hands. Oseney has gone, but Wolsey and Henry VIII together made in Christ Church a college and a cathedral of St.

Frideswide, though Henry, it is said, had a mind at first to let Oseney form the new see. Of the original Saxon church a little masonry (though archæologists are not even agreed upon that) still remains. If true, they are the relics of an Oxford which existed long before the schoolmen arrived, though these appear to have flocked there in the time of the Norman kings. Oxford then is distinctly of monastic origin—and Saxon monastic at that.

CATHEDRAL CITIES

After Oxford, it seems appropriate to turn to Cambridge. Dr. Cecil Headlam well remarks that the universities "were a gradual and almost secret growth." Certainly much of the history of both towns is buried in legends, those of Cambridge often so wild as to approach the farcical. Both were once compact medieval cities, walled and fortified, though the stranger, familiar with Oxford, who first contemplates the lovely and majestic prospect of the collegiate buildings of Cambridge from the "backs," may well speculate as to other origins and with justice, for the colleges there developed outside the town. In the records, however, of both university towns the one thing that emerges clearly (though Cambridge claims a Roman origin) is the fact of the monastery coming first, with the subsequent framing of systems of teaching that had their beginnings in cloistral schools.

Some of the other great cathedral-monastic institutions like Durham and Ely developed on different and very remarkable lines, both of these creating towns, though Ely has always remained the smaller. Durham, "half church of God, half castle against the Scot," still reflects the days when the prince-bishops led armies in the field, the vast cellarage of the priory buildings providing ample barrack storage. The Bishop of Ely also

218

ᛁCHFIELD CATHEDRAL

The three spires of the cathedral are a famous Midland landmark. The birthplace of Dr. Johnson, this city is a modern commercial centre as well as a place of historic importance. The begrimed red-sandstone fabric of the cathedral is remarkable in being almost all of Gothic style, for it was built mainly between 1200 and 1350. There is a tradition that it was the see of the diocese of the Anglo-Saxon kingdom of Mercia in the seventh century. Certainly there have been bishops of Lichfield since Saxon times.

BOSTON STUMP, LINCOLNSHIRE

One of the landmarks of the Fen country, the tower of Boston parish church is here seen across the River Witham. The tower is a noble specimen of Perpendicular Gothic architecture. Boston in the thirteenth century was the leading English seaport, the river silted up and by the seventeenth century the town was ruined. Dredging has made it once more an active seaport. The town of Boston, Massachusetts, in the United States of America was founded in 1630 by citizens of this town.

was a great ruler, literally a Monarch of the Fenland, with a fine house in London, the chapel of which still exists Durham's coalfields have no doubt brought it modern prosperity, but it was the castle and the cathedral-monastery which created both the town and its university.

Norwich, which is of Roman origin, was a great town in the Middle Ages and with York and perhaps Coventry coming next only to London. Even now its many and widely separated churches imply a great population, close packed as they are in narrow streets and alleys. It still remains a large city and has never lost its importance though new streets have been cut through its ancient lanes. How has Norwich developed? Cathedral-monastery and castle combined as elsewhere but other factors have contributed to its importance Its sea-borne trade, its woollen manufactures, the fertility of the county of which it was the capital, all bore their part. Norfolk people, it should be remembered, still claim priority in food production.

After these come many towns, not cathedral cities but in the development of which the abbey was primarily responsible. Of these St. Albans probably comes first. The town, of course, takes its name from the proto-martyr St. Alban who suffered at Roman Verulamium near by. A town grew up on the new site in the wake of the great Benedictine foundation and bears its name It was of Saxon origin, rebuilt in Norman times largely out of re-used Roman brick and remains to this day one of the most remarkable churches in existence Its estates were vast, indeed it disputed long with Westminister as to which was the premier English abbey. At the Reformation the townsfolk bought the church, which was not, however, given cathedral rank till 1877. Like all places

KING'S GATE, WINCHESTER

This picturesque glimpse of Winchester is near the southern end of the cathedral close, lying under St. Swithun's Church. It was part of the defences of the medieval walled town. Through the arch can be seen College Street, leading to Winchester College, and the narrow entrance to Kingsgate Street.

within five-and-twenty miles of London, it has grown rapidly of recent years but it still conveys the impression of its monastic origin.

Like St. Albans, the beautiful old town of St. Edmundsbury, Bury St. Edmunds as it is called today, had to wait for its cathedral honours which were not given till 1913. Here, too, we sense the fine flavour of a medieval past combined with Georgian dignity conveyed by fine old eighteenth-century houses. Here unfortunately no Reformation scheme was carried out for a new bishopric, and its noble church, one of the most outstanding monastic buildings

in Christendom, remains today brutally wrecked. The present cathedral is an ancient parish church (St. James's), one of two equally entitled to the honour. Everything about this sweet and dignified Suffolk town (its two little rivers rejoice in the names of the Linnet and the Lark) speaks of its venerable origin. Its name is that of a Saxon king murdered by the Danes, but he was afterwards canonized, while its Benedictine monks were instituted by King Canute himself. Indeed, St. Edmundsbury figures more than most towns in the thoughts of the average Englishman, while Carlyle. in *Past and Present*, has

221

paid a sympathetic tribute to its Abbot Sampson, a fine twelfth-century figure and a great organizer.

A great abbey, however, did not necessarily cause more than an insignificant town to spring up. So grand a foundation as Glastonbury, with a history unique in Christendom and which to a devout Englishman is one of the most sacred spots in Europe, led only to the creation of a small town. Selby (Benedictine), the most famous of the Yorkshire abbeys and one still in use, did the same, as also did Hexham in the north and Christchurch, Hampshire, in the south. Some abbeys nevertheless may be considered the cradles of modern British watering places, for instance, Torquay, Tynemouth and Whitby. Brighton even grew round a little cell of Lewes Priory still remembered in a little street called after its dedication to St. Bartholomew. Scarborough's castle and its most ancient parish church (St. Mary's, originally monastic) will claim between them to be the parents of that great northern resort. Nunnery churches, however, were less prolific. The original buildings as often as not were placed in obscure villages which have continued so, but Romsey, Shaftesbury and Wilton are exceptions, and the very noble church of the first happily remains.

BENEDICTINE ABBEYS

Other abbeys, like Sherborne and Wymondham, call for mention and it is impossible to ignore Bristol, the medieval maritime importance of which as well as its modern greatness have developed independently of religious foundations. Two other great modern towns, however, must not be omitted, since both are of Benedictine monastic origin — Birkenhead and Coventry. Coventry was the more important, for it was perhaps the fourth largest town of medieval England, coming next to Norwich, York and London. Its legend of the lady on the horse may be an invention of the seventeenth century, but the Lady Godiva was a real personage who, with her husband, Leofric, Earl of Chester, had "built herself an everlasting name" by the foundation of a great Benedictine abbey just before the Conquest (1043). Coventry was also a bishopric, united to Lichfield, but the great church was destroyed at the Reformation and the cathedral, formerly the parish church of St. Michael, became such only in 1918, to be in turn partly destroyed in the Second World War, as great a loss by enemy action as that of any medieval building in England.

RURAL INDUSTRY

Another great church, Holy Trinity, lies hard by and a third with a noble spire is at hand, the whole making together the best example in England of grouped medieval architecture. Had the original cathedral been spared (its scanty ruins lie near the great churches), the ensemble must have afforded in medieval architecture one of the grandest sights in England. It is still, even with its ruins, almost without a rival.

Neither medieval England nor the England of the Renaissance possessed anything like what would now be called industrial towns. As in all civilized states there were manufactures, but these manufactures were carried out equally in small communities, villages and even in solitary country houses as in the towns. It must be remembered also that not until the Industrial Revolution did rural sights and sounds in so many English cities become the far-off thing they are today. It is also worthy of note that ribbon development, that is to say the erection of rows of buildings along main roads, was a thing feared as far back as the days of Elizabeth (there was

GLASTONBURY ABBEY, SOMERSET

Glastonbury has not grown much beyond its medieval limits. Yet it is one of the most historic places in all Britain and the abbey is the only link between early Celtic Christianity and the revived monastic movement under the Anglo-Saxons. It is probable that Glastonbury Abbey was founded in the third century and there is a tradition that the first church in Britain was built there by Joseph of Arimathea. The abbey was re-founded under a Benedictine abbot in the tenth century, after which it flourished continuously until the dissolution of the monasteries by Henry VIII. The medieval town of Glastonbury grew up round the abbey and became an important centre of commerce. The photograph shows a part of the remains of the ruined abbey church from the materials of which many houses in the present town were built.

even repressive legislation). "Merrie England" was the land of the farmstead more than of the factory.

Medieval England nevertheless possessed its manufactures and among them that of textiles was unrivalled in Europe, a pre-eminence it has always retained. A hundred little towns were once centres of a flourishing cloth industry, like Lavenham, Suffolk, where a row of picturesque weavers' cottages remains, while Worstead, a Norfolk village, has given its

name to a whole class of finely spun fabrics. Sometimes a mechanic like John Smallwood, better known as "Jack of Newbury," by skilful organization of others' labours became a manufacturer on a larger scale. Such men were known as clothiers, a word that has since changed its meaning. Hogarth's typical industrious apprentice, Smallwood married not his master's daughter but his master's widow, led in person a hundred and fifty of his workmen to

223

Flodden Field, entertained Henry VIII, and with his son built the existing church. The Cloth Hall in Newbury still stands, appropriately turned into a museum for its trade has gone. It may be added that one of England's pre-Reformation textile manufactures was nunnery-wrought needlework, vestments of such supreme excellence that Popes have been known to demand them for their own use.

INDUSTRIAL DEVELOPMENT

So important and, as we may well believe, so well organized an industry underwent great development from the sixteenth century onwards. The greatest change took place perhaps when many of the more energetic and skilful Yorkshire farmers turned woollen manufacturers. They produced their own wool and bought more if they wanted it. The spinners were their wives and daughters whose work at home preceded that in the factory. The cloth halls indeed were fed from solitary farms as well as from villages and town dwellings. Yorkshire, of course, had no monopoly, other districts also enjoyed a reputation for high quality for which the reasons are often obscure. Climate and skill may go together, while some hidden cause, as in the waters of the Cotswold streams, may account for the super-excellence of the scarlet superfines of Gloucestershire.

Next to cloth comes iron. Few travellers in Sussex as they traverse "the wooded, dim, blue goodness of the Weald" realize that that delightful country was once the seat of the principal English iron industry. The last furnace (at Ashburnham) was not extinguished until 1828. The explanation of the closure of the Sussex ironworks was, of course, the proximity of coal to iron ore which created such towns as Middlesbrough. It is interesting to note, however, that no colliery town of any size has as yet appeared in Kent. Coal-mining there has so far wrought much less change in the landscape than in the north.

A glance at a century-old gazette reveals two interesting facts; the number of small manufacturers that have faded out as well as many which still happily continue, and the larger ones whose recent growth has been so great that their ancient origin is forgotten. Chichester, for instance, had a suburb, St. Pancras, in which every house is said once to have been occupied by a needlemaker. That trade was killed by the Redditch article, not that it was better but because it could be produced at a third of the price. Taste, sentiment and excellence have probably combined for the happy survival of Banbury buns, Shrewsbury cakes and Melton Mowbray pies; and it is to be hoped that the memory of these picturesque little industries will not perish. Sometimes manufacturers, ancient and modern, jostle each other very oddly, none more so perhaps than at St. Helens where plate glass, flourishing there from the eighteenth century, contends with pills and chemicals.

DEVELOPMENT OF TOWNS

The quarries of the Isle of Purbeck both of marble and of freestone, created the town of Portland. The marblers were of special importance in medieval days as their exported lengths of marble, drums or shafts of a standardized size were transported far and wide. For centuries a Derbyshire village Chellaston, exported, even to continental countries, its alabaster carvings. Other marbles were worked extensively in Sussex, Surrey and Kent, but created no centres of population and now even the actual quarries are forgotten. Chiddingfold, in Surrey, once had an important glass industry which, however did not lead to the erection of a town

AERIAL VIEW OF COVENTRY

The city that, during the Second World War, gave its name to a new word in the English language, to "coventrate," is rising again from the devastation which followed intensive enemy bombing. This aerial view shows in the right foreground a vast area of desolation and behind it the roofless walls of the cathedral. The main fabric was destroyed by fire during the bombardment, though the spire, which rises nearly 300 feet high, survives intact. To the left of it is the almost equally lofty spire of Holy Trinity Church. In the background there are the chimney stacks belonging to the factories which have thrived since the motor-car industry attained a national importance. Owing to its good communications and position on the edge of the Black Country, Coventry has become a centre of heavy engineering as well as of the motor-car industry.

Saltaire is perhaps at once the most remarkable and the most romantic example of a modern town called into existence by a manufacture, and that a waste material, alpaca. This town, appropriately named after its founder, Sir Titus Salt, came into being in 1853, and was then rightly esteemed as a model foundation with some score of amenities for the thousands of workers employed. That great historian, Dr. Mandell Creighton, justly compares Saltaire with Kirkstall Abbey, both great foundations in a Yorkshire valley, one of the nineteenth, the other of the twelfth century and equally creditable to both.

With Saltaire may be compared Bournville, a town created out of cocoa in a Birmingham suburb, and Port Sunlight, near Birkenhead, from soap and other toilet products. No less remarkable, but with greater danger to other beautiful things, may become the development of great motor industries at Cowley, a suburb of Oxford. Other instances are Coventry, famous of old for its ribbons, then for cycles and now for motor cars, Northampton for boots and shoes, Leicester for hosiery and so on.

The Pottery towns—their individuality and even existence familiarized by Arnold Bennett—Burslem, Fenton, Hanley, Longton, Tunstall and Stoke, with many smaller places, became one great county borough in 1910. Its names are ancient. The mother town, Burslem, manufactured pots in Tudor times or earlier. Staffordshire in fact, though perhaps in a less degree than Yorkshire, epitomizes England. It is not only the headquarters of earthenware but also of silk (Leek), and of beer (Burton-on-Trent) and of everything that can be made of metal from anchors to ferrules, from chains to motor-car chassis. A mere catalogue of Lancashire's industries would fill pages; but every county makes something.

As travellers well know there is an increasing tendency to plant factories in the country. Most garden cities and suburbs now have their more or less discreet manufactures. Even sport has created towns for the Englishman. Newmarket was born of horse-racing three centuries and a half ago; Ascot, Doncaster, Epsom are all more or less dependent upon it. Large towns have arisen around railway works, notably Crewe and Swindon, with Derby to a smaller extent and Ashford to an even

APPLEBY, WESTMORLAND

Appleby is the county town of Westmorland and one of the smallest county towns in England, with a population of about 2,000. It has escaped the spread of modern industry and has not changed its character greatly since medieval days, when its life centred on the castle and the Horse Fair, which is still famous throughout the northern counties. The photograph shows a typical narrow street in the old part of the town.

PORT SUNLIGHT, CHESHIRE

This photograph shows the entrance to the Art Gallery, on the right, and a number of the attractive houses which help to give Port Sunlight its distinctive character. It was built as a model village for the workers in the soap works of Lever Bros. and was founded in 1888. It is thus an earlier experiment in town planning than Letchworth or Welwyn Garden City, which latter is shown on page 245. The success of this home-planning scheme was due in part to the careful spacing of the houses and the selection of a style which, though in the half-timbered manner, yet incorporates distinctive modern features. Port Sunlight is on the Wirral peninsula.

lesser degree. At Worcester a huge sauce manufactory arrests the eye equally with the cathedral tower. The city's historians tell us that its inimitable porcelain was started in the eighteenth century as relief work for unemployed clothworkers whose descendants nowadays make gloves.

In trying to describe what was once in reality the workshop of the world it is clear many things have been omitted. That is unavoidable in the space available. It should be remembered, however, that once the smoke and dirt disappear from manufacturing, and some other form of energy, electric or atomic, takes the place of coal, there is no reason why once again manufacturing processes shall not be as welcome as in medieval times. There is, even today, a cleanliness, austerity and sometimes even a grandeur, which the south of England does not realize, about the rectangular brick masses of the cotton mills in Lancashire and of the woollen ones in Yorkshire, often in stone.

To understand the origin and development of the market towns it is essential to know something of the trading conditions that fostered them. Which came

GUILDFORD, COUNTY TOWN OF SURREY

Guildford was founded on the River Wey, where the ancient highway, now called the Pilgrims' Way, forded the river. A Norman castle was built overlooking the ford. The medieval town grew up round the castle, which lies to the right of the steep High Street shown in the photograph. The tower of Holy Trinity Church can be seen near the top of the hill.

first, the market or the town? Neither perhaps; rather was it a concourse of people that rendered both possible. It has already been shown how many towns, great and small, came into being. The Roman military station developing into a city, towns springing up around abbeys as at Bury St. Edmunds and Westminster, round the castles of the feudal lords as at Guildford or Shrewsbury. In all these cases buying and selling ensued as an inevitable factor of

civilized life. The lord of the manor was also lord of the market, his steward became the village innkeeper, his domestic chaplain the parish priest.

Long before there arose an actual market, that is an assemblage for buying and selling at a given time and at a settled place, there was a great deal of itinerant trade. Doubtless the first regular merchants were the "dark Phœnicians" who trafficked along the prehistoric highways of Britain. This in

228

a way has lasted down to the present time. The "credit draper," a lordly individual travelling in his own car, is the lineal descendant of the solitary pedlar and his pack, though such men must often have travelled in company for the sake of security. Shops were in existence at all times. Medieval ones were noisome little dens often arranged so that the shutters, when lowered, could be utilized as outdoor counters with their wares open to inspection from passers-by, but probably none survives in England today. Trading in the open air, which still flourishes, must always have been very extensive and to mark the spot, and perhaps to bless it, various ancient market crosses were built. Most were simple crosses and nothing more. Others which survive at Chichester, Malmesbury, Salisbury and elsewhere were often elaborate and beautifully carved as well as designed for shelter.

OPEN-AIR MARKETS

The market then came into being from the patronage of the great, that of the lord of the manor, of the abbot of the monastery or even by the king's royal mandate. The references to markets in Domesday prove that they were institutions of long standing, even Alfred the Great, who figures so creditably in the story of the island civilization of Britain, founded markets. As time went on it was inevitable from the growing power and wealth of the guilds that public ownership of the markets should follow and that the united guilds of the towns should control all trade. Something of the kind was rigorously enforced in medieval England, when, however, lack of craft competence was more often the reason for refusal to grant the necessary permission. As town planning grows, however, it is certain the position of the shops and the shopping centre will more and more be con-sidered from the point of view of the town or district as a whole. Nevertheless, undue interference with natural business relations will inevitably lead to systematic evasion, contempt of law and authority, and to the age-long practice of smuggling, a thing likely to increase with the progress of civil aviation.

ANGLO-SAXON ORIGIN

It may be remarked that a market held only once or twice a year is called a fair. These institutions, which often faded out in the nineteenth century, have been revived of late with striking success as markets for livestock sold by auction. Steyning, a little Sussex market-town, is a case in point. On the other hand there are instances, as at Hove a century ago, of complete failure to establish markets. Londoners will remember, too, the market built by Lady Burdett-Coutts in Hoxton, a magnificent Gothic Hall which still exists but proved to be unwanted. This is a case where private enterprise, though generously undertaken, has proved a failure, though it should be remembered that the most famous market in the English-speaking world, that of Covent Garden, is still, strangely enough, in private hands.

Smaller English market towns, happily still to be numbered by the score, retain their charm, apart from the church, which is often its greatest ornament. What, for instance, can surpass the beautiful old Yorkshire town of Beverley, with its wide, open spaces, one for a market, its mellowed red brick architecture and its two noble churches of the first rank? Though many such towns, especially in the Midlands, have grown out of recognition as manufacturing has increased, many remain unspoilt. Some examples are retained in every English county, each faithfully reflecting the geological conditions of its environment. One great, wide High

Street is a constant feature and when curved, as in Chipping Campden, is particularly lovely. The great width is sometimes due to the fact that an intermediate row of houses has been swept away.

The comfortable market towns of Kent and the substantial stone-built ones of the fine, open Cotswold countryside are among the best architecturally and in the latter district the names of such places as Chipping Campden and Chipping Norton (Cheapside has a similar derivative) prove their trading origin. (Anglo-Saxon *cēap* — bargain, sale). The position of the market-place varies; it may be in the widened High Street or today in the yard of a railway station or an open space near the church. In medieval times, market days and Sundays often coincided, the hours of divine service and chaffering alternating.

To conclude with the different contents of the market in medieval and even Stuart times, most textiles were then coarser and all livestock smaller. There was too much salt meat most of the year, but it was not inferior in quality. Some things, however, were absent, such as tea and coffee, sugar and potatoes. Good sherry went under the name of sack and there was plenty of it. Ales and beer would present the greatest contrast, medieval strong ales must have well deserved their name.

In Roman Britain the port was merely a military station. In this way, for

CHIPPING CAMPDEN, GLOUCESTERSHIRE

Chipping Campden is built throughout of Cotswold stone, though its buildings date from all periods between the sixteenth century and the present day. On the left is the market hall and on the right the High Street. The first part of the town's name, as in Chipping Norton, Chipping Sodbury, and others, indicates that it was a market town before the Norman occupation.

MERMAID STREET, RYE, SUSSEX

Medieval seaport and one of the original Cinque Ports Confederacy, Rye has been left high and dry on its hill two miles or more away from the sea, owing to the silting up of the Rother estuary. Though thus deprived of its ancient trade and importance, it has survived as a picturesque reminder of times past. Its cobbled streets, its timber-framed white-washed houses and its quaint mixture of architectural styles dating from the sixteenth to the nineteenth centuries are like nothing else in England. This view of Mermaid Street gives a good impression of the little town which has revived part of its former prosperity by catering for large numbers of holiday makers.

instance, Southampton (Clausentum), developed with Winchester (Venta Belgarum), one day's march or less inland, being safer there in case of hostile raids. In the same way were born Canterbury, Chichester and Exeter. Many other towns arose near the coast but not on it. If one glances at a map of Roman Britain one will see hardly a town on the coast. Roman genius would not have planted a Lincoln or a York, either as a colonia or a city of the second rank, on an open coast. Anderida and the Kentish ports are exceptions, not being specially connected with other towns, but, after all, they were small places.

Though English history is largely that of its maritime achievements, harbours did not always come into the picture. The last great invasion of the island came in flat-bottomed boats in autumn days upon the beaches of Sussex. The Allied invasion of Normandy on a June night in 1944 offers an extraordinary parallel, with tanks instead of the little carts depicted in the Bayeux Tapestry. There were harbours, nevertheless, at all times, such as the famous Cinque Ports —Hastings, Romney, Hythe, Dover and Sandwich, with Winchelsea and Rye added afterwards. These were flourishing in Saxon times, but Dover (Dubrae) and Sandwich (Rutupiae or Richborough) claim a Roman origin. On the coast where William the Conqueror landed were the little havens of Pevensey, Bulverhythe, the two Hastings, and Old Winchelsea, the last swallowed up in a February gale. All save Rye have indeed vanished or found other uses, as Seaford, a harbour till the Ouse found a new outlet at Newhaven. Even Brighton once had a harbour, its site (Pool Valley) the present busy terminus of country bus traffic. Farther along is the Shoreham river, the Adur, the mouth of which has shifted over a distance of ten miles since the first Roman galleys appeared there, to the picturesque Arun which has created Littlehampton, a survival of many villages since swept away, then to Chichester

RIPON, YORKSHIRE

Cathedral city and ancient market town, Ripon is one of the most distinguished places in the north of England. The market still attracts trade from hundreds of square miles of agricultural country. In the far corner of the market-place is the Wakeman's House, a building which dates from the thirteenth century, when the Mayor of Ripon was called the Wakeman, a title which continued until 1604. In the background is the modern town hall.

LIVERPOOL, GREAT PORT OF THE NORTH-WEST

The third largest city in England and one of the dozen greatest ports in the world, Liverpool combines numerous modern industrial and commercial premises with fine shopping streets and crowded residential areas near the docks. Comparatively insignificant before the Industrial Revolution, Liverpool has increased rapidly in size and has attained its present position partly by virtue of being the natural port of entry for raw cotton and the natural exporting centre for the finished products of the great Lancashire cotton industry. This photograph of the water front shows on the left the Royal Liver building. On the summit of the tower of this modern office block the liver bird can be seen, thus perpetuating the legend that the city's name is derived from the mythical bird, apparently a kind of eagle, which appears in the city arms. In the foreground is part of the landing stage, which is more than 2,500 feet long, a floating structure on pontoons which is connected with the shore by numerous bridges. This part of the landing stage is used by the Mersey ferry steamers.

Harbour with its treacherous tides, avoided if possible by nervous yachtsmen. Why have these all decayed? Probably because the earth's surface everywhere is either rising or falling, but mainly because the internal silting of every river renders constant vigilance necessary, and often hard work as well to keep a harbour open.

For ancient ports on the east coast one seeks in vain. There was no cross "German Ocean" traffic with the Low Countries and Scandinavia in Roman times and if there had been such ports they would long since have disappeared. Medieval Dunwich has tumbled into the sea—churches, cliffs and all, some of it within living memory. The Yorkshire port of Ravenspur has utterly vanished. Returning to the south, Chichester

233

Harbour suggests that of Poole, which it resembles not a little with its colony of bungalows and its villas at its mouth. Westwards, Bridport must rank as another "port of stranded pride." Farther west the traveller comes to two little harbours of great fame in the Middle Ages, so pleasant and cheerful that it seems a libel to use the word decayed, Dartmouth and Fowey. Dartmouth still retains the memorial to a merchant who in 1390 "took thirty-four shippes laden with wyne to the summe of fifteen hundred tunnes." In the same century the gallants of Fowey helped not a little to lay the foundations of England's maritime greatness, forerunners as they were of Drake and Hawkins, Frobisher and Cabot. Salcombe Harbour with its many branches is perhaps the most beautiful of all.

INFLUENCE OF PORTS

From these little towns, and a host of others where it is so pleasant to linger on sunny days, we turn to the great cities to which the seven seas brought power in the eighteenth and nineteenth centuries and continue to do so today. It is appropriate to begin with London, Britain's greatest town in Roman times as now. Sailors, incidentally, speak of London River, not of the Thames. Few Londoners can realize the vastness of the port and none but those who have threaded the hundred-mile windings of its tidal waters with diminishing green country on either bank. Nowhere, not even since the Manchester Ship Canal was constructed, can ocean-going steamers penetrate so far inland into England, a fact which ensured its future greatness even in pre-Roman times.

Liverpool may no longer rank as England's second city in mere size but its maritime pre-eminence is assured. What has made Liverpool? It had less than one hundred thousand inhabitants at the beginning of the nineteenth century. The importation of raw cotton and the export of the finished article are mainly responsible with a hundred other staples of commerce including, one must say, Negro slaves. It started with a fine natural harbour and a central position for both inland and overseas traffic. All towns in the great industrial north and many in the Midlands feed Liverpool, as did almost the first railway, the "Manchester and Liverpool." The Mersey naturally brings one to the great Manchester Ship Canal, of which the jubilee was reached on January 1, 1944. It is a fine experience to see the square miles of docks at Salford with their great ocean-going steamers fifty miles inland, even if many miles on the outward journey are traversed before the first blade of grass appears.

Kingston-upon-Hull, to give its full title, derives its name from one of the greatest of English monarchs, Edward I, who in 1296 himself selected the site of a new port which has steadily advanced in importance until it ranks today, after London, Liverpool, Glasgow and Southampton, as one of the most important in the kingdom. Geographically it is to the east coast what Liverpool is to the west, curiously alike yet dissimilar, as every traveller knows.

OVERSEAS TRADE

The splendid natural harbour of Southampton, with its four tides daily, its approaches protected by the cliffs of Vectis (Isle of Wight), must always have appealed to the instincts of the navigator. Easy of access, easy of defence (though it was rarely attacked), its convenience as a port of call for the craft of many nations has led inevitably to the great modern developments now making it accessible to even the largest vessels.

Bristol, not so great a port despite the

modern development of Avonmouth, must always have profited by its spring tides which rise to a great height. It is sad to dismiss this grand old city with ships in its very heart and lovely terraces of houses on the surrounding downs in a few words, but mention must be made of its *Great Western*, one of the first two British steamers to cross the Atlantic (in 1838), and earlier still of its unfortunate prominence in Negro trading.

A brief catalogue only can be given of some of the rest; of Glasgow and Leith with their glorious mountain and loch approaches; of Newcastle-upon-Tyne with other Tyneside ports and those developed by the coalfields of the north; Grimsby, the greatest fishing port probably in the world; Immingham, the

GLASGOW, CHIEF INDUSTRIAL CENTRE OF SCOTLAND

This aerial view of Glasgow shows the River Clyde where it flows through one of the busiest commercial districts. In the right centre is St. Enoch's Station, behind it the Central Station. Along the river in front of St. Enoch's Station is the Custom House Quay, flanked by some of Glasgow's most important commercial buildings, including the Custom House, just in front of the farther railway bridge. Reading from the top of the picture towards the camera the following bridges can be picked out—King George V Bridge, just behind the railway bridge, and Glasgow Bridge just in front of it, the Suspension Bridge, the Victoria Bridge and, in the foreground, the Albert Bridge, with the Court-house on the farther bank of the river between it and the St. Enoch railway bridge. In the extreme right foreground is Glasgow Green.

BLACKPOOL, LANCASHIRE

One of the large modern holiday towns, Blackpool was no more than a small village a hundred years ago, but today has a population of more than 100,000, with an annual summer influx of twice that number of visitors. It is as a week-end and holiday resort for the industrial population of Lancashire and especially of the cotton towns that Blackpool has gained its vast modern prosperity. This photograph shows part of the splendid sands which are flanked by a promenade stretching for more than seven miles.

great dock which was opened only in 1913; Great Yarmouth and Lowestoft, big fishing ports and watering places in one. Mention must also be made of the great naval arsenals of Portsmouth and of Plymouth's triple towns and its lovely entrance where one wishes, in return perhaps for the *Mayflower's* leaving there, all Americans arrived to-day; of Falmouth, famous port of call; Cardiff with its vast acreage of docks and miles of quays; Swansea; Milford Haven, where whole navies can ride in

safety; Barrow-in-Furness, again with great docks, called into being by the adjacent ironworks. Truly this small island is not without greatness in the way of ports and harbours as in some other things.

Long before inland townsfolk took lodgings by the sea they flocked to "spaws" as they were called (the spas of today), for the sake of drinking the waters; to Bath, Cheltenham, Harrogate and Tunbridge Wells. Scarborough in the north, too, was famed for its healing springs and even Brighton had its well at Hove, which the corporation has recently filled in, pulling down the well house because, it is said, small boys clambered on the roof. Royalty and physicians alike boosted spas. George III patronized Weymouth, his son (afterwards George IV) Brighton for gaieties, though a Dr. Russell had the priority in prescribing sea bathing. The idea of drinking, however, was paramount, and this worthy physician, no more empirical probably than other doctors today, even prescribed sea water as being beneficial for drinking as well as for bathing.

Not even the rise of Britain's great industrial towns has been more phenomenal than that of her seaside resorts. Ramsgate and Margate seem likely to become one great town, Brighton and Worthing greater still. Already a huge population extends from Christchurch to Poole with Bournemouth in the centre. Blackpool with its grand air, its many miles of sands and side-shows, serves vast areas of Lancashire and Yorkshire. Rapid transport enables Brighton on the south coast, with its suburbs, and Southend on the east, to become dormitories for Londoners.

THE PARADE, HOVE, SUSSEX

Hove today forms a continuous whole with Brighton. But it is a separate borough and mainly residential, in contrast with Brighton, predominantly a shopping centre and holiday resort. This photograph of the front makes an interesting contrast with that of Blackpool, shown on the opposite page. The broad promenade and the sea front, the wide road and the varied styles of modern architecture displayed in blocks of flats, hotels, and private houses are common to both. As at Blackpool, growth has been most rapid during the last hundred years, though the fame of Hove in the Regency period when it became a fashionable watering place is well shown by the fine rows of Regency houses which are to be seen in the older part of the borough.

Southport fulfils a like function for Liverpool, Weston-super-Mare for Bristol.

Indeed, so extensive has been this creation of new settlements on the coast that there are vast stretches where houses seem almost continuous. Elsewhere there have been some disastrous experiments, of which Peacehaven, the ridiculous name of a bungaloid and villa speculation on the top of a cliff with a glorious view, is perhaps the worst.

It may be added that the seaside resorts, though possessing much in common, offer also many points of difference as well as curious illustrations of English character. One rejoices with little warrant in the prefix "aristocratic," others parade an intellectuality not wholly genuine. Most are really alike in their catering for public amusement, as an intelligent foreigner visiting, say, Blackpool or Brighton, Margate or Southend on an August Bank Holiday might well find.

TOWN PLANNING

To a certain extent the planning of towns goes back everywhere to the time when fixed sites were given to the temple of the tribal god and to the house of the tribal chieftain. Admittedly it was very limited but we soon find the market-place added. In Greek towns this was generally overlooked by the temple and surrounded by a colonnade for perambulation and discussion. Commerce took place in the open centre under the sky but was enclosed by structures for the communal life of the mind. So in Roman towns, the temple overlooked the forum at one end and the basilica at the other, the whole being surrounded by columned walks as in Greece. All this, which in Rome extended hundreds of acres, was for communal life, the market-place generally being elsewhere. Roman towns, however, had another determining factor—that of defence. They followed the square plan of the Roman camp with two main streets leading to the four gates and crossing in the centre. These streets remain in many English towns, as in Gloucester and Chichester.

MEDIEVAL DESIGN

In medieval towns as such there was not much planning in the modern sense, though Winchelsea is an exception. If there was a cathedral its shape, and especially that of its cloisters, meant a certain squareness and spaciousness in the centre; and the market-place, generally a square, had its lines and position dictated, no doubt, by those of the cathedral and its cloister. The other determining factors were the city walls, but as these generally followed, for defensive purposes, the contours of the land, they did not lead to regular planning. The medieval towns of Britain are full of winding lanes which, indeed, are part of their charm even if they do not contribute to their hygienic qualities. The City of London before the Second World War had many such lanes now largely destroyed. It must not be thought, however, that in medieval times the houses were as close together as they are today, nor were without gardens. Such towns had to be ready to withstand a siege and for this purpose if for no other the medieval town contained many gardens, some few of which, like the churchyards, remain today as open places. The walls, however, were a restriction on building and soon the towns were built right up so that in the end the medieval town may be considered almost as dense and unhealthy as the early Victorian one with its fifty to sixty houses to the acre, its scarcity of drains and the almost total absence of fresh water in the houses. It left behind, nevertheless, many beautiful

EDINBURGH, CAPITAL CITY OF SCOTLAND

This view of Edinburgh shows the long straight stretch of Princes Street on the left, the Princes Street Gardens and the Castle Rock. The Scott Monument can also be picked out beside Princes Street in the middle distance. In the right background is the range of bare hills known as the King's Park, rising to its highest point at Arthur's Seat. Other buildings which stand out clearly include the Royal Scottish Academy and the National Gallery of Scotland, which are facing the camera on the rise known as the Mound, half-way down the Princes Street Gardens. Behind the Castle Rock there is the 160-feet-high lantern tower of St. Giles's Cathedral. Historically Edinburgh has grown up round the Castle Rock, which has been fortified and inhabited almost continuously from the seventh century. Princes Street is considered one of the most handsome streets in Europe: the scheme of which it is a part was begun about 1760.

things like the old High Street of Edinburgh with its defile of tall houses, the Rows in Chester, the many medieval streets in York, and perhaps, too, the grand curve of the High Street at Oxford, lined with its colleges, would not have come about but for a medieval origin. It is indeed such an origin which often causes the breaks in classical symmetry, like the sudden appearance of a garden and trees in Whitehall itself, that gives these towns their peculiarly English character.

With the Renaissance many of Britain's architects like Inigo Jones visited Italy and returned not only with the detail of classical architecture but with certain town-planning ideas. There the prince's palace had led to a symmetrically designed forecourt and approaches as well as to large internal courtyards. Both these ideas were at once applied at home. Inigo Jones built the piazzas of Covent Garden and the church there, of which the magnificent portico overlooks it, and no doubt set out the lines of the surrounding houses. These indeed may form the first English square, though Lincoln's Inn Fields, in which he built Lindsey House, must have been laid out about the same time. Sir Christopher Wren, following him, designed the magnificent approach from the river to Inigo Jones's Queen's House at Greenwich, which, while it could not have come about without preceding Italian and French ideas, is nevertheless a more imaginative piece of architectural planning and composition than either of those countries can show. While, perhaps fortunately, there are no completely designed towns like Versailles or Mannheim, where the palace of the prince dominates the whole layout, or even a little town like Richelieu at the gates of a chateau which it was put there to enhance by contrast with the magnificence of the owner's house, there do exist plenty of examples of fine vistas, such as Wren's at Hampton Court leading to the Palace or, to take a later example, that of the Mall leading to Buckingham Palace. These, however, did not affect the town as a whole or even a large section of it.

EIGHTEENTH-CENTURY BATH

For the above examples of such planning it is essential to go to Bath in the early eighteenth century where the heart of the town was deliberately replanned in his spare time by a Yorkshire surveyor, John Wood. Going to a surgeon named Gay, of Hatton Garden, who owned the centre of the town, he took the plan of a new "spine" to the town, advisedly called Gay Street, with a square on one side called Queen's Square and leading to the famous circle of houses called the Circus, but with only three roads leading into it so that wherever one enters it there is an arc of houses on the opposite side. One of these roads leads to the Crescent, bigger and finer still, which was carried out by Wood's son. Within the lines laid down one walked within a perfect scene of classical architecture from one Roman shape to another. Although, too, in each design the houses were the same externally, each varied internally. Here then was a new town-planning idea, that of a classical form adapted to a certain level of society. It was only democratic within that limit. William Pitt, Thomas Gainsborough, the painter, and Dr. Oliver, of biscuit fame, all lived in the Circus together but met, if they did, in the Circus garden, only because they paid similar rents. In this way a difference was made from the unenclosed village green which all could use.

USE OF OPEN SPACES

This idea of squares and crescents for the richer inhabitants spread everywhere in English towns. London has whole districts of such, like Belgravia, Bayswater, Bloomsbury, Pimlico, and Islington, all with a fine, sedate architecture but all at one time with locked gardens, at present, however, mostly open because without railings. The Robert Adam layout of similar squares next Princes Street, Edinburgh, is another and very fine example architecturally but with the same social distinction. It should be remembered, however, that as London and other big towns grew they absorbed many villages in their march and that these villages all had open greens and that these

240

greens have generally remained so to-day; Turnham Green, Kew Green, Camberwell Green are examples.

Sometimes, of course, the green has disappeared and only the name remains, as in Bethnal Green, or in little strips as at Islington and Paddington. It is these communal greens, especially in the poorer parts, which saved London and some other towns in the Industrial Revolution and in those Victorian days when the ambition of landlords and others seems to have been to cram as many houses on the land as possible either for the rent they brought in or for nearness to work. Hence the long, monotonous streets and areas, sometimes miles square in the northern manufacturing towns like Preston, without a break, for no village green happened to come in the way or if it had been there once it had been enclosed earlier.

Hence, too, the reaction which came about in the early part of this century for greater open space and more light and air everywhere and finally for the fully planned town that is aimed at

BELFAST, CAPITAL OF NORTHERN IRELAND

A great modern city with a proud historical record, Belfast today is a most interesting mixture of modern buildings (many of them in the classical style), broad thoroughfares and extensive residential areas, where are the homes of hundreds of thousands of workers engaged in the chief industries of Northern Ireland, including the linen industry and shipbuilding. Here are the City Hall, seen on the right in the picture, in a modern rendering of the classical style of architecture, and past the block of offices known as Ocean Buildings a glimpse of the important dock area of the city.

HUB OF THE CAPITAL:

One of London's great traffic centres, Piccadilly Circus is in the heart of the theatre-land of the metropolis, only a few hundred yards from Leicester Square. The monument known as Eros is in its old home again on the plinth at the centre of the traffic roundabout. The steps of the monument are the traditional market-place of London

PICCADILLY CIRCUS, LONDON

flower sellers. In this photograph traffic converges from the eastern end of Piccadilly on the left and from Regent Street in the centre; on the right of this is Glasshouse Street and on the extreme right of the picture is the entrance to Shaftesbury Avenue. The uniformity of building on both sides of Regent Street is the result of careful planning.

everywhere today, largely maybe as a result of the enemy's bombing during the Second World War. Just as the Great Fire of London led to endless plans for the rebuilding of that city in the seventeenth century, so the "blitz" has done the same.

REGENCY ARCHITECTURE

Before turning to the garden city and the town-planning movement of this century it must be remembered that in the early worst part of the nineteenth century there were big, if rather pompous, planning movements for sections of the town, as that for Regent Street and Regent's Park in London, and for the Brunswick Square and Terraces in Hove. As in the first two cases, these are often due to the Regent and his architect, John Nash. Old Regent Street leading from the Regent's palace in Waterloo Place consisted of palace-like building after building stretching in design from side street to side street, all in the broadest classical architecture and of a height to let sun into the street. The palaces were in plastered brick, repainted every spring, and formed one of Britain's finest streets. It is gone now and commonplace buildings have replaced the palaces, but one can get an idea of their Roman grandeur from some of Nash's terraces which are still left in Regent's Park. The Regency era stimulated by a monarch truly interested in architecture was a great one, the like of which has not yet returned, in spite of new streets since cut and built, as Kingsway in London and Corporation Street in Birmingham. The town-planning achievements of the twentieth century, great as they have been, have been sociological rather than architectural in scope.

Many philosophers have in the past produced schemes for ideal cities, but the first to put a plan on paper to scale was probably Richard Newcourt, a Somersetshire worthy, after the Fire of London. His plan for London with a rectangle given to each parish may in some ways be rather mechanical and absurd but he did consider the town as a whole. It was not till 1898 when Ebenezer Howard published his book *Tomorrow*, or really till he republished it in 1902 as *Garden Cities of Tomorrow*, that the possibility was formulated of a new town owning and controlling all the land it stood on, as well as of having a green belt round it with all the functions of residences, industry, shopping and schools separated but conveniently placed. Although Letchworth and Welwyn Garden City grew out of that book and are flourishing today with many advantages other towns lack, probably the chief result of Howard's book was in the loose building of Britain's suburbs, with eight to twelve houses to the acre instead of forty or fifty and in the Garden City movement generally.

PRESENT-DAY DEVELOPMENT

On the impulse of these ideas for greater space everywhere the town in England has been rapidly eating up the country and with the growth of motor transport at an ever greater and greater rate. Obviously with such disintegrating forces and ideas at work, as well as with the continued existence of slums and slum conditions in nearly all the great towns, it was high time that the study of town planning, sociologically as well as architecturally, should be undertaken. This was first started in Britain in 1909 by the University of Liverpool when, with the help of the first Lord Leverhulme, a Department of Civic Design, a better term because more inclusive than town planning, was founded in the School of Architecture there with an endowed professorship, lectureship and quarterly journal.

From the teachers and students of this school, as one can see today, nearly all Britain's town planners, like Professor Adshead, Sir Patrick Abercrombie, Professor Holford, Alwyn Lloyd and others, as well as the city architects like those of London and Manchester and the planners of colonial towns, have come. With them and others have grown up the new ideas of traffic circulation, of density, of playgrounds, of the separation of living from industry except in the smaller trades, and of the hundreds of other things like the proper placing of schools, shops, theatres and every kind of institution that goes to make the town plan of today. Sir Patrick Abercrombie has replanned or is replanning, for instance, Dublin, Sheffield, Hull, the Clyde Valley, Plymouth and, most of all, London, both the London County Council area with the London County Council Architect and that of Greater London. Other schools of architecture have, of course, followed, and town planning, with the purpose of the ideal composition of the neighbourhood unit and all it implies which underlies it, is today a new subject of study everywhere. With the increase in speed of traffic not only have non-stop arterial roads been invented and developed by Sir Alkar Tripp and others, but the corresponding but opposite idea of quiet precincts with no wheeled traffic on the lines of the Inns of Court. All these things are being embodied in the plans of towns now being prepared. When these are carried they should indeed be not only places of historical interest but, as towns should be but so rarely are, examples of the finest works of man.

WELWYN GARDEN CITY, HERTFORDSHIRE

Welwyn Garden City was one of the two earliest experiments in modern town planning on a large scale, the other being Letchworth, also in Hertfordshire. The aim of the originators of Welwyn Garden City was to produce a new town spaciously laid out with its own industrial area and a controlled residential district. After a period of doubt the scheme proved successful, though the Garden City was not so self-contained as its originators had hoped, as many of its citizens became daily travellers to London. It was founded in 1919 and soon reached a population of 7,000. In this photograph is seen the Park Way, one of the main thoroughfares, with flanking gardens and tastefully arranged rows of dwelling places nestling amid trees which grew on the original site.

PAGEANTRY IN A LONDON CUSTOM

On November 9 each year a new Lord Mayor is elected for the City of London, and on that day he goes to the Law Courts to be sworn in, travelling in his famous coach, and escorted by pikemen. This event, the Lord Mayor's Show, is made the occasion of a great procession through the streets of London, a tradition which dates back many centuries. Here the Lord Mayor's Coach is seen going down Ludgate Hill towards the Law Courts.

Custom & Tradition

THE traditions and customs of an old and long-civilized country are as precious a part of that country's national heritage as are the great events and heroic lives which make up its recorded history. Old tales and legends, ballads, folk-songs and customary celebrations often shed a clearer light upon past happenings than the written word, for they show the event, not as it appears now, but as it appeared at the time. Many traditional customs have their origin in those early days before the light of Christianity dawned, when paganism and semi-magical fertility religions still held sway. Others preserve a memory of medieval habits of life long since forgotten and discarded, or of striking events which made a deep impression on the minds of those living at the time. For this reason alone they deserve attention, since they facilitate an understanding of the past; and even if they did not, they would still be worth preserving for the sake of their intrinsic beauty and charm.

Many surviving manorial and civic customs are of considerable age and interest. In medieval times land was often held by the rendering of a particular service to king or overlord, or by the presentation of some object, such as a rose, a falcon, or a sheaf of arrows, as quit-rent. These ancient tenures still exist in many districts. Some feudal dues are regularly discharged, while others may lapse for years because they are not demanded. Unless they have been specifically abolished, however, they remain in force and may be revived.

The Dukes of Wellington and Marlborough annually render a flag to be hung in Windsor Castle, the first for Strathsfieldsaye on Waterloo Day, the second for Blenheim Palace on the anniversary of the Battle of Blenheim. These are comparatively modern examples of quit-rents; the majority of those surviving today spring from much earlier times. When King George VI visited Launceston Castle in 1937, he received from his Cornish tenants a curious medley of goods, including a pair of greyhounds, a grey cloak, spurs and a salmon-spear. In exchange, each tenant was given a white wand as a token that due payment had been made. In the same year, at Holyrood, the owner of Braeside offered the king a napkin and a basin of rosewater in which to wash his hands, this being the service by which that estate had been held for centuries. At Wyfold Court in Oxfordshire a red rose is due to the sovereign whenever he visits that district on May Day and a piece of land known as the Playcroft, which John of Gaunt gave to the commoners of Hungerford, is similarly paid for by a rose given whenever it is demanded.

In London two quit-rents are paid each year by the City Corporation for some land in Shropshire called The Moors, and for a forge which has now disappeared but which once stood on the site of Australia House. On an

CROWN QUIT-RENT

*The Solicitor to the Corporation of the
City of London is chopping faggots
with a billhook in the presence of the
King's Remembrancer in payment of
rent for The Moors. Large horseshoes,
rent for a forge which stood on the site
of Australia House, are on the table.*

agreed day between Michaelmas and
Martinmas the City Solicitor brings a
billhook and a hatchet to the Law
Courts and with them chops two small
faggots in the presence of the King's
Remembrancer. The latter then says
"Good Service," and the tools are
handed over to him. This pays for The
Moors. As rent for the forge six large
horseshoes and sixty-one nails are given.
The billhook and hatchet are new every
year, but the nails and horseshoes are
used again and again, being kept by the
King's Remembrancer during the year
and returned to the City in time for the
ceremony. Another old London quit-
rent, dating from 1346, is paid on Midsummer Day, when the vicar of All-
Hallows-by-the-Tower brings a single
rose on one of the church cushions and
presents it to the Lord Mayor.

At Ratby the grass of a field called
the Wether is sold every year to pay for
two meals on Whit-Monday, the first a
lunch at Enderby and the second a
dinner at a Leicester inn. Any surplus
money from the sale is given to local
charities. Legend says that John of
Gaunt once saw the villagers dancing in
Ramsdale Meadow after mowing and
stopped to dance with them himself.
Then he said he would give them a ewe
for their ram, and a wether whose fleece
would provide a yearly feast. This he
did, in the form of three fields known as
the Ewes, the Boot and the Wether.
With them he gave detailed instructions
as to how the festivities were to be
managed, and much of his programme
is still carried out. A special caterer is
elected to provide a lunch of salads,
cheese, cakes and ale, and a dinner which
always includes a calf's head. After
lunch the grass is sold, and then the
caterer and seventeen other men ride
into Leicester to dine and drink John of
Gaunt's health in brandy.

A number of parishes in Knightlow
Hundred pay Wroth Silver on St.
Martin's Day to the Duke of Buccleuch
in order to preserve the right of driving
cattle across his land. Their representatives come to Knightlow Hill before
sunrise and there, in the presence of the
duke's steward, they throw their money
into a hollow stone, saying "Wroth
Silver" as they do so. Afterwards they
are given breakfast at the Dun Cow Inn
at Dunchurch. The amount the Duke
receives is far less than he spends on this
occasion, for no parish pays more than
2s. 3½d. The custom, which is believed
to go back to Anglo-Saxon times, is
rigidly enforced, and non-payment is
punishable by a fine of £1 for every
penny due, and the provision of that
almost legendary animal, a white bull
with red ears and a red nose.

The people of Wishford also preserve
an ancient privilege by a picturesque
ceremony held on May 29. In order to

ANNUAL PAYMENTS

The Vicar of All-Hallows-by-the-Tower (right) is presenting the Lord Mayor of London with a freshly plucked rose— an annual penalty imposed over four hundred years ago for building an obstructive bow window in Seething Lane. Although the observance of the ceremony no longer has meaning as a penalty it is carried out with conscious feeling for the maintenance of old customs, and serves to underline the authority of the Lord Mayor. The collection of Wroth Silver is an English custom which almost certainly originated in Anglo-Saxon times. Below, representatives of the parishes are seen dropping their "silver" (actually about twopence for each parish) into the hollow stone which has been used for the purpose from time immemorial. This is a custom which has been rigidly observed for many hundreds of years.

maintain the right to gather wood in Grovely Forest, they rise before dawn and cut oak boughs, after which they march through the village shouting "Grovely! Grovely! and all Grovely!" More branches are then brought from the woods and set against the doors of the houses, and at noon there is a procession which includes four women carrying faggots on their heads. Originally the boughs were taken to Salisbury, where the people danced with them before the cathedral, but this part of the ceremony was suppressed in the nineteenth century. A curious detail of the Grovely custom is that the wood must be gathered "by strength of people"; it must not be brought in horse-drawn carts or motor cars, but handcarts and bicycles are allowed, since human strength is needed to move them.

In this village also the grass of two fields is let on Rogation Monday by a kind of sunset auction known as Midsummer Tithes. The parish clerk goes to the church at five minutes to seven, and walks up and down the churchyard path for as long as the sun remains above the horizon. During that time would-be tenants make their bids. Immediately the sun sets the clerk strikes the gate

OAK APPLE DAY AT WISHFORD, WILTSHIRE

On Oak Apple Day, May 29, the people of Wishford hold an ancient ceremony to maintain the privilege of gathering wood in Grovely Forest. Before dawn they cut oak boughs and later march through the village street.

with the church door-key and the last man to bid before he does so claims the grass until the following November.

Manorial Courts still function in many districts and do much useful work. At Ashton-under-Lyne the Court Leet meets regularly to consider road repairs and rights of way, and to appoint its mayor, high constables, pounder, ale-taster and jurymen, as it did in medieval times. In the New Forest the Court of Swainmote sits at Lyndhurst to protect the pasturage and turbary rights—that is the privilege of digging turf on another person's land—of the foresters and to deal with game offences and similar matters. Another Verderers' Court sits

in the Forest of Dean. At Cricklade the Reeve Leet regulates the local grazing rights, while in London the Savoy Liberty has its own court which is responsible for the good order and safety of every dwelling within the Liberty.

One of the most interesting manorial survivals is at Hungerford, where the town government is still in the hands of an elected constable, portreeve, bailiff and court of feoffees. Here the famous Hocktide ceremonies are held on the Tuesday after Easter Week. They begin with the blowing of a horn at eight o'clock in the morning, after which the bellman goes round to summon the commoners to the court meeting. Absence from this meeting is punishable by a fine of one penny. The constable and officers for the coming year are then elected, and after a civic lunch, strangers and new commoners go through the ordeal of "shoeing the colt." A hammer and nails are brought in, the stranger's foot is seized, and a "blacksmith" pretends to drive in nails until release is bought by a round of drinks. Anyone hardy enough to refuse this ordeal is fined £1, but needless to say, no one ever does refuse!

The most picturesque feature of Hungerford's Hockday is the Tuttimen's parade. Two elected tything-men set off at nine o'clock in the morning carrying long staves called tutti-poles which are adorned with ribbons, nosegays, and an orange. Accompanied by the Orange Scrambler with his sack of fruit, they visit all commoners' houses and claim a coin from every man, and a kiss from every woman. For each kiss an orange is given, for each refusal a penny is paid. After lunch the rest of the oranges are carried outside the court-house and are scrambled for by a large and happy crowd of children.

In Ripon a horn is blown in the market-place every night at nine o'clock by the Mayor's Hornblower. Originally this was done by the Wakeman, then the principal officer of the city, but in 1604, when the last Wakeman became the first Mayor, an official Hornblower was appointed. Ripon's inhabitants claim that this custom, once a form of curfew, goes back to the time of Alfred the Great.

Another cathedral city remembers its past in two interesting ceremonies, one dating from the early fifteenth century and the other from Edward VI's reign. Lichfield once had to provide fourteen

COURT LEET AT ETON
Held in the School Hall at Eton, this Court Leet meets to deal with regulations governing the common land within the Manor of Eton, and to confirm the appointment of the Bailiff of Hayward. All owners and tenants may attend.

HUNGERFORD HOCKTIDE CEREMONY

The Hocktide ceremony at Hungerford is connected with summoning the commoners to a court, at which local officers are elected. Here, the Orange Scrambler, accompanied by the two Tuttimen, is distributing oranges.

suits of armour for the national defence, and these were annually inspected on Bower Hill by the Court of Arraye. This inspection still takes place in June at the ceremony known as Lichfield Bower, though now the suits are worn by young lads instead of men-at-arms and knights. The second custom is the Sheriff's Ride. In Edward VI's reign Lichfield's sheriff was required to perambulate the city once in every year, and this duty was confirmed by a charter granted in 1664. Accompanied by forty or fifty horsemen, he now rides right round the city on September 8, halting at every boundary mark, or place where a mark once stood. This is a purely civic perambulation and has nothing to do with beating the parish bounds at Rogationtide, a rite still performed at Lichfield as elsewhere.

In Preston the ancient glory of the medieval Guilds-Merchant is commemorated every twenty years by the celebration known as Preston Guild. In the Middle Ages the trade of every important borough was regulated by these powerful guilds which controlled all buying and selling, wages, working-hours and the price and quality of goods. How strong they were in their heyday is shown by the fact that London's Lord Mayor is still elected by the seventy-seven Livery Companies of the City and has been so elected since 1376. These Livery Companies still flourish, with their crowned masters and wardens, their traditional banquets, and their cherished privileges, like that shared by the Vintners' and Dyers' Companies of owning swans on the Thames.

In other towns the guilds have mostly declined or vanished, but Preston's Guild-Merchant still provides one of the most distinctive festivals of the borough. It takes place in August or September and lasts for several days, with balls and ceremonies of all sorts, and a great procession in which all the trades of the town take part. The Guild Court meets to confirm old rights and enrol new members, for, though most of the privileges of membership have disappeared, it is an honour to be enrolled.

Some interesting customs spring from the doles and gifts provided by the charitable of other centuries. At St. Bartholomew the Great in Smithfield twenty-one poor widows go to a certain tombstone on Good Friday and there kneel to pick up a sixpence laid upon the stone. Afterwards each one receives a hot cross bun and half-a-crown. No one knows the origin of this charity, for the papers concerning it were burnt in the Great Fire of London.

The Tichborne Dole is distributed on March 25 in the form of flour from wheat grown on twenty-three acres of land called the Crawls. A bin is set before the door of Tichborne Church and prayers are said for Lady Mabella Tichborne who founded the dole in the reign of Henry I. The flour is then blessed and distributed to every man, woman and child in the two villages of Tichborne and Cheriton. Legend says that when Lady Mabella was dying, she begged her husband to set aside some land to provide bread for the poor. He was evidently unwilling but, instead of refusing outright, he took a faggot from the hearth and said she might have whatever land she could encircle before it burnt out. In her weak state it seemed impossible that she could fulfil this harsh condition, but she struggled from her bed and, since she could not walk, crawled round the land which has ever since been known as the Crawls.

The Biddenden Dole began with two sisters, Eliza and Mary Chaulkhurst, who left twenty acres of ground to provide an annual dole of bread and cheese. They were twins who died within a few days of each other; the date of their death, and therefore of the dole, is usually said to have been about 1100. Bread and cheese is now annually distributed to the poor on Easter Monday and in addition about a thousand

THE HORNBLOWER OF RIPON

After blowing a blast at each corner of the Market Cross in Ripon, the Hornblower goes to the residence of the Mayor and blows three blasts at the front door, as seen in this picture.

Biddenden cakes are given to all who are present.

At St. Cross Hospital, near Winchester, bread and ale are given every day to any who ask for it. This Wayfarers' Dole is more than eight hundred years old; it was begun when the hospital was founded in the early twelfth century and it has gone on ever since. It was intended to assist travellers of whatever degree, and today those who come to the porter's lodge for refreshment are still given ale in an ancient horn and bread on an old carved platter. No question is asked, and the only distinction made between one wayfarer and another is that those who really are in want receive somewhat larger portions.

By far the most interesting, because the most ancient, surviving customs are those seasonal rites which mark the different stages of the agricultural year. Many of them go back to a period long before the Christian era, and spring directly from old fertility cults and pagan ceremonies intended to make the crops grow and the cattle increase. They have survived in Great Britain chiefly because of the wise and understanding policy adopted by the early missionaries who preserved as far as possible the established customs of their new converts and sanctified them by giving them a Christian meaning. Pagan temples were freed of their idols and were re-consecrated as churches; healing or wishing wells

PRESENTING THE TICHBORNE DOLE

The Tichborne Dole of flour is presented to every inhabitant of the villages of Tichborne and Cheriton on March 25. Here flour is seen being given to a villager after being placed on the ceremonial table in front of Tichborne Church.

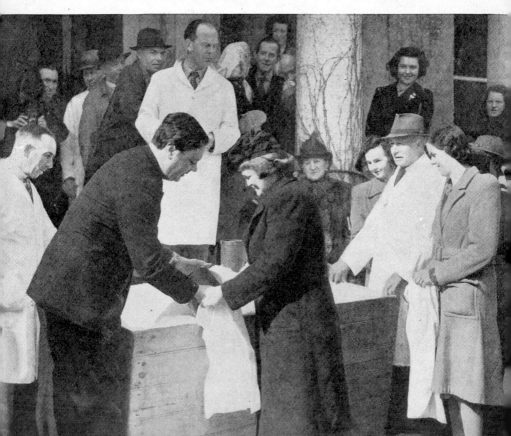

were dedicated anew to saints, and time-honoured customs were absorbed into the celebrations of Christian Holy Days. The greater feasts of the pagan year were replaced by the major feasts of the Church, and lesser anniversaries by minor ones, so that traditional festivals remained to gladden men's hearts, but with a new reason for rejoicing. Thus the Church which, in its first missionary fervour, might have destroyed so much that was beautiful and interesting in rural life, did in fact preserve it; and today many of the oldest pagan customs are so closely associated with Christian rites that their origin is hardly realized by the majority of those who see or take part in them.

The underlying idea of fertility rites was the desire to ensure, by magical or religious means, the good harvest upon which the life of the community depended. In primitive times sacrifices were offered to the gods of the soil, and ritual dancers strove to make the crops grow by imitative magic, leaping high into the air to make them tall, or enacting the death and resurrection of the seed as it lay in the ground. Traces of these old rites are still to be seen in mumming plays and in some figures of sword- or morris-dances.

With the advent of Christianity, such methods naturally ceased, and instead the fields and cattle were blessed by the priests. So also were some of the tools used. Plough Monday formerly was an important date in the agricultural year, when the ploughs were taken to church to be hallowed and were then dragged all round the village by the men who normally drove them. Usually there was some sort of feast afterwards and, in the north of England, sword-dancing and a mumming-play. Only a ghost of this festival now remains. In some parts of the country ploughs are still blessed. Sword-dancing continues in Durham

GOOD FRIDAY CEREMONY

At the Church of St. Bartholomew the Great, Smithfield, widows are seen picking up their buns from the tombstone in the churchyard. They also receive a small sum of money. The charity dates from at least 1600.

and Yorkshire, and at Swaffham Prior and some villages in Cambridgeshire and Lincolnshire children with blackened faces parade the streets with an old plough. But these fragmentary survivals are now the only reminder of this once general holiday and in most places the day passes almost unnoticed.

In many districts, however, the crops are still blessed. When the bounds are beaten in Rogation week a short service is often held in a specially selected field. At Cannington in Somerset every allotment and field is visited, and after a service in one of them, the procession returns to the church singing the Litany. Similar ceremonies take place at Twyford and Sonning and in other parishes. On the coast, where fishing counts for more than agriculture, the boats are sometimes blessed during the beating of the bounds. At North

255

THE WAYFARERS' DOLE

The Hospital of St. Cross near Winchester is the scene of a very rare survival known as the Wayfarers' Dole. Here, at the porter's lodge, bread and ale are being offered to a wayfarer by one of the pensioners.

Shields a service is held on the quayside, and both here and at Cullercoats the clergy sail out into the harbour to bless the craft anchored there. At Hastings, Mudeford and other places, the sea itself is blessed, and so are the boats and nets used by the fishermen.

The benediction ceremony at Norham-on-Tweed is particularly impressive, for here it is not performed during the spring perambulation but in the depth of winter and in the dark of the night. It marks the opening of the salmon net-fishing season. At a quarter to twelve on February 14 fishermen from both sides of the border assemble in their working-clothes for an open-air service that is timed to allow the first boat to be launched punctually at midnight. In its present form the custom is only about fifty years old but it seems probable, in view of the antiquity of the Tweed fisheries and the once general habit of

blessing boats, that it is a revival of an older rite which, like so many others, had been allowed to lapse.

One other fishing custom must be described here for the sake of the light it throws on pre-Christian methods of ensuring a good season. At Burghead in Morayshire the Clavie, a cask or barrel, is annually burnt on New Year's Eve with a wealth of ceremonial detail that has nothing to do with Christianity. Led by their "King," in whose family the kingship has been hereditary for several generations, the boats' crews fill a sawn-down barrel with tar and faggots and fix it to a six-foot wooden pole. In this work no metal tools are ever used except the nails, which are specially forged for the occasion and hammered in by a large stone. This in itself is a mark of extreme antiquity, a harking-back to the early Iron Age when the more ancient stone was still used for ritual purposes. When all is ready the "King" throws a glowing peat into the barrel, and the flaming Clavie is then carried up from the beach to the Doorie Hill. Formerly every fishing-boat was visited first, but this is no longer done, though luck is brought to the fishermen's families by throwing lighted faggots into the open house-doors as the procession passes. On the hill-top the Clavie is wedged into an ancient stone altar and pails of tar are flung over it, making a roaring beacon that can be seen for miles around. When it begins to break up, the "King" and his assistants hack it to pieces, the spectators scramble amongst the glowing rivulets of tar for luck-bringing fragments. These are carefully preserved throughout the year, and some are sent overseas to local fishermen who have emigrated.

Not every parish blesses its fields and fisheries, but the majority continue to beat their bounds every year. For many centuries this custom served a practical as well as a religious purpose. When few could read, it was important that boundary lines should be well known to all so that, in case of dispute, the local people could vouch for them without the aid of the written word. Boys, therefore, were taken round to every mark and whipped there in order to impress the situation of each upon their youthful minds. If the boundary was a ditch or river, they were thrown into it, if a hedge, they were dragged through it. By the end of the day they had good reason to remember the parish marks, and memory was further assisted by a reward of money, cakes, or some other gift.

Today, people are more merciful, and it is the bounds, not the boys, which are beaten with long wands carried for the purpose, though in St. Clement Danes' parish, London, one lad is still let down

MUMMERS AT FREEFOLK, HAMPSHIRE

Mumming is a custom which preceded the coming of Christianity to Britain and represents ritual dances carried out in prehistoric times as fertility rites to ensure a good harvest. Below, mummers are seen in traditional costumes.

BEATING THE BOUNDS

Very many parishes in all parts of the country still preserve the custom of beating the bounds. Above is shown a part of the ceremony of beating the bounds of the manor and parish of Hendon, where the custom of taking schoolboys to the various boundary marks in order to impress their position on the youth of the parish has been revived, though the methods adopted are more humane than those customary in bygone days.

by his heels to reach a certain mark in Temple Gardens. In Oxford the boundary lines of two parishes run through college quadrangles, and there the boys scramble for pennies thrown to them by the Fellows. At Lichfield, choir and clergy carry elm-boughs in procession and halt at eight places on the route to hear the Gospel read and to sing a Psalm. Then they return to the cathedral where the green branches are laid round the font. Some parishes beat their bounds only once in three years. St. Mary's, Leicester, is one of these, and another is the Tower of London, where those who take part are reminded of past sorrows by the presence of the Yeoman Gaoler carrying the axe which

once preceded prisoners on their way to and from their trials.

Interesting as are the ecclesiastical boundary ceremonies, none can rival the purely civic celebration known as Hawick Common Riding, which takes place annually in June. This is more than an ordinary beating of the bounds. It commemorates both the tragic defeat of the Scots at the Battle of Flodden Field in 1513, and a victory won soon afterwards by local men from a company of English soldiers. The marches are ridden by the young men, led by their elected chief known as the cornet; numerous other processions wind through the streets with much playing of bagpipes and the singing of

AT THE TOWER OF LONDON

What was formerly a practical demonstration has, in some ceremonies of beating the bounds, become a matter of show and pageantry. The ceremony at the Tower of London is carried out only once in three years. The Yeomen of the Guard take part, as also the Yeoman Gaoler, who carries the axe with which he once preceded prisoners on their way to and from their trials.

KNIGHTS OF THE GARTER AT WINDSOR CASTLE
Six hundredth anniversary of the foundation of the Order

WELL DRESSING AT TISSINGTON
On Ascension Day the wells of Tissington in Derbyshire are blessed. For this ceremony the wells are dressed with panels designed by local craftsmen.

traditional songs; at night there are banquets and various other festivities.

On the evening before the opening day the cornet receives from the provost a blue-and-gold flag which he carries in all the processions. This is a replica of the one captured from the English by Hawick Callants at Horneshole. To Hawick people it is the symbol of defiant and enduring courage in the face of great odds. Blue and gold ribbons flutter all over the town, repeating its colours. Among the many processions connected with the Riding is one in the early morning, when the company go to the moat and sing a hymn as the sun rises. This, coming so near midsummer, is a reminder of primitive sun-worship and may well derive from it. And in the

Riders' most famous song, the chorus begins with the odd line "Terribus yr Teri-Odin"—words which have no obvious modern meaning but seem to be a direct survival of Norse paganism, an invocation of the great gods, Odin and Tyr.

The battle of Flodden Field is also commemorated in the Selkirk Common Riding which takes place soon after that at Hawick. Tradition has it that of all the young men who rode away from Selkirk, only one returned. He brought with him a banner and this, or one which is said to be the same, is still carried during the Riding.

Pure water is of such vital importance to mankind that it is not surprising to find wells and springs being honoured from very early times. Legends of all sorts surround healing and wishing wells, where saints or indwelling spirits were once invoked and where, even now, quite new pins, thrown in by some half-believing votary, can often be seen in the water. In several counties well-dressing still goes on during the parish perambulations or on some other important anniversary. The most famous ceremony of this kind is at Tissington in Derbyshire. Here, on Ascension Day, the five wells of the parish are beautifully decorated with pictorial panels, showing biblical subjects, designed by local craftsmen. The makers take a justifiable pride in their handiwork, producing a different design for each well every year, and keeping it secret until the panels are ready to be set up at dawn on Ascension Day. During the morning a service is held in the church, and then clergy and parishioners go round the wells to bless the springs and give thanks for the priceless gift of water. Similar festivals occur at Endon, Belper, Wirksworth, Baslow and elsewhere; at Buxton there is a very elaborate celebration in which the mayor and corporation take part and a festival queen is crowned by the mayoress after the springs have been blessed.

Few people, even in these days, can have any real conception of what the coming of summer meant in olden times, or the consequent importance of May Day. With it the season of warmth and plenty began, and everyone rejoiced wholeheartedly. Young men and girls went to the woods on the previous night to gather green branches; a young tree was set up in the village to serve as a maypole, and garlands of flowers were carried to every house so that all might share in the luck of summer. A king and queen of May were crowned, the sweeps and milkmaids had their own special processions, in the Isle of Man the followers of the May Queen and the Winter King had a mock fight in which the latter was always defeated. The ritual driving out of winter was the key-

note of a number of spring customs, but at no time was the triumph of summer so definitely celebrated as on May Day.

May queens are now usually school-girls, and the May king has disappeared altogether, though once he was as important as his consort. The May-birchers have gone, too, and so have the horns that sounded so vigorously at daybreak. But the spirit of the festival is by no means dead yet, and many old customs are still kept up. Street may-poles can be seen in numerous villages, some set up for the occasion only and some permanent shafts, like those at Welford and Barwick-in-Elmet. At Flore, near Weedon, a large floral crown is taken by the senior schoolboys to every house in the parish; at Charlton-on-Otmoor flower-covered crosses are carried round and a special carol is sung, while the clipped yew cross in the church

SOUTERS' DAY AT SELKIRK

Selkirk Common Riding is a commemoration of the Battle of Flodden Field, the tradition being that, of all the young men who rode away from Selkirk to Flodden only one returned bringing with him a banner believed to be the one carried by the standard-bearer in the present-day ceremony.

PADSTOW HOBBY-HORSE

The weird form of the Padstow Hobby-horse is shown in this picture of the May Day revels. The precise origin of the Hobby-horse is unknown, but it probably originated in pre-Christian times.

is freshly decorated with blossoms. In Oxford the boys of Magdalen College School sing a Latin hymn at sunrise on the top of Magdalen Tower, and immediately afterwards the morris-dancers run through the streets and dance at various points. A somewhat similar ceremony is held in Southampton, on the top of Bargate.

At Padstow a very ancient rite begins at midnight when the Hobby-horse appears with a band of blackfaced followers and visits all the houses, greeting the householders by name. Throughout the day the Horse gambols and prances, drinks from the Traitor's Pool and, at intervals, dies a ritual death and rises again. The universal desire to explain the half-understood has produced a legend to account for this celebration, namely that, in the eighteenth century, French troops landed nearby and fled without a shot because they mistook the scarlet-clad mummers for soldiers. This story adds local colour to the festivities but it does not explain their curious pagan details. Minehead and Dunster also have Hobby-horses, the latter a strange ship-like creature with masts and sails in the centre and a cow's tail behind. Here is a traditional custom slightly modified by the memory of an historical event. The horse is as genuine a hobby-horse as his fellows elsewhere, but his ship-like form is a local peculiarity dating from 1722, when a ship was lost with all hands off Dunster on May Day eve and only a cow was washed in from the sea.

Sometimes May Day ceremonies are held on later dates, often on May 29, when they are combined with the rejoicings of Royal Oak Day, the anniversary of Charles II's restoration in 1660. Knutsford's famous Royal May Day can be at any time during May or even in June. At Barwick-in-Elmet the celebrations are on Whit-Tuesday. Here the eighty-foot maypole is taken down at three-yearly intervals to be repainted and regarlanded, and is then set up again under the direction of three elected Pole Men. At Castleton in Derbyshire the bell-ringers choose a Garland King who rides round the village on May 29 accompanied by another man who wears women's clothes and is now called the Queen, though once he was styled simply "the woman." On the King's head is an enormous bell of flowers which reaches to his waist and is surmounted by a posy that is also called the queen. After the procession the heavy garland is hauled to the top of the church tower and left there, while the posy is laid on the war memorial in memory of other bell-ringers who once took part in the proceedings and can now do so no more.

One of the loveliest survivals of old May-rites can be seen on May 8 at

Helston, where the Furry is danced through the streets at seven o'clock in the morning, at half-past ten, and again at noon. The whole town takes part in this ancient ceremony, from the young people who go out at dawn to gather green branches to the town officials who lead the invitation dance at midday. The dance itself is a long procession that winds about to the music of a traditional song whose words state clearly that all concerned have been to "fetch the summer home." At noon the dancers all wear their best clothes, morning dress for the men and gay summer frocks for the women; they stop to knock at every door and whenever they find one open, they dance right through the house, in at the front and out at the back, to bring the luck of summer to those who dwell within. This, of course, is the underlying idea of all the garlands, crowns, crosses and posies that are carried round on May Day, and also of the green branches brought in at dawn. In the same way the guise-dancers of St. Ives used formerly to enter houses early in January to ensure a happy New Year for all. Helston tradition says that Furry Day celebrates a victory gained by St. Michael over the Devil when he forced the latter to drop a stone from which the town gained its name. A boulder in the Angel Hotel yard was long pointed out as the Hell-stone in question, but it was broken up in 1793 and no trace of it now remains.

Many other colourful customs mark the year's slow progress from spring to autumn. Some parishes still have their club-walks at Whitsun, though most of these once-important rural clubs have now disappeared. In Preston, Warrington and many other north-country

DANCING ROUND THE MAYPOLE

This is a typical scene during the May Day revels in an English village, with children dancing round the maypole at Little Gaddesden in Hertfordshire.

towns, Walking Day, with its charming processions of Sunday-school children, provides a general holiday at Whitsun or the patronal festival. In Manchester there are two such days, each with its procession that takes over three hours to pass a given point, the Church of England and Nonconformist children "walking" on Whit-Monday and the Catholics on Whit-Friday. In London, children carry small grottoes made of shells on July 25, the feast-day of St. James of Compostella whose emblem was a shell.

HARVESTING CEREMONIES

Many old harvest customs have been swept away by mechanical reapers and binders; the Lord of Harvest is no longer needed to lead the reapers, and few harvesters now "cut the neck" with scythes thrown from a distance at the last patch of standing corn. But Harvest Home suppers are still quite common, and in many parishes "corn babies" are made from the last sheaf and hung in farm kitchens or the church porch until next year.

The word "wakes" has now acquired a secular meaning for most people because of the Lancashire and Yorkshire Wakes Weeks when mills and factories are closed and everyone goes away to Blackpool or elsewhere. Formerly, however, the word meant the patronal festival of any parish. The parishioners watched, or "waked," in church on the previous night; then the great rush-bearing carts trundled in with their loads of sweet-smelling reeds and the rest of the day was spent in dancing and games. Until the middle of the eighteenth century the unboarded floors of churches were covered with rushes, and these were renewed on Wakes-day and the greater festivals. Now, of course, this is no longer necessary, but in several parishes rushes are brought in once a

year and left on the floor for a few days. At Shenington grass is laid down on Trinity Sunday, at Glenfield and Wingrave new-mown hay. At St. Mary Redcliffe, Bristol, rushes are strewn on Whit-Sunday when the Lord Mayor comes to hear a sermon provided for in 1493 by the will of William Spensor, and flower-posies are placed in every seat.

At Warcop the custom had lapsed completely until a new vicar partially restored it. Now the choirboys bring in reeds on St. Peter's Day and young girls come to church wearing the old flower-covered crowns that their predecessors wore at bygone Wakes. But at Grasmere the rushbearing has gone on uninterruptedly for centuries, though not always on the same date. For more than fifty years it has taken place on the Saturday nearest August 5, the feast of St. Oswald, to whom the church is dedicated. Here the rushes are twisted into intricate traditional patterns—harps, crowns, gates, serpents, St. Oswald's Hand and many more. Led by the clergy the villagers carry them round the parish and then take them to the church where, after a service, they are left until the following Monday. Then they are fetched away by their owners, another procession is held and the day finishes with races and games.

ATHLETIC CONTESTS

The celebrated Grasmere Sports take place a little later, on the third Thursday in August. Wrestling is the principal feature of these sports, but athletic contests of all sorts are included. In the same month, or in September, the still more famous Highland Games are held at Braemar. In ancient Scotland and Ireland such games were occasions of great ceremony, when the young men of every tribe assembled to display their skill before the chiefs and take part in what was both a national and a religious

TORRINGTON MAY FAIR

At May Day celebrations in this town in North Devon, the people sing and dance through the streets. Butchers, bakers and other tradesmen leave their shops open and join in the dancing throng in the square facing the town hall, where music is played, usually by a naval band.

267

MAY DAY REVELS AT PAIGNTON

Of all the traditional folk ceremonies of Britain, May Day revels are the most numerous and the most picturesque. The importance of May Day lies in the fact that it represents the coming of summer, and is, therefore, especially in primitive societies, a fit time for rejoicing. Here, folk dancing is in progress at the May Day revels at Paignton in Devonshire.

festival. Today the finest athletes of each clan come to Braemar to compete in running and jumping, tossing the caber, putting the weight and throwing the hammer. The King is frequently present, and the most splendid spectacle of the whole gathering is the long march past of the clansmen as, with drums beating, pipes skirling, and ancient weapons flashing, they pass before the saluting base. The Braemar Games are perhaps the best known outside Scotland but they are not the only ones of their kind; there are similar gatherings at Fort William and Blair Atholl, at Dunoon and Bridge of Allan.

The Welsh Eisteddfodau also spring from ancient tribal assemblies, though they are, and always were, concerned with artistic rather than physical prowess. They are gatherings of bards, the recognized poets and musicians of Wales, and of those who aspire to bardic degrees. The first Eisteddfod of which there is any account took place on the banks of the Conway in the sixth century but others are known to have been held in the fourth century and the Gorsedd, or assembly of bards, goes back to pre-Christian times. In their present form they date from the beginning of last century when they were revived after a long lapse.

Winter also has its festivals, most of which were formerly connected with fire-worship and the hope that springs

MAY QUEEN'S PARADE

The May Queen nowadays is usually a schoolgirl, and the May King has practically disappeared from modern celebrations. As this picture shows, the tradition of the May King is translated into terms of two schoolboy courtiers who accompany the queen in the May Day procession.

anew at the Winter Solstice. The first day of the pagan year was November 1, and on it was held the Feast of Samhain which the Church has changed to the Feast of All Saints. In early times bonfires blazed then on every hill and open space, as they still blaze, five days later, for the anniversary of the Gunpowder Plot. This latter event has so completely overshadowed the earlier celebrations that in most places they are entirely forgotten. In Lancashire and Derbyshire, however, memories still linger of Hallowe'en bonfires and of burning brands carried round the fields on the following day. These fires were meant to fertilize the earth; cattle were driven through them to protect them from murrain, and young people leapt over the dying embers for luck. In Christian times they were sanctified by their association with the souls in Purgatory. As the fires were lit, prayers were said for the departed, and though this custom is now everywhere extinct, the name Purgatory Field still clings to some northern pastures where the rite was formerly practised.

The allied custom of Souling lingers on in Cheshire and Shropshire, though in a much-corrupted form. In pre-

AT THE BRAEMAR GAMES

Formerly a national and a religious ceremony, the Braemar Games remain an important event in the Scottish calendar, and are visited by the finest athletes of each clan. The games represent a modern interpretation of medieval tribal assemblies. The photograph shows a competitor tossing the caber.

Reformation days the Soulers used to collect alms on November 2 to pay for Masses for the dead, and when religious beliefs changed, the custom persisted in a modified and somewhat meaningless form. Bands of men and boys went about singing traditional songs and were rewarded with money, ale, and soul-cakes baked specially for the occasion. Sometimes they were accompanied by the Hodening-Horse, a man covered with a sheet and carrying a horse's skull on a pole. This Horse was a survival of old fertility rites anciently associated with autumn and the end of harvest, and in some districts the skull was strenuously fought for by rival companies of men and afterwards given a ritual funeral. Hodening survived until the end of last century, but it has gone now; and all that remains of the twin practice of Souling rests today in the hands of children who, in these two counties, go about singing on All Souls' Day and receive fruit or pennies from the householders they visit.

THE GUNPOWDER PLOT

But if Souling and Hodening have declined, the celebrations of Guy Fawkes's Day have not. The ancient fire-festival still flourishes under a new guise and on another date. In most places bonfires are cheerfully lit without much memory of Guy Fawkes and none at all of earlier reasons for rejoicing. In Lewes and Bridgwater, however, the anniversary is treated very seriously. There are torchlight processions, fireworks, bonfires, and burning effigies of Pope and conspirator; but in addition there are religious services and "No Popery" banners to remind the townsmen of the day's true meaning. In Lewes there are six bonfire societies of respectable age which take charge of the proceedings and are responsible for seeing that no damage is done. London, too,

remembers the Plot by a traditional search through the Houses of Parliament just before Parliament meets. Carrying candle-lanterns and ignoring the electric light the Yeomen of the Guard inspect every corner and cranny and not until they are satisfied that no conspirators are hidden anywhere is word sent to the King that it is now safe for Parliament to meet once more.

YULETIDE FESTIVALS

Christmas customs are so well known that it is hardly necessary to describe them here. Some are very old, as might be expected when it is remembered that this lovely feast of spiritual beginnings has replaced another festival, that of the Winter Solstice, when the sun starts again on his upward climb and the light begins to strengthen. As is customary today, houses were decorated with greenery at the Roman Saturnalia and at the Norse Yule. Santa Claus, whose real name is St. Nicholas, traces his descent from that other gift-bringer, Odin, who drove through the sky at Yule and rewarded those who honoured him. And the mummers who still go about at this season in several districts present a primitive death-and-resurrection drama which combines ancient magical vegetation rites with the later legend of St. George, now usually re-named King George in unconscious flattery of the four monarchs who together reigned for more than a century.

Christmas formerly lasted for twelve days, beginning on St. Thomas's Day when women went "a-Thomassing" for gifts of corn, and ending on Twelfth Night. The holiday included New Year's Day which, in England and Wales though not in Scotland, was early overshadowed by the two great feasts on either side of it. January 1 was the first day of the Roman year, and was celebrated in pre-Christian times by wild rejoicings

GUY FAWKES'S NIGHT

Celebration of Guy Fawkes's Night takes many forms in various parts of the British Isles, but most organized events include lighting the bonfire and burning the effigy of Guy Fawkes or some other notorious character. In the photograph above, garlanded torch-bearers are walking in procession through the streets of Edenbridge, Kent, escorting the Guy to the place where it is to be burnt.

that included dances in the open led by men dressed in animal-skins. These rites were frowned upon by the early Church, and Christians were urged to take no part in them and to observe the day as a fast. In the eighth century, however, the heathen anniversary became the Feast of the Circumcision and thereafter formed part of the Christmas holiday. Only in Scotland did it retain its original importance as one of the principal winter festivals and this character it still bears there.

NEW YEAR CUSTOMS

In the north of England one old custom connected with New Year is carefully observed. The First Foot goes round with gifts of coal, food, or money, knocking on the doors of his friends' houses immediately after midnight to bring them luck. No one is admitted until this auspicious visitor has called. Superstition demands that he should be a man, if possible a dark-haired man. If no regular First Foot is available, the milkman or the postman is pressed into service, though these lack the gifts that ensure warmth, food and money throughout the year. On no account must a woman be the first visitor, for if she is, nothing but bad luck may be expected for the ensuing twelve months.

Twelfth Night, being the last day of the holiday, was formerly an occasion of much feasting. Wassail-bowls containing a mixture of ale, sugar, spices, cream and roasted apples were carried round the houses, and in some places to the cow byres also. In Herefordshire bonfires were lit in the fields and flaming brands carried at great speed over the ground as a ritual fertilizing. A relic of the wassail-custom still lingers in Devon and Somerset where the apple trees are wassailed either on Twelfth Night itself or on Old Twelfth Night (January 17). To ensure good crops the people go at night to the orchards and pour cider round the roots of the trees, adjuring them in song to bear "hats full, caps full, three score bushels full." Toast soaked in cider is laid in the tree-forks, and shots are fired through the upper branches.

The song which the apple-wassailers sing is traditional, as is the Furry Song at Helston and that sung by the Riders at Hawick. There are other songs, also traditional, which are not joined to any particular occasion. These are the melodies that have been preserved by the patient work of Cecil Sharp and his fellow collectors who took them down from the lips of old men and women and afterwards published them. Many are beautiful, both in words and music; others are of lesser merit, but all are interesting, since they spring from the minds of simple people and for generations have been handed down orally from father to son.

TRADITIONAL SONGS AND DANCES

The names of their composers have been lost in the mists of time, and the songs have become the common heritage of the whole people. Unhappily, they are now being rapidly submerged by the flood of modern music and are no longer part of every rural singer's repertoire. The same is true of country-dances. These survive, but they are not now danced as a matter of course at village merrymakings, and to many people the Sir Roger de Coverley is often the only one known. Morris- and sword-dances, however, are still vigorously alive in various parts of the country. Between these and country-dances there is a sharp distinction which is, perhaps, not always realized. Country-dancing was, and is, a social delight, to be enjoyed by any one and at any time. Morris- and sword-dances, on the other hand, were performed only at set

273

seasons, by highly skilled male dancers wearing a special costume. They were, in fact, ritual dances, closely allied to the mumming-plays and derived, like those plays, from ancient religious rites. They were not pastimes but ceremonies which only certain people could perform, and every figure and evolution had its clearly defined ritual meaning.

Those figures naturally altered in the course of centuries, but traces of their origin can still be seen. Some morris sides formerly blacked their faces, as the fool still does in numerous districts. This, or some other form of disguise, appears again and again in ancient dances and in some mumming-plays; at Overton and Longparish the present-day mummers wear elaborate head-dresses with long paper streamers that completely cover their faces. In many sword-dances there is a figure strongly suggesting human sacrifice. The swords are woven together to form the lock or rose which is placed on the neck of one dancer; then the component swords are sharply drawn away and the victim falls to the ground, to be revived in some variants by the Besom-Betty or the Doctor. Occasionally there is a death after a fight, as in the mumming-play, and here again there is usually a magical resurrection. In morris figures the ritual drama is less obvious, but the numerous sunwise circles, the stamping, leaping, stick-clashing, and waving of handker-chiefs are all reminders of those mimetic rites by which primitive man sought to make the crops grow, the fruit-trees bear, and the sun gain in strength.

SWORD-DANCING

Sword-dancing takes place round about Christmas, very often on Plough Monday which is the first Monday after the Epiphany. It survives in full vigour in several north-country districts and can be seen at Grenoside, Earsdon, Whitby, Handsworth and elsewhere. The eight dancers wear a special dress, which varies with the different teams, and carry long or short swords of wood or flexible steel. With them go other characters, such as the Besom-Betty, a man dressed in woman's clothes and carrying a broom, the Fool, the Musician, the King and Queen, and sometimes a Hobby-horse. This vigorous and exciting dance is also found in the Shetland Isles, but it has no connexion with the well-known Scottish sword-dance which consists of intricate figures danced by a single performer over crossed swords on the ground.

MORRIS-DANCING

The morris, which flourishes chiefly in the Midlands, is usually a summer dance, though in some places it is performed at other seasons. In Thaxted, for instance, it begins on Easter Monday, and at Little Downham a Plough Monday dance survived until a few years ago. At Oxford the Headington troupe dance on May-morning and at Whitsun; at Bampton the dance is also given on the morning of May Day and on Whit-Monday. Here, as in many dis-tricts, the dancers wear white shirts adorned with ribbons, white trousers, bright-coloured bell-pads on their legs and flower wreaths on their hats. They are accompanied by a Fool carrying a bladder on a stick and a sword-bearer with a large cake on the point of his sword. At Abingdon a Morris Mayor is elected in June by the householders of Ock Street, and is "danced in" after election, first through that street and then in other parts of the town. This is supposed to commemorate a fight in 1700 between the Ock Street men and the rest of the citizens, a fight followed by the roasting of a whole ox whose horns are still preserved and carried by the morris team in some of their dances.

MORRIS-DANCERS AT BAMPTON

Morris-dancing is another survival of primitive rites and dances carried out before the Christian era to ensure fertility. Bampton in Oxfordshire is one of the great centres of morris-dancing. This photograph shows a figure of the dance in progress, the dancers clad in their traditional costume.

TWO TRADITIONAL GAMES

The quaint custom of bottle kicking is observed at Hallaton every Easter Monday. It is one of the many traditional "games" played at fixed times, the origin of which is unknown. The "bottle," a small beer barrel holding five pints, is kicked through the streets by the villagers of Medbourne and Hallaton with the object of getting it across their respective boundary brooks. On the right, a member of the victorious side is seen holding the barrel aloft whilst sitting on top of the Butter Cross at Hallaton. At Haxey, near Doncaster, on January 6, another game is played in the streets each year when the male villagers struggle for the "hood," a long roll of canvas. Whoever carries it to a certain inn wins a shilling. Below, the "Fool" is seen being toasted before the game.

At Abbots Bromley in Staffordshire the Horn Dance takes place every year. The actual day is determined by the date of Wakes Sunday, always the first Sunday after September 4, the dance taking place on the following Monday. This curious dance represents a hunt and is held by some to commemorate the granting of some forest rights in Henry III's reign. The six principal dancers take the part of the deer, the other characters those of the hunters. Dressed in red and green clothes of antique cut, the deer-men carry reindeer skulls whose branching antlers overtop their heads and give a realistic impression of horned men. They are followed by two musicians with accordions and triangles, Robin Hood on a hobby-horse with snapping jaws, Maid Marion, a Fool,

and a man with crossbow and arrows. After a preliminary dance in the market place, the "deer" run off, pursued by the others. Their course takes them right round the scattered parish; every house, farm and cottage is visited and the dance is performed again and again.

Perhaps enough has been said in this brief summary to show how persistent and how varied are the ancient British traditions. Many, it is true, have already been lost, and others are even now in danger. Time, forgetfulness, and changing modes of life are constantly fighting against their survival.

But happily this is only one side of the picture. In countless places the old rites still go on as freshly and vigorously as ever, adapting themselves from time to time to modern conditions and often absorbing new legends and characters but remaining in essentials what they always were. Such customs, dances, games and ceremonies are a part of the British heritage which can ill be spared, and if by bringing about an understanding of their meaning and by sympathizing with the performers, they can be saved from oblivion, invaluable links with the far past and much that is lovely and friendly in present-day life will be preserved.

HORN DANCERS OF ABBOTS BROMLEY

This dance is an imitation of a hunt and is danced throughout the neighbourhood of Abbots Bromley in September. Here the dancers, accompanied by the accordion and triangle, are performing in the grounds of Blithfield Hall. The six principal dancers represent deer, and the other characters the hunters. This is a later example of ritual dances as opposed to country dancing, the former in most cases being a survival from a period of primitive religious observance, but sometimes, as here, owing its origin to much later events.

CRAFTSMANSHIP IN STAINED GLASS

Pictorial designs in coloured glass probably do not date back before the ninth century, but by the Middle Ages craftsmen were making extensive use of them, particularly for decorating churches. The window shown, of relatively modern design, is in Westminster Hall, formerly the hall of Westminster Palace built by William II to replace the palace of Edward the Confessor.

Heritage
of Craftsmanship

GOOD craftsmanship is found everywhere, in towns as well as villages, but it is in the country and the country towns that it finds its greatest freedom of expression. The organization of a large urban factory does not encourage the fine creative skill and the pride in good work carried through from beginning to end that is to be found in smaller enterprises. Uniformity of workmanship and faithfulness to plans produced by somebody else are what the large manufacturer wants from his workpeople; and these, while they produce their own high standards, leave little scope for individual artistry. The independent craftsman has much more opportunity to express himself through his materials and a far older tradition of fine work to maintain; and it is perhaps not too much to say that he enjoys his work more and feels a deeper responsibility for it than the average maker of mass-produced factory goods can ever hope to do.

The heyday of British craftsmanship was in the Middle Ages, when the work of Englishmen was known all over Europe for its excellence. English embroidery was far-famed, and so were the illuminated manuscripts, the alabaster carvings, the stained glass and fine wood- and metal-work produced in Britain. It is to the craftsmen of those days, working unhurriedly by hand and without mechanical aids, that so many of Britain's magnificent cathedrals are due, the lovely angel-roofs of East Anglian churches, the noble screens and intricately carved choir stalls, and all the beautiful church ornaments and windows that survived the activities of Cromwell and others who expended a great deal of time and energy in smashing up church ornaments and destroying much of the decoration.

After the Reformation there was a noticeable decline, caused partly by the loss of Church patronage and partly by the weakening of the powerful craftsmen's guilds. More potent in its effects, perhaps, than either of these was the gradual rise of the professional artist. In the Middle Ages there was no clear distinction between the artist and the craftsman. It frequently happened that both worked together in one workshop even when the duties of each were not undertaken by one and the same person. But with the appearance of the professional architect, sculptor or painter, came a cleavage hitherto undreamt of between the designer and the handworker. The one, rising in the social scale, tended to interest himself more and more in the fine arts alone, the other to sink to the status of a mere executant.

Nevertheless, throughout the long

pre-industrial era, the craftsmen held a very important position in the community. Their work was as essential to the well-being of a predominantly agricultural country as was that of the farmers themselves, for if the latter tilled the soil, the former made the tools with which they did it. Local skill and materials loomed large in village economy when bad roads and poor transport cut off one parish from another to an extent almost inconceivable today. It was, in fact, to its own sons that every small community was forced to look for most of its requirements. It was then that the strong local traditions of style and workmanship grew up to meet the needs of different districts; and then, too, arose that still-surviving unwillingness to be satisfied with anything less than the best which distinguishes the true craftsman from the man who works only for money.

NATIVE CRAFTSMEN

With the materials nearest to hand the native builders raised the great barns, the cottages and little manor-houses that so often look as though they had grown where they stand, fitting into the landscape as naturally as a tree. Native craftsmen made the simple furniture for farm and cottage, the shiplike carts that carried the corn from field to granary, the gates and hurdles that protected the stock. Nearly all the needs of the isolated villages of those days were fulfilled by them. Their work was often strictly utilitarian in aim; they sought primarily for practical usefulness rather than for beauty, yet beauty constantly crept in as an inevitable result of the close union of hand and eye and spirit with the materials used and the purpose for which the finished article was intended.

Today the independent craftsman no longer holds this supreme position, and he is unlikely ever to do so again. He has to contend with the competition of machine-made and imported goods, with changes of taste and fashion, and the lamentable results of the pre-war decline in agriculture which caused so many migrations from the country to the towns. But happily the long tradition, with its pride in good material and fine work, has not yet broken down, and it is fostered with admirable efficiency by a number of organizations.

THE LOCAL SMITHY

There are in England today about one hundred thousand skilled blacksmiths, many of whom are master-smiths who have passed the extremely stiff examination in metallurgy, horse-anatomy, diagnosis and practical ironwork required of them by the Master Farriers' Association. In earlier times, before acute agricultural depression had undermined so many rural trades, there were far more. Almost every village then had its flourishing smithy whose master was an important local figure, and whose brightly glowing fire and musical clanging of iron on iron were sure magnets for all the children and disengaged adults of the place. In the bad years many of these workshops disappeared. Small farriers were unable to afford modern equipment or welding plant and impoverished farmers could not find them sufficient employment to keep them going. A single smith and his assistants had to do the work of a much wider area than their predecessors of two or three generations back, and new forms of work had to be undertaken to counteract the decline in farming needs. Today the industry is once again prosperous, for the revival of agriculture has brought more work to the forge than existing smiths can cope with, and steps are being taken to ensure a much-needed flow of young men to the trade.

Most people think of a rural smith

280

BLACKSMITH'S FORGE AT LACOCK, WILTSHIRE

Lacock village, one of the most historic in southern England, has been restored and is preserved by the National Trust. The forge, like the village, retains much of its medieval appearance, but the work of the craftsman who labours there is today more varied than ever before; he may sometimes shoe a horse, but more often he will repair farm machinery or even help to design and manufacture some contrivance to meet a local need.

FARRIERS AT WORK

Because the fitting of a shoe is at least as important for a horse as for a human being the farrier needs not only skill but special knowledge, particularly if the animal's foot is damaged or diseased. Before one can be termed a master-smith examinations

IN A SUSSEX FORGE

must be passed in horse-anatomy and diagnosis as well as in metallurgy and practical ironwork. Many forges such as the one at Bexhill in Sussex shown above, still operate in various parts of the British Isles, particularly in agricultural areas.

283

CONSTRUCTING A SIGN IN WROUGHT-IRON

In demand not merely to carry out repairs but to design and create new articles, the blacksmith is a local personality. When a bracket, a sign, a pair of hinges or even gates of wrought-iron are required, his inventive power is as welcome as his technical skill. Above is shown an ornamental sign being made.

chiefly as a man who shoes horses, and this is still an important, though by no means the only, branch of his work. A good shoeing-smith requires considerable knowledge of horses as well as the ability to work exactly to the hundredth of an inch with heavy tools and materials. He has to know everything about the formation of a horse's foot, how to fit the shoe so as to preserve normal shape and growth of horn, and how to deal with feet that are damaged or diseased. When the horse arrives at the smithy, the old shoe is first examined and the foot carefully inspected and cleaned. If everything is in order, a shoe in stock will probably be used, either one bought ready-made from a wholesaler, or one made by the smith himself in his spare moments. Such work can be done very quickly by a skilled craftsman, especially if the horse comes regularly to the forge and is not nervous. But if the foot is damaged or diseased the job will take much longer, for a new shoe will have to be made and the foot may have to be treated before the shoe can be put on. Horseshoes are made in a variety of shapes; some are specially designed to correct faults, and all are made and fitted in such a way as to permit foot-expansion and natural horn-growth. On proper shoeing depends much of the horse's health, and a good farrier often has to devote as much, or more, of his time to veterinary work as to the actual manual labour on the anvil.

VARIETY .OF WORK

Shoeing, however, is only one of his many occupations. The great variety of work done by the ordinary blacksmith is not always realized outside rural areas. To the country smithy come farmers with agricultural implements to be repaired and orders for small pieces of new machinery, shepherds needing buisting irons for earmarking sheep, local

motorists wanting luggage-grids or other contrivances for their cars. The wheelwright sends his wooden wheels to have the iron rims shrunk on, the ploughman his drags and harrows to have the spikes, called tines, sharpened. Sometimes the local innkeeper requires a frame for a new sign, or the rector some ornamental ironwork for the church. In the dark recesses of the workshop goods of all sorts may be seen from plain hinges and splints to fine brackets with designs of leaves and flowers, weathervanes, and occasionally a pair of ornamental gates ordered by some landowner with sufficient taste and money to value good craftsmanship. At one time Oxfordshire blacksmiths specialized in wrought-iron gates, and some fine specimens were produced at Weston-on-the-Green, Churchill and elsewhere. Most of them are privately owned and still adorn the parks or gardens of country houses, where they indicate the high standard of modern work.

TRAVELLING TINKERS

The tinsmith is another craftsman who still manages to make a living in spite of mass-production and the cheap tin goods to be found in all multiple shops. Some districts have their own tinsmith, but much of the work is in the hands of travelling tinkers who wander from place to place in carts or vans, carrying their tools with them and working in the open air. Because they are wanderers they are sometimes viewed with suspicion by the respectable; the Vagrancy Laws have borne hardly on them and they are now fewer in number than they once were. But in the districts where they do flourish, they supply a definite local need and do much good, honest and useful work.

Some tinkers specialize in particular forms of tinware, as in mining areas,

285

where the pannikins used by colliers to carry food or cold tea are regularly made by them. Others supply housewives with such useful articles as baking-tins, washing-up bowls, milk pans, Dutch ovens, toasting forks and pot lids, and do all sorts of repairs. Cooking pots, babies' baths, oil cans for motor cars,

WOOD CARVING

Wood carving is one of the oldest of the traditional crafts. In the Middle Ages the English wood carvers had no superior in Europe; today, even in the making of a child's toy, a high standard of craftsmanship is maintained.

sandwich cases, small repairs to cycles and gadgets of many varieties all come within the travelling tinker's scope. His tools consist usually of a light tinsmith's anvil—the leg of which is driven into the earth to steady it while he works—soldering irons, shears and mallet, a bossing hammer, rimming tools, and the oil stove which in most cases has replaced the old brazier and bellows. His materials he obtains from wholesalers; his workshop is the tent which he carries in his cart. His is a free and healthy life, and it is a useful one. He makes goods that are needed and, since he usually travels up and down a defined area, his work must be good if he is not to lose trade on the return journey. If in the name of progress he is finally crowded off the roads altogether, the country will be definitely the poorer, not only by the loss of honest hand-made goods, but also by the loss of one more way of life that encourages a free and independent spirit.

Wood craftsmen are many and various, ranging from the maker of clothes pegs, who is often a gipsy, to the carpenter, wheelwright or cabinet-maker whose trade has sometimes been carried on by the same family in the same place for generations. It was the country wheelwright, working to satisfy local needs, who evolved the traditional farm wagon in all its varying forms, each one perfectly adapted to its purpose and lovely as a ship in its fine proportions and bright decorations of scarlet, blue and green. Mechanization and agricultural depression bore hard upon the followers of this ancient craft. They saw their trade gradually deserting them, their daily work shrinking to a mere matter of occasional repairs. But even on the most highly mechanized farm the motor lorry can never entirely replace the horse-drawn cart, and with the general revival of husbandry the

THE WORK OF THE WHEELWRIGHT

Three stages in making a wheel for a cart are shown here. Top right, the wheelwright is shaping the spokes, which have been fitted into a cast-iron hub, before applying the outer rim. Top left, the ends of the iron tyre, previously bent into shape in a sort of mangle, are being welded together before the heated tyre, as shown below, is fixed to the wheel itself.

wheelwright has come into his own again. His workshop is once more a busy centre of industry and today, like the blacksmith, he is more troubled by lack of skilled assistants than by any dearth of employment.

The carpenter was never in such a bad position as his brother craftsman, for his work covers a much wider and more varied field. Wherever houses are built, there the carpenter will be, working on the roof and constructing doors, window-frames, and other fixed wooden parts of the building. The farmer looks to him for new gates and fences, hen coops, ladders and wheelbarrows and repairs of every kind. The general trade of a country workshop may include such diverse jobs as making wooden pumps or well-heads, repairing mill-wheels and the sails of windmills and oast-houses, or making dovetailed boxes, corner cupboards, or pieces of ornamental woodwork for special orders. Some carpenters make furniture, as their ancestors did before them, and many undertake repairs to old pieces, bringing to this delicate task all the careful skill that springs from an innate love and understanding of wood. Usually the village carpenter is also the undertaker, whose coffins of elm or oak are made to

RURAL WOOD CRAFTS

Hurdles are in demand in rural areas for making sheep pens, and also for fences for gardens and parklands. Ancestors of the worker in the picture on the right have been making hurdles in Sussex woods for three hundred years. The man on the left is making a wooden sledge—a method of transport still used in some remote farm districts, particularly in North Wales, where the terrain is too rough for the use of ordinary farm carts.

CRAFTSMEN IN THE WOODLANDS

Working among the trees which furnish their raw material, in rough, temporary shelters which are moved from place to place as the trees are felled, skilled woodsmen produce a range of goods which includes fence stakes, hop-poles, gates, ladders, tent-pegs and wooden clogs. The photograph shows a tent-peg maker at work in a beech wood in Oxfordshire.

measure instead of being ordered by standard sizes, as they are in the larger towns. This is a task to which the country craftsman gives ungrudging labour and infinite care, for it is often the last service he can render to someone personally known and respected in life.

Some wood craftsmen work in the woods, amongst the trees that provide them with their raw material. Such men are usually itinerant workers who move from place to place as the supply of timber dictates, carrying their own tools with them and erecting rough temporary sheds in the clearings to serve as workshop and shelter. Their trades vary

considerably. They may produce palings or fence stakes, pit props, hop poles, or more elaborate articles such as gates and ladders. But they are all skilled woodmen who know how to select and fell the best trees for their purpose, and how to split, trim and shape the wood.

In the Buckinghamshire beech woods thousands of tent-pegs are turned out in a season by men who carry through the entire operation, from felling to packing, on the spot. Brush-back slats are sometimes made in the open, and at one time wooden roof tiles were so made in the Surrey and Sussex woods. Another outdoor craft which often serves as a sideline for coppice and other workers is the making of walking sticks. Thorn or ash sticks are very popular in farming circles, and they are quickly made from straight pieces of wood. If the wood is bent or twisted, it can be straightened by hanging the green stick from some convenient height and weighting it with stones, or by steaming it over a fire. A rub on the grindstone removes any roughness and gives it a finish, and when the ferrule is added it is ready for sale, either locally or to a firm which specializes in such wares.

One of the oldest surviving woodland industries is that of the charcoal burner

SURREY RURAL INDUSTRY

At Chiddingfold on the borders of Surrey and Sussex one family has been making walking sticks for over one hundred years and here a craftsman, using a specially constructed vice, is seen bending the sticks to form the crooked handle. The wood is natural cross-head ash and is grown in extensive plantations nearby.

who still works along much the same lines as his remote predecessor of Norman or Saxon times. His carefully built hearths, with their evenly distributed logs piled into a sunken pit and covered with straw and earth, require constant watching, so that he is forced to live near them in a temporary hut until the work is done. A slow even heat is necessary; the fire burns for days together and during that time the charcoal burner tends the hearths at all hours, arranging his meals and sleep to suit his work rather than his own convenience. In spite of change and progress, the best charcoal is still produced in this slow, unhurried manner. In early times it was widely used for all kinds of blacksmith's work, for armour-making and iron smelting and, when hops were first introduced, in oast houses. It is still needed for a variety of purposes and is used by welders and florists, distillers and artists, by the makers of gunpowder, jewelry, biscuits and toothpowders, and for purifying water in reservoirs.

The chair bodgers of the Chilterns sometimes work in the beech-woods, though most prefer a shed near their own homes. These are the craftsmen who supply the Wycombe chair factories with chair legs made from hand-riven timber turned upon a lathe. Most modern workers now use an automatic lathe but a few still cling to the primitive home-made pole lathe which has not changed its form for centuries. It consists of a flexible pole joined with string to a treadle below, the pressure of the treadle and the spring of the pole causing the chair leg to rotate on an iron spike against the cutting tool held by the turner. The work done by the Chiltern craftsmen is amongst the best of its kind, for only hand-split wood is used, and the chair legs so made are far stronger and better than those turned from sawn wood.

CHARCOAL-BURNING

Charcoal is the residue of burnt vegetable matter, especially wood. This traditional craft, which has been carried on in Britain for many hundreds of years and in areas where wood is plentiful, consists in cutting the wood into suitably sized lengths, stacking it as shown in the photograph, and burning it. Wood charcoal thus obtained is used mainly for fuel, though it also has industrial value as a purifier. These burners, near Marden in Kent, continue to work as their forefathers have done throughout the centuries.

A lighter form of pole lathe was formerly used in bowl turning. Wooden bowls and platters were customary tableware in simple households before the days of cheap china and they are still produced by craftsmen in a number of districts. In Cardiganshire wooden spoons and ladles are made by independent workers, who also make milking stools, dippers and other dairy necessities. The spoons vary in shape in different districts and are often very attractive, those for table use being slender and delicate, with fine bowls and handles, quite unlike the ordinary thick spoon used in cooking.

Clogs are not as much worn, even in the north of England, as they once were, but there is still a great demand for them amongst colliers, millhands and all those whose work keeps them standing in damp places. Many are, of course, factory made, but of late years there has been a tendency for this ancient trade to revert to craftsmen working on their own. The wooden soles are often made by gipsies who either sell them to the finisher, or who are employed by a regular clogger to fell his trees, split the

TIMBER-CUTTING ABOVE THIRLMERE

The Lake District possesses considerable reserves of timber which were drawn upon extensively during the Second World War. In this romantic setting above the waters of Thirlmere workmen are cutting timber into suitable lengths for pit props which are used as supports in coal mines. It is a skilled craft now aided by the use of machinery. Recently fresh afforestation of the Lake District has been proposed by the Forestry Commission, a change which would alter the aspect of the landscape as it has done in some other parts of Britain, notably in the Breckland district of Norfolk.

292

IN A CLOG-MAKER'S CAMP

The making of clogs, like that of tent-pegs, is a highly specialized rural industry. But whereas the bulk of Britain's tent-pegs are made in Chiltern beech woods, almost the entire needs of Britain for wooden clogs are met from the products of rural camps in the Forest of Dean district of Monmouthshire —in which district charcoal burning also is practised on a large scale. In this picture, on either side of the rough lean-to workshop in which they are made, the clogs are stacked ready for "export." The majority of the clogs are sent to Lancashire where they remain popular in cotton-spinning towns.

wood into blocks, and cut the soles from them. Irons are frequently made by blacksmiths and fitted to the curved wooden soles by the clogger. The work is not as simple as it appears to those who watch the rapid way in which the craftsman shapes the soles and forms the wood, iron and leather into one united whole. The skill lies in the proper curving of the wood, and in shaping the iron so that it gives the necessary bend to the foot in walking; the thickness of the iron also varies with the type of clog and the requirements of the wearer. A well-fitting clog, made to measure, is extremely comfortable and can withstand continual damp, for the iron raises the foot above the wet of cobbled yards or dairy floors, and the wood remains smooth and dry in conditions that would cause even the thickest leather to deteriorate.

Thatching is a very ancient art in which country folk have been skilled for countless generations. Straw or reeds drawn from local cornfields or reed beds provided one of the earliest coverings for small dwellings, and at one period even churches and manor-houses were thatched. In the pre-industrial era the great advantage of this form of roofing lay in the fact that the materials were ready to hand and did not have to be brought great distances over bad and sometimes impassable roads, and even today there is much to be said for it. A thatched house is warm in winter and

THATCHER AT WORK IN BERKSHIRE

This photograph shows the skill which is needed to repair a thatched roof. The thatching material (often dried reeds) is fixed securely to the edge, each "bundle" overlapping its neighbour so as to minimize the risk of displacement or of water percolating through. Then the whole roof is "bound" round the edge to prevent slipping. A roof thus covered will last for many years.

RENEWING THE THATCH

The thatcher at work in this photograph, is stitching the thatch mats into position with a patent needle. This method of making fast the thatch is used in roof and rick thatching alike and is a highly skilled operation.

cool in summer; the rooms are pleasantly quiet, for the thick covering deadens sound, and the trim roof, with its creamy or silvery tones and its soft outlines, adds greatly to the appearance of the building. The colour varies with the materials used, the type of work with the locality. Strong local traditions have grown up in most areas but, within their limits, the skilled worker has plenty of opportunity for individual expression, so that it is sometimes possible to recognize the handiwork of a particular craftsman merely by looking at the roofs he has made or repaired.

It is a common mistake of townspeople to suppose that all thatching is the same wherever it is found. This, however, is an error which any observant person can correct for himself simply by travelling through the country and noticing the different styles. Almost every region has its own way of thatching. In the west of England a thick, soft thatch, made from specially grown wheat-straw, is common; in Kent and East Anglia the long, tough local reeds are used, and in Wales a dark close thatch is made of rushes. North-countrymen sometimes use ling heather gathered from the surrounding moors and this is also done in Scotland. Some Leicestershire houses have thatched porches as well as roofs, and in parts of Devon and Buckinghamshire the tops of the walls are thatched as an additional protection against damp.

A well-made roof, with its straw or reed bundles correctly slanted from eaves to ridge and well secured to the rafters and each other by tarred twine or osiers and double-pronged "spiks" of split withy, will last for years as an enduring memorial of the thatcher's skill. Rick thatching, on the other hand, is not intended to last for more than one season, but it calls for as much knowledge and shows almost as many variations of style as roofwork. Ricks and stacks are thatched with rye-, wheat-, or oat-straw, with reeds or rushes, or with the specially grown wheat-straw known as Somerset reed. Binder twine is commonly used for the roping, but some thatchers still prefer the softer hand-twisted straw ropes.

The manufacture of these ropes is an art in itself which requires long practice before the knack is learnt. The straw is teased with a stick held in the left hand and rapidly twisted into a rope between the thumb and first finger of the right hand. The steadily turning stick winds it into coils, and as the straw is paid out the loose ends catch and draw out others before they are themselves tightened into place. Very thick, short coils of this type are sometimes used for new-born calves and foals; beds were formerly made from them for the extra labourers who came to help with the harvest, and shepherds still occasionally fashion such beds for their own use in the lambing season. Longer and more perfect ropes are made with a swing hook and require two workers, one to turn the hook and the other to add fresh straw as the coil lengthens.

In some districts the completed rick is ornamented by a "dolly" in the form of a bird, a coronet or a boat. These "dollies" have a long history and, are related to the kern-babies that once formed an important part of all harvest celebrations. Usually the kern-baby was a simple sheaf of corn dressed in women's clothes to represent the Corn Spirit, and this primitive type can still be seen in a few farm-houses at harvest-time, and in the churches of Little Waltham, Essex, and Whalton, Northumberland. Sometimes, however, it took other forms, one of which survives in the curious spiral corn pyramid that hangs in the church porch at Overbury in Worcestershire. It is these more elaborate conceptions that are dimly remembered in the ornamental devices on ricks, though the man who makes

WITHY CUTTERS AT WORK

The growing, cutting and working of withies is an important rural industry in many parts of Britain. This scene is at Wickmoor near Langport, on the River Parrett in Somerset, but it might equally well be in Norfolk or the Vale of York, or near the banks of any English river where the willow flourishes. The withies are cut in handfuls with a sickle, and then bound in bundles for convenient handling. Often the withy bundles are stacked on boats which are poled, rowed or towed along the streams, a very convenient method of transport. They are used extensively in chair-making and hurdle-making.

MAKING LOBSTER POTS

These fisherfolk at Budleigh Salterton in Devon are making lobster pots from withies similar to those seen in the picture on the previous page. These lobster pots have to be of considerable strength, as the lobsters which they are designed to trap may weigh up to ten pounds, and in parts of the coast where they are used the sea bed is rocky. The making of lobster pots, like the making of nets, is a craft handed down from father to son.

them today probably does so without any ritual intention, simply because "it has always been done" in his village. The "dollies" are often beautifully designed and made. A favourite variety is the cock made of barley, a fine upstanding bird with a bushy tail and crest erect; another is the harvest crown of plaited straw set upon a pole. Nowadays they are more rarely seen than formerly. Shortage of labour and other difficulties have swept away many such pleasant manifestations of skill, but these shining gold birds and coronets can still be found in numerous dis-

tricts; and in some places where they have vanished from the ricks, they have reappeared on the tops of thatched houses.

Many of the older straw crafts have disappeared. Bee skeps are still made in spite of the modern beekeeper's preference for wooden box hives, and in some regions church hassocks are fashioned from twisted straw, not infrequently by gipsies. The old beehive chairs, with their draught-resisting hoods, are rarely made now, and the plaiting and braiding industry which, as recently as the end of last century, kept hundreds of women working in their homes for the Luton hat factories, has practically ceased.

But if straw-work is dying out, willow- and rush-work still continue. At the beginning of the present century osier-growing was so important an industry in some districts that local schools closed at certain seasons to allow the children to help in stripping the rods. In recent years it has declined through lack of labour and the increased cost of draining the land, but large quantities of osiers for commercial use are grown in Somerset, where the watery moors of Athelney and Sedgemoor are specially suited to their cultivation. Some Berk-shire and Gloucestershire basket makers still own or rent their withy-aits, as at one time nearly all such craftsmen did; others buy their raw material from farmers, cutting and stripping the rods themselves, or get them ready cut from a firm which undertakes to buy the finished baskets. The rods are cut in spring, stacked, seasoned and, if they are for white work, are peeled by women and girls; if the harder-wearing buffs are required, they are tied together in bundles and thoroughly boiled. For garden furniture unpeeled willows are generally used, being more weatherproof than the peeled varieties; watercress hampers are also made from unpeeled

BASKET-MAKING

These basket makers are employed in a workshop near Castle Donington in Leicestershire. Primitive in appearance, these rural workshops, of which there are many in Britain, house craftsmen whose skill in making many and varied types of baskets is unrivalled, and whose craft has not as yet been superseded by machine methods. The photograph shows two of the stages of manufacture and a stack of the finished products.

rods and so are the square baskets needed in the Vale of Evesham and other fruit-growing areas.

Baskets are of many types, from the ordinary shopping or garden baskets to the spelks used for coaling ships or lifting potatoes and the special baskets used at Covent Garden. Though shape and pattern vary according to use, the method of making is much the same in every case. The worker sits on the floor with a lapboard between his knees, pegs the flexible rods into a frame, and weaves them firmly into the desired shape. A skilled craftsman can work very quickly with his bodkins, mauls, knives and cleavers round him, and the rate at which he passes through the complicated processes of slaighting, staking, weaving, plaiting, top-walling and finishing seems almost magical to the uninitiated observer.

Other basketry products are indoor furniture, the crab- and lobster-pots used all round the coast, eel-hives, fish-kiddles, trade carriers of all sorts, and the Sussex trugs made of willow cleavings fitted on to a frame of split ash or chestnut wood. All these are hand-made, and so are the hurdles of split wood and woven willow common in the south of England. Basketwork cannot be adapted

MAKING BESOMS

One of the ancient crafts associated specially with the gipsies, the making of besoms is now widely dispersed in the countryside as a village craft. Here in a Carnarvonshire workshop the craftsman is splitting hazels for binding the besoms as shown in the completed articles propped against the bench on the right. Brushwood, which forms the basis of the broom, is seen on the left.

to machinery, and what the British craftsman has to fear most is not the competition of the machine, but that of his fellow-craftsmen in other countries, particularly Holland and Belgium.

Rushwork is an old and widespread craft, for rushes have always grown plentifully in England, especially in the eastern counties, Cheshire and Hampshire. Flourishing village industries exist at Micheldever and Longstock, where the sedge is cut about the end of June, dried in open sheds, and plaited and sewn into baskets, Moses cradles, floor and table mats. In Cheshire rushes and sea grass are used to produce comfortable and extremely hard-wearing chair bottoms and stools. Plaited mats are made in Anglesey from marram grass, and so are whitewash brushes and brooms.

Besom-making is another ancient trade that is unlikely to die out as yet for large numbers of besoms are required in the ironworks of the Midlands and South Wales, in collieries, and in factories of various kinds. In north Hampshire and along the edges of Sherwood Forest they are made of seasoned birch twigs; in the north of England and Wales they are often of ling heather or marram grass. The twigs or heather stalks are sorted into bundles of the correct size and tightly bound together with withy or cane which is then securely tucked in with a tool known as a hundred putter. For the wholesale trade the brooms are sold apart from their tails; for retail sales the besom-maker uses cleft ash or beech stakes with pointed ends which are thrust into the top of the bundle, hammered in against a stone and firmly secured with a peg or nail.

Leather provides plenty of opportunities for the skilled craftsman. In most country towns there is a busy saddler's shop where saddles and harness of all types are made, and almost every kind of

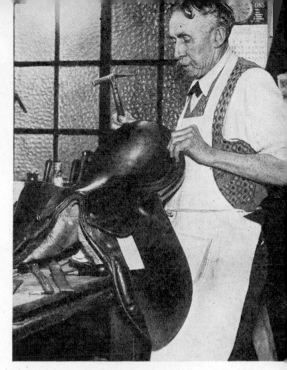

SADDLER AT WORK

To make a saddle which is comfortable both to the rider and to the horse is a craft which needs much skill and patience. In the days when the horse was the main form of transport, the local saddler was kept in full employment on this article alone, but today he makes handbags, suitcases, and many other kinds of leather articles.

leatherwork is undertaken, with the exception of bootmaking and bookbinding. The term "saddler" is really far too narrow to describe the work of this craftsman, who does indeed make saddles but who also produces a host of other necessary articles required in the daily work of farm and rural homestead.

Some modern saddlers specialize in making racing saddles or trap harness, while others spend most of their time working for a particular hunt. Most, however, can and do turn their hand to any branch of their trade, and make a great variety of goods, from horse and

VILLAGE COBBLER

The village cobbler is one of the craftsmen whom modern industry has not put out of business. The need for his services is just as great as ever—in fact it has increased in proportion to the increase in population during the last hundred years. The times are certainly past when the cobbler not only repaired but made shoes, but here and there in country villages there are still cobblers who make clogs or boots for specially heavy wear. This cobbler's shop is at Congresbury in Somerset, but its like exists in almost every village.

pig gear to women's handbags, from gloves for hedgers and ditchers to buffetts for muffling church bells. Many veterinary surgeons have a number of their appliances made by local craftsmen working from detailed instructions; blacksmiths have their bellows made or mended by them and shepherds their tackle. The ordinary saddler may be called upon to supply a ball to the local football team, the canal bargee with towing harness, the traveller who has a taste for good baggage with solid trunks

and suitcases; while for the general customer the saddler makes straps and anklets, leggings cut to measure, dog collars and leads, shopping bags, satchels, purses, and cases for guns, cartridges, field-glasses and bottles.

Country workers of all sorts depend upon the saddler for many necessary goods, and no one more so than the farmer, for whom he makes the diverse types of harness used for field work as well as the lighter harness for traps, riding saddles, whips, and belts for threshing and churning. Harness-making calls for considerable knowledge of differing agricultural needs dictated by local conditions and the breed of horses used. Horse collars alone, simple as they appear when finished, demand much specialized skill, for the types vary with the soil and contour of the region, and every breed of horse, from the great Clydesdale to the small Welsh pony, needs its own special make. In hilly districts, for instance, a light close-fitting collar is necessary to ease the strain of climbing; in the flat fields of the Midlands something heavier and thicker is customary. The saddler's success depends upon a clear understanding of local requirements, upon accuracy of eye and hand to secure the all-important good fit in harness and not least upon physical strength. Much of his work is very heavy and a strong arm is essential for such tasks as stitching leather collar facings with raw hide, or beating and pressing home the drawn stitches.

The village cobbler is another leather worker who flourishes everywhere and probably always will, but the country shoemaker is now less often seen. In the Lake District and in Scotland it is still possible to have stout mountain or shooting boots made by hand and in Northamptonshire it is quite a common thing to find shoes made by bespoke shoemakers, many of whom had their early training in the great boot factories of that district. It takes longer to buy one's footwear in this way; the craftsman is particular in his choice of leather and does not mind keeping his customers waiting till he finds exactly what he wants. But if patience is sometimes necessary, it is worth it in the end, for the finished article is a comfortable, perfectly fitting shoe which will long outlast the factory-made varieties.

Gloveing, like straw plaiting, is mainly a feminine industry. The skins are cut and stretched by men, but the sewing, pointing, finishing, button-holing and padding are done by women who work either in the factory or in their own homes. England has long had a reputation for producing the best heavy gloves, as opposed to the lighter French makes, and this reputation was largely built up by the patient fingers of part-time workers in the days when gloveing was almost entirely a cottage industry.

MAKING GLOVES

Although the various parts of a glove may be prepared and cut out by machinery, the best English gloves are still stitched by hand. The photograph shows an elderly worker stitching and using a "donkey," which holds the pieces securely in position.

In Worcestershire and Somerset many outworkers are kept busy by the large manufacturers who supply them with ready-cut skins, thread and usually, when machine-sewn gloves are required, with the necessary machines. Smaller factories, like those at Woodstock and Chipping Norton, also employ a number of local women who give three or four days in the week to sewing at home and spend the rest of their time in household duties. In this way many a married woman, who could not give full time in the factory itself, can add to the family income whilst preserving her independence and having sufficient time to look after her house and her children.

Home gloveing flourishes in Dorset, at Sherborne, Sturminster Newton and several other places. At Netley Marsh in Hampshire fine hand-made gloves are produced, cut from only the very best skins. These really beautiful gloves have a more than local reputation and are sold all over the world, wherever first-class handiwork is appreciated. Knitted

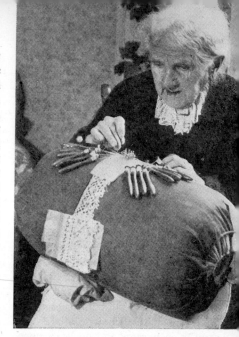

LACE-MAKING

Lace-making is one of the artistic crafts which has been counted an accomplishment by wealthy and poor alike for many hundreds of years. The above photograph shows a bobbin lace-maker at work at Maidenhead, Berkshire. On the left is a worker seen making lace curtains, a craft in which the intricate designs cannot be reproduced by the use of machinery.

gloves have been a Hampshire speciality for a long time, and those made there are still considered to be the best of their kind. In the eighteenth and early nineteenth centuries children were taught to knit at a very tender age. It is said that in one year, 1796, the children of Bentley turned out over two thousand pairs of yarn gloves and sixty pairs of worsted gloves, in addition to those made by their parents. The price paid was fourpence a pair and "most of this sum was given to the workers." Modern ideas of education and child welfare have happily made impossible such strenuous work by the very young, though within living memory girls of five or six helped their mothers with the simpler parts of the gloves, such as the cuffs. Today there is no glove-making in Bentley but it still goes on at Burley and Crowe Hill, and at Kinson and Cheselbourne in Dorset.

English hand-made laces are well known for their beauty and delicate workmanship. A hundred years ago almost every cottage in the various lace-making districts contained at least one worker, sometimes two or three; lace schools flourished and countless children were trained in them until the majority were swept away by the Education Acts of the late nineteenth century. Since that time the effects of poor pay, changes of fashion and the flood of foreign and factory laces have caused a sharp decline in the industry, so that today there are comparatively few workers to carry on the old tradition and preserve the old designs. In recent years much has been done by the various lace associations to encourage this ancient craft; and it is largely to their untiring efforts in organizing the business side, securing prompt and regular payments, and advising the lace-makers in their choice of patterns, that we owe the continued existence of the fine Buckinghamshire point laces, the net ground work of Devon and Dorset, the Guipure-type Honiton laces, and the delicate, filmy Tambour lace made at Coggeshall.

Lace is still produced in Buckinghamshire and to a lesser extent in Oxfordshire and Bedfordshire. Tradition says that Catherine of Aragon taught the cottagers this art when she was living at Ampthill Park. She probably fostered it, if she did not actually introduce it. Another tradition says it was first brought to Britain by Flemish and Huguenot refugees in 1568. English workers have always been quick to learn new crafts from foreign visitors, and to adapt them subtly so that in time the alien trade comes to bear an indelibly British stamp. The "bays and says" of Essex and the famous Spitalfields silk came to us in this way; and if the Scottish straw-plaiters can hardly be regarded as foreigners, they were at least strangers when they taught their trade to Luton women in the early years of James I's reign. Flemings and Huguenots may well have had something to impart to the early native lace-makers, but some sort of bobbin work seems to have been known in Great Britain long before, for a Harleian MS. of Henry VI's reign refers to it.

Many traditional Buckinghamshire patterns used by modern workers have

COGGESHALL TAMBOUR LACE

Working at an intricate pattern, this lace-maker at Coggeshall, Essex, is using the wooden frame fitted with a revolving spindle which is peculiar to this method of lace-making.

attractive names like Waterlily, Rose, Lovers' Knots, and Box of Knowledge. They are pricked on to a parchment spread over a pillow supported by a wooden pillow horse. The threads are kept in place by brass pins and are woven together by the movement of the bobbins. These bobbins are now usually of plain wood or bone, but the older ones were more varied. They were frequently made of brass or copper, ivory or glass, and some, called butterfly bobbins, were inlaid with pewter. A few had coloured beads set in the spiral mouldings, and all had "jingles" of gay beads strung on a wire loop at one end. Those of bone or wood were usually made at home, or by the village turner; they were favourite gifts between friends, and were often adorned with carved mottoes, the letters of which were coloured red and black. "Suffer me not O Lord to wast this Thy day in sin or folley," runs one inscription on a bobbin now in Cardiff Museum; but more usually the mottoes were of an amorous nature, such as "Love the giver," "A present from my true love," or more sadly, "It is hard to be slited by one as I love."

HAND LACE-MAKING

The modern pillow-worker's outfit consists of a pillow and its stand, bobbins and a bobbin-winder, pins, thread, parchment, needles to unite the different parts of the pattern, a bobbin case, a pincushion and the necessary designs. The old lace-makers' light is rarely used now. Once, however, when cottage illumination was restricted to candles, it was a very necessary adjunct to night work. It was a large glass globe fixed in a leaden cylinder with a round base which stood on a table near the pillow horse. Near it a lighted candle was placed in such a way that its rays shone directly upon the glass and were reflected on to the pillow.

The available light was thus increased and the cost of additional candles saved, an important consideration in the days when even a quick and industrious worker could earn little more than a penny an hour.

TRADITIONAL WORKMANSHIP

Coggeshall Tambour lace is less well known than Buckinghamshire or Honiton lace, but it is quite as beautiful. The craft is said to have been taught to the inhabitants of this Essex village in the early years of last century by a French émigré named Drago. For many years it flourished both in Coggeshall itself and in the surrounding villages till the blight of decay fell upon it, as upon the other hand-lace crafts of England. By the beginning of this century it had almost died out and the surviving workers were turning their hand to the manufacture of coarse lace curtains and similar undistinguished products. In 1910, however, the hand-lace craft was revived by the devoted work of two ladies who reorganized the industry, trained young workers, and set up a high standard of workmanship on the old traditional lines. From that date till the outbreak of the Second World War, many beautiful pieces of lace were produced by local women, from simple collars and handkerchiefs to elaborate christening robes, fans, chalice veils, and the like.

Tambour lace is made on a foundation of net stretched upon a frame which, being originally shaped like a tambourine or small drum top, gave its name to the lace. Modern frames are no longer made in this form; they consist of two parallel bars of wood with movable crossbars and a revolving spindle attached, on to which the cotton thread is wound. No parchment is used to guide the stitches. The workers keep the pattern beside them and vary it from time to time as they copy, so that

SPINNING IN IRELAND

In the Middle Ages almost every farm-house through the length and breadth of Britain had its spinning-wheel, where sheep's wool was converted into threads for weaving, after which the weaver, who lived in the town, would make the thread up into clothes for the family. In fact, the basis of the great woollen boom of the fourteenth, fifteenth and sixteenth centuries was the farm-house craft, which became just as important to the prosperity of the country as farming itself. This photograph was taken in a cottage in Ireland, where today numerous spinning-wheels continue in use the finished design often has pleasant individual touches. The pattern is worked in chain stitch with a fine crochet hook. Special stitches are used for the fillings, and these have traditional names like Smuggler, Neat, Eyelet, and Honeycomb. The resulting lace is as beautiful and filmy as the Brussels variety. It is hoped that, with the return of normal conditions, the industry, badly hit during the years of shortage brought about by the Second World War, will revive. It would be a tragedy if it did not, for Coggeshall can claim to have been the first, and later the only, place in England where hand-made Tambour lace was produced.

Such spinning and weaving as is now done in England is a modern revival of a craft that was once almost universal in this country. The art of making cloth by distaff and loom is one of the oldest known to man and, like pottery making, it has been practised since the dawn of civilization. Before the Romans came to Britain our forebears fashioned garments from wool and flax and dyed them with saffron and other vegetable dyes, and throughout medieval and Tudor times English cloth was one of

SCOTTISH HAND-LOOM WEAVING

Weaving, by which is meant the process of making cloth on the loom, is, like many other traditional crafts in Britain, of very ancient origin. Like pottery, weaving was certainly carried on in prehistoric Britain, for fragments of woven material have been found in ancient encampments. This hand-loom is at Bunavoneddar in the Hebrides, where the industry is carried on independently in cottage homes and the mills send out agents to collect the products.

the foundations of English prosperity. Until the middle of the eighteenth century every competent housewife could spin and card wool and make dyes for her own fabrics from plants and lichens, shells, seaweed or soot. Household linens and everyday garments were spun at home as a matter of course; weaving was sometimes done there also, but more usually the yarn was sent to a professional weaver who worked in his own cottage or travelled about from village to village.

TRADITIONAL TEXTILE ART

The Industrial Revolution changed all that. When ready-made fabrics became cheap and plentiful, the ordinary Englishwoman lost her skill as a spinner, and the handloom weaver was driven out of business. What remains of the old craft today is the work of weavers who specialize in the production of beautiful and distinctive cloths from yarns which are often hand spun and hand dyed. Handlooms are used in a number of places, notably in Gloucestershire and at Ditchling in Sussex where a colony of craftsmen turn out woven fabrics in lovely patterns and colours. Their work has a character all its own, and though their output is necessarily limited, it commands a firm and growing market amongst those who appreciate fine workmanship and really good design.

In Scotland, Wales and Ireland there has been no such break in tradition as in the sister country. The old textile arts never died out, and the famous Harris and Donegal tweeds, the Shetland homespun shawls, and the unshrinkable flannels and blankets made in the small Welsh mills, are the work of craftsmen whose families have produced such goods for generations. Spinning goes on in many highland and Irish cottages, on wheels of the Norwegian type at which the worker sits, or the older big wheels

before which she stands, as she spins. The finished yarn goes to the local weaver, one of whose looms will keep many spinning wheels turning to supply it. In the Aran Isles a very ancient type of weaving survives in the making of brightly coloured belts, or *crois*, which the men wear. They are made at home of strong thread in five colours. No loom of any kind is used. The warp threads are passed round the weaver's foot, and in this primitive manner are woven into the distinctive belts made in this locality.

Before spinning, the wool has to be scoured unless it is to be spun "in the grease," and it is then carded to loosen the fibres. Carding is very hard work and most of it is now done at the mills rather than by hand. When it is undertaken at home small wooden "hands," shaped like rough battledores and studded with iron bristles, are used. Formerly this task was made an occasion for the gathering of neighbours and the singing of old songs, as fulling still is in the highlands, where the woven cloth is shrunk and thickened to music.

DYEING TWEEDS

Dyeing can be done before or after carding. In the western Highlands and the Shetland Isles, natural-coloured wool from black sheep is often used, without the addition of any colouring matter, to give fine sepia tints to the cloth. But for other shades a variety of plants are employed, including madder, bracken, onion skin, rowan, blackberry, elder bark and lichen. It is the crotal used in Harris tweeds that gives them their distinctive smell, as of hemp or peat smoke. The plants are gathered at different seasons, according to the parts used: roots and bark are generally collected in the autumn, lichens in the winter or after heavy rain, and berries as soon as they are ripe. When dyeing begins, the dyestuff is put into an iron pot and covered by a pierced board which is weighted down with stones. On this board the wool, which has been washed and treated so as to fix the dye, is laid and constantly stirred as the water boils and the colour wells up over it through the holes. A thorough rinsing, followed by slow drying, completes the process. Natural dyes give much softer and lovelier shades than ordinary commercial dyes, and it is to their use that most handwoven cloths owe their distinctive and beautiful range of colours.

Knitting is a traditional art in Scotland and Ireland where the old patterns are still used in the production of jerseys and hose. Along the coasts fishermen's stockings and socks are made from undressed wool which is more waterproof than the dressed variety, and fine hose of all kinds is produced in many parts of the highlands and western Ireland. The thick, undyed socks made for seamen and farmworkers have found their way into urban markets also, where they are bought by sportsmen for wearing under fishing and ski-ing boots.

Fair Isle jerseys, made in Fair Isle itself or in the Shetlands, are famous all

WEDGWOOD POTTERY-MAKING

Though nowadays only surviving locally as a rural craft, various phases of pottery-making remain highly skilled operations carried out by craftsmen many of whom learned the secrets of their trade before pottery-making became centred in the factories; for there is a strong family tradition in pottery and father has handed on the craft to son for generation after generation. Modern Wedgwood pottery carries on the tradition of its founder. Here, in a Stoke-on-Trent workshop, a craftsman is applying decoration to a china jug.

over the world. The traditional patterns are said to have been learnt from survivors of the Spanish Armada, but it seems probable that they are really of Norse origin and were known in the islands long before the sixteenth century. A plainer type of jersey is made at Appledore in Devon from unbroken lengths of strong worsted. These jerseys have no seams and are knitted, like stockings, in a circle; they are much prized by seamen for their damp-resisting qualities and are not infrequently fashioned by the sailors themselves.

Quilting survives in Wales and Durham where very fine work is done from patterns known and used for centuries. The quilts are made of linen, silk or cotton and are lined with scoured sheep's wool which is kept in place between two pieces of material by the stitches forming the design. Plain diamond quilting is the groundwork of the various patterns, all of which are now highly conventionalized. In Durham the favourite designs are the feather and the shell; in Wales they use the Tudor Rose, the wave, pear, leaf and scroll and, for bridal coverlets, the crown. Diamond quilting was originally used for padding under armour, and was later turned to more domestic uses, such as petticoats and bedding. In the seventeenth century quilted work became extremely fashionable, and it is interesting to note that the designs used to ornament the bedrooms of wealthy Caroline householders were the same as those now used by the quilters of Durham and Wales.

Many other crafts are carried on in the villages of Britain. Pottery, like glass-making, is now mainly centred in the large urban factories, but there are a number of country workshops where this fundamental craft is followed in the traditional manner. Earthenware and pottery goods are made in Devon,

POTTER AT WORK

Pottery is the general name given to ware which is made by moulding and baking clay. The origins of the craft are lost in obscurity. Certainly there were potters in prehistoric Britain and in Roman times. Hand-made pottery is manufactured in villages, particularly in southern England, and here an old-fashioned cider bottle is being moulded on the ancient "kick drive" potter's wheel at a century-old pottery in Winchcomb, Gloucestershire.

Cornwall and Sussex, at Hamworthy and Verwood in Dorset, and at Buckley in Flintshire, where they specialize in attractive pie dishes and kitchen-ware. Flower pots are made by hand in the Cotswolds and several other districts, while heavy stoneware for farm use is produced in the north of England. Tiles and drain-pipes are made in a variety of places and brickfields are found all over the country.

Bricks were made in Britain during the Roman occupation, but the art was lost when the Romans withdrew and was not re-introduced until about the thir-

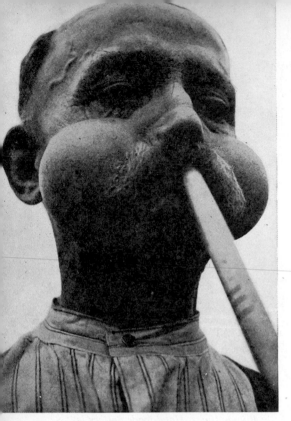

family for at least two hundred and fifty years.

Simple pottery has been made in Great Britain since the dawn of history. Neolithic women fashioned round-bottomed bowls and jars with glossy surfaces and rough ornamentations of pricks and finger-tip impressions. In the Bronze Age more elaborate beakers and food vessels were made of fine, hard, reddish paste adorned with dotted lines and geometric patterns in horizontal bands. Until the seventeenth century, pottery goods were not widely used for tableware; wooden or pewter platters, horn mugs and metal tankards were the rule in simple medieval and Tudor houses, with silver and imported Venetian glass for the really wealthy. Fine porcelain was not made in Britain until a comparatively late date. John Dwight experimented with stoneware in the reign of Charles II and produced an improved glazed variety, but it was not until the middle of the eighteenth century that the lovely Bow and Chelsea, Worcester, Derby and Wedgwood chinas first appeared. They were never country products in the sense that earthenware was and to some extent still is; but much fine craftsmanship was needed for their making, and today a good deal of individual handwork goes on inside the factories, notably in free-hand painting and brushwork, which is often done by girls.

Parchment is made at Havant from sheepskins, for drum heads, banjos and similar goods, and vellum from calf-skin. The work is almost entirely hand done, the only machine used being for splitting the skins. Soft toys are made at Brockenhurst and Broughton in Hampshire, and this craft is taught and fostered in a number of other places by the Women's Institutes.

Fishing nets are made all along the coasts, and boats are still built by local

GLASS BLOWER

This is a portrait of a craftsman. The blowing-iron he is using is five feet long and must be kept rotating: with it the skilled craftsman can make hollow glassware of infinite variety.

teenth or fourteenth century. Medieval bricks were, of course, moulded by hand. In some country brickfields they are still so made from the puddled clay and dried in long, low sheds before being fired in kilns. In the larger commercial fields machinery is used, but hand-moulding is found both convenient and profitable in many smaller ones. At Old Basing in Hampshire hand-made mullions and twisted chimneys are produced, as they have been in this locality for centuries; and here, too, the secret art of making dew ponds, known also in Sussex, has been carried on by one

VITAL INDUSTRIES

Though not village crafts in the same sense as many of those illustrated in this chapter, both brick-making and glass-blowing are industries of vital importance to the nation's economy, and industries which employ many thousands of workers. On the right a workman is seen removing the mould after placing the brick on the "off-bearing" barrow. The art of blowing glass (below) as opposed to the older method of moulding it was probably invented by the Phœnicians of Sidon about the beginning of the Christian era. Since that time the art has been continuously followed in almost every civilized country. Old English glass, as elaborated in the later Middle Ages, includes some of the loveliest examples in the world. The craft is one of those which have found a permanent place in modern industrial undertakings.

SHEEPSKIN-CURING

Old-fashioned ways of curing sheepskins rank among surviving village crafts especially in Yorkshire and Gloucestershire. This photograph of a curing shed at Knaresborough, Yorkshire, shows how tension is maintained by cords attached to a rectangular wooden frame, and how the "moon knife" is used.

craftsmen, in spite of the competition of the larger boat-building firms. On some rivers rafts and coracles are made, the latter on lines almost exactly similar to the coracles used by our remote ancestors, though the materials have changed with the passage of centuries. A curious seasonal industry is the gathering of birch twigs at Hurstbourne Tarrant for vinegar making. The twigs are sent to London where several old-established firms use them in the brewing of vinegar. In the same county, at Chilbolton, a unique craft is followed by a single family whose members make Mid-Lent wafers for Mothering Sunday from a secret recipe. The irons used are known

to be at least three hundred years old, and are kept in Winchester Museum during the year and are returned to Chilbolton in time for their seasonal purpose. They are formed of two round iron plates pivoted on long handles; these plates are heated in a wood fire, and the batter is then poured on to the lower one and pressed into shape by the upper. Nowadays the wafers are used locally instead of simnel cakes, but it is believed that at one time they were distributed after Holy Communion to the worshippers who came to the parish church on Mothering Sunday from the various outlying chapels-of-ease. From their nature they appear to be of pre-

Reformation origin; the recipe now used has been handed down for more than two hundred years and is never revealed to anyone outside the maker's family.

It is not possible here to describe in detail the fine work turned out by the many artist-craftsmen in various parts of the country who produce fine silver-ware, pottery, textiles, and hand-printing. Their work is perhaps nearer to the medieval tradition of craftsmanship than that of the country workers with whom this brief sketch is principally concerned, but it has not the same continuous history. It springs from the great revival of handicrafts sponsored by William Morris and his followers in the late nineteenth century. Morris, who was himself a master of many crafts, had a passionate belief in the spiritual worth of handwork. He distrusted the standardized perfection of the machine and the extreme division of labour that went with it, and he saw clearly that hand-work had an immense social value in that it gave to the worker a sense of pride and fulfilment which no other form of work could give. With this in mind he founded his famous firm which specialized in stained glass, wallpapers, chintzes, carpets, carvings and metal-work, and later the tapestry-weaving works at Merton and the Kelmscott Press. His influence was enormous, both at home and abroad.

The modern artist-craftsmen not only make but also design their own products as well as design much factory-made pottery, silver, glass and textiles. Art and machinery do not always go well together, for creative freedom is the ideal of the one and standardization that of the other. But the increasing use of attractive designs in mass-produced goods has an enormous future importance, and it has already done much to

BOAT-BUILDING

All along the coasts of Britain small groups of craftsmen are still making boats and, to the uninitiated, their methods appear somewhat primitive. Small yachts, fishing vessels, dinghys and other craft are made entirely by hand. This workshop in the Isle of Wight specializes in small sailing craft.

raise the level of British factory workmanship and to bring beauty into the countless articles required for everyday domestic use.

Nevertheless, it is the country craftsman, the independent worker by hand or small machine, who is the real guardian of Britain's traditional skill rather than the artist-designer of the Cotswold and other schools. He has, as a rule, no "artistic" education to guide him, only the innate love of good work and good material which inspired his forebears. He has also their adaptability, which enabled them to learn from foreign immigrants, and now enables him to adopt readily new tools and new methods when occasion demands. Some rural crafts are indeed doomed in this age of mass-production and speed, but many are still firmly entrenched and others need only a little encouragement to survive. They still have a valuable contribution to make to the national life; and their disappearance, should it ever come about, will be a tragedy not only for those who love old things and old ways, but for all who prize responsibility and independence of spirit, virtues essential to good craftsmen.

CHAIR-MENDING

A specialized craft, chair-mending is traditionally carried on by gipsies. Now that the number of gipsies throughout Britain has decreased and gipsy camps have disappeared from many parts of the country, it has become a village craft which is plied by craftsmen going from door to door. The home of the chair-making craft is in the villages in the Chiltern Hills in Buckinghamshire.

Index

318

Acknowledgements

The publishers wish to thank the following for permission to reproduce copyright material: The National Gallery for the frontispiece, plates V, VIII and XIII, and paintings on pp. 154, 156, 157 and 167; the Tate Gallery for plates VI, XVII and XVIII, and paintings on pp. 159, 165, 166, 169, 173 and 175; the Victoria and Albert Museum for plates IX, XIV and XVI; the Birmingham City Art Gallery for plates II, VII and XII, and paintings on pp. 163 and 168; the Manchester City Art Gallery for plates I, IV, X and XI, and paintings on pp. 171, 172, and 178; the Norwich Castle Museum and Art Gallery for plates III and XV, and the painting on p. 164; Sir Muirhead Bone for his painting on p. 176; Walter Howarth, Esq., for the painting by Walter Sickert on p. 174; Mrs. Nevinson for the painting by C. R. W. Nevinson on p. 177; the Controller of H.M. Stationery Office and the Director General of the Ordnance Survey for the photograph on p. 64; the Air Ministry Geological Survey for the illustration (Crown copyright reserved) on p. 97; the Government of Northern Ireland for the photograph on p. 241; Messrs. Aerofilms, Ltd., for the photographs on pp. 9, 38 and 77.